The Demands of Justice

T0244393

TAMIKA Y. NUNLEY

The Demands of Justice

Enslaved Women, Capital Crime,
and Clemency in Early Virginia

The University of North Carolina Press *Chapel Hill*

This book was published with the assistance of the Fred W. Morrison Fund of the University of North Carolina Press.

© 2023 The University of North Carolina Press
All rights reserved
Set in Arno Pro by Westchester Publishing Services
Manufactured in the United States of America

Library of Congress Cataloging-in-Publication Data
Names: Nunley, Tamika, author.
Title: The demands of justice : enslaved women, capital crime, and clemency in early Virginia / Tamika Y. Nunley.
Description: Chapel Hill : The University of North Carolina Press, [2023] | Includes bibliographical references and index.
Identifiers: LCCN 2022037194 | ISBN 9781469673110 (cloth ; alk. paper) | ISBN 9781469673127 (paperback ; alk. paper) | ISBN 9781469673134 (ebook)
Subjects: LCSH: Discrimination in criminal justice administration—Virginia—History— 19th century. | Women slaves—Legal status, laws, etc.—Virginia—History—19th century. | Women slaves—Legal status, laws, etc.—Virginia—History—18th century. | African American women—Legal status, laws, etc.—Virginia—History—19th century. | African American women—Legal status, laws, etc.—Virginia—History—18th century. | Female offenders—Virginia—History—19th century. | Criminal law—Social aspects— Virginia—History—19th century. | Clemency—Virginia—History—19th century. | Virginia—Race relations—History.
Classification: LCC E445.V8 N86 2023 | DDC 305.48/896073075509033—dc23/eng/20220830
LC record available at https://lccn.loc.gov/2022037194

Cover illustration: Slave pen in Alexandria, Virginia, 1860s (glass, stereograph, wet collodion). Civil War Photographs, 1861–1865, Library of Congress Prints and Photographs Division.

Portions of chapter 3 were published in a different form as "Thrice Condemned: Enslaved Women, Violence, and the Practice of Leniency in Antebellum Virginia Courts," *Journal of Southern History* 87, no. 1 (February 2021): 5–34.

For Thavolia Glymph

Contents

List of Illustrations ix

Prelude xi

Introduction 1

CHAPTER ONE
Virginian Luxuries 25

CHAPTER TWO
Poison 53

CHAPTER THREE
Murder 87

CHAPTER FOUR
Infanticide 115

CHAPTER FIVE
Insurgency 145

Conclusion 181

Acknowledgments 191

Notes 193

Bibliography 217

Index 231

Illustrations

Virginian Luxuries 27

Lucy Parke Byrd 51

Dance in Lynchburg, Virginia 55

Enslaved Girl 58

Colton's Virginia 61

"Lumpkin's Jail" 142

African American cabin 171

Map of the city of Richmond 172

Slave pen 186

Prelude

In the summer of 1619, sweltering heat and humidity wafted between the stiff breezes that swept Point Comfort as the *White Lion,* and just days later the *Treasurer,* landed on Virginia's shores. The Dutch vessels commandeered by Englishmen carried African people forcibly brought to the colony after having been taken from a Portuguese ship that already bore the losses of nearly half of the human "cargo" shackled to the *Sao Joao Bautista.*[1] To Europeans, these people were the bounty of an Angolan-Portuguese war. The muster, or census taken the following spring, listed fifteen men and seventeen women, confirming trends of increasingly more female captives as the historian Jennifer L. Morgan identified in research on the fifteenth- and sixteenth-century slave trade.[2] Women captives who exist in the extant record included Margaret, Isabella, and Angela (listed as Angelo). These women survived warfare in their African homeland, the turmoil of the Middle Passage, and a privateering raid only to be faced with disease and the attacks of neighboring Natives defending their claims to land.[3] Their experiences signal a state of constant warfare that shaped the transatlantic slave trade and the dynamics of colonization. While their status remained relatively vague in Virginia, largely attributed to their designation as "servants," the nature of their captivity and sale underscored the distinctive commodification of Africans sold into lifelong bondage to provide labor for the Portuguese, Spanish, Dutch, English, and French imperial outposts in the Americas. Isabella arrived on the *White Lion* and became the servant of Captain William Tucker, Margaret worked on a plantation owned by Edward Bennet, and Angela arrived on the *Treasurer* and worked for Captain William Peirce.[4] While little is known of any of these women and their fellow captives, historians can identify African-descended people who served a term of service, arranged for their freedom, and owned land during the early decades of the seventeenth century. The ethnic fluidity of social dynamics, or the rather underdeveloped nature of race, in the early decades of the colony paint a very different portrait than what we might associate with racial slavery in antebellum Virginia. The mutability of their legal status eventually shifted to one firmly based on ideas of race and gender.

The forced passage of Africans to the British colony reflected the series of seizures that shaped the Atlantic world as Europeans claimed bodies, land, bounty, and resources that positioned them to usurp the possibilities for competitors in the rapid currents of colonization. Margaret, Isabella, and Angela experienced the warfare waged by the Portuguese in West Africa, the English on the seas, and witnessed the conflict that followed in Virginia with Opechancanough and the Powhatan people who launched an assault on the colony. Europeans were not the only actors who brought transformation to the Chesapeake. Native American polities established a presence that long predates the arrival of the British. They defended their claims to land that Europeans seized from them and made colonization a precarious venture. In addition to Native Americans, African-descended people appeared in increasing numbers by the mid-seventeenth century. Scores of Africans arrived, and their lives began to look different from the lives of those who arrived aboard the *White Lion* and the *Treasurer*. Centuries later, enslaved people approached the fortress erected at that same site, Point Comfort, to seek refuge and offer their labors in service to the Union government. In the seventeenth century, Africans landed in Virginia as the charter generations, laboring, toiling, and resisting amid the rhythms of colonization and global commerce.[5] But there, on the shoreline of Virginia, over two hundred years later, Black people pitched their stakes to claim freedom, selfhood, and survival. These moments provide one of many sets of chronological bookends to understanding racial slavery in Virginia—the oldest and largest slave state in the Union. But to understand the span of time between the arrival of Africans in Virginia and the Civil War one must begin with African-descended women.

The Demands of Justice

Introduction

How does a person treated like chattel express and enact a human ethic? What does an individual who is deeply devalued insist upon as her set of values?
—Tiya Miles, *All That She Carried*

Decades after the *White Lion* and the *Treasurer* appeared on the shores of what became Virginia, in 1662 colonial slave law legally recognized enslaved women and their progeny as the property of a slaveholder. Prohibited from full citizenship, political inclusion, and legal testimony against white people, enslaved women were viewed in relation to their ability to perform the skilled, reproductive, and sexual labor required of them.[1] Their commodification within the violent system of slavery and the slave markets meant that these women appeared in records as tithables, chattel property, currency, and assets tethered to their reproductive possibilities. Many of the stories we tell about enslaved women correctly point us to the oppressive systems they were subjected to, but these systems did not exist without the calculated intentions and ambitions of Anglo-Americans, nor did they go unchallenged by the people affected by them.

The Demands of Justice examines the lives of enslaved women accused of capital crimes to understand how slavery and its corresponding laws and social customs worked to criminalize them and limit their access to legal justice. Treated as legal property with the human capacity to commit crimes, these women and girls did not possess the same rights of white men and women and free Black people. The conditions of slavery that legislators codified in law meant that the contours of the criminal justice system posed limits to the manner in which enslaved women and girls might seek redress through the courts. If they were raped, beaten, or maimed by white Virginians, they could not avail themselves to justice in the courts. Justices understood the cruelties that made slavery a system notorious for violence. Ever aware of the contradictions between the noble principles of liberty that the United States championed and the realities of lifelong bondage that fueled the labor demands of the nation, lawmakers sought to create a legal system that both empowered the authority of slaveholders and carved out the possibility for a more benevolent feature of the law—clemency. The historian Walter Johnson explains that "this peculiar mixture of ostensible moderation and outright threat was called paternalism."[2] In instances where enslaved women and girls violated the law and qualified for executive clemency, the best possible outcome relegated them to a return to the conditions that drove them to such actions or sale to another slaveholder. The women and girls here engaged in acts of resistance, which the courts recognized as transgressive actions committed outside the parameters of the law. Even petitions from locals, who explained the brutal conditions or unusual circumstances that shaped a particular case, did not rescue an enslaved woman from the gallows or the domestic slave trade. So, then, what is justice under such a system? I explore this question in the pages that follow, with a focus on enslaved women and girls in nineteenth-century Virginia who found themselves in conflict with white Southerners that began outside of the courts.

In the intimate spaces of rooms, kitchens, farms, cabins, and the nooks and crannies of estates that dotted the diverse landscapes of the commonwealth, enslaved women and girls made decisions, for reasons of their own, that changed their lives forever. The nature of enslaved women's gendered labor in these spaces, reproductive and sexual exploitation, and criminalization shape the focus of this study to understand the relationship between gender, slave law, and justice. To examine the lives of enslaved women and girls reveals not only the manner in which their gendered experiences of bondage informed the crimes they stood accused of but also the ways their actions expressed a social economy of right and wrong. In other words, the actions of enslaved women and girls might translate into a critique of the rights that white Virginians possessed to maim, beat, violate, and extract from enslaved women's and girls' lives, bodies, and labors. Denied a trial by a jury of peers, they arrived to the courts and stood before a panel of local justices; people who barely knew them determined their guilt. Before they arrived at court, they were people who loved, worked, cried, shared stories with kin, and discovered strategies of survival, but the society they lived in also viewed them as legal property and the law maintained the expectation that, regardless of the cruelty they might experience, they remain subject to the authority of the people who enslaved them. This is not a history that romanticizes the actions of enslaved women and girls, and, additionally, I will not take up space to discuss the merits and nuances of the early legal system. I arrive at this work to think seriously about what these actions might mean and what they tell us about alternative considerations of justice not yet realized in the legal system but manifested in the decisions of enslaved women and girls.

This book examines the forces of human will that lawmakers, slaveholders, and locals went to great lengths to subdue, mainly the alleged crimes that enslaved women committed against slaveholders and the threat that such incidents posed to white members of local communities in Virginia. The power dynamics between the enslaved and the enslaver, and the bystanders of plantation households and locales, reveal not only the manner in which these places were contested spaces but also the degree to which the early colonial, and later American, legal system worked to manage and oversee such dynamics. Enslaved women responded to the conditions of bondage in a number of ways that might bring them before the courts and jurists of Virginia. In these legal encounters, we see not only a system that worked to define and affirm a commitment to legal paternalism, that upheld the rule of law and made slavery viable, but also decades of responses made by the countless enslaved women accused of capital offenses. *The Demands of Justice* examines how these responses constituted the makings of an intellectual history of enslaved women's articulations of justice.

In *All That She Carried*, the historian Tiya Miles asks, "How does a person treated like chattel express and enact a human ethic? What does an individual who is deeply devalued insist upon as her set of values?"[3] Sources from the archives dress the enslaved up in numbers, figures, calculations, lists, and estimations to enact the logic of chattel slavery. The criminalized actions and behaviors of enslaved women throw these methods off and impose their presence and ideas in ways that inspire more questions than the sources can answer. In "Mama's Baby, Papa's Maybe," literary scholar Hortense Spillers framed the consequences of slavery as the "veritable descent into the loss of communicative force."[4] The silences provoke important questions about the violence of the archive and the subjection of enslaved women on slave registers, lists of returns and transactions, and hastily assembled trials that often exclude their words and testimony.[5] But to uncover this history is to contend with an imperfect archive and a set of records that reinforces the silence of Black women. The voices of enslaved women accused of capital crimes appear muffled, silenced, and between the lines of legal forms, trial records, auditors' accounts, executive papers, and receipts for transportation and compensation for the loss of property. These records, then, appear in fragments, as many Virginia county records were destroyed. What remains are the pieces of information that one could only decipher, piece together, or imagine as a whole. The literary scholar and social theorist Saidiya Hartman grapples with these silences by deploying "critical fabulation," or the convergence of critical theory, history, and narrative fiction, to begin to piece together the gaping absences in the archive.[6] This project does not employ critical fabulation to its fullest possibility, but the basis on which the concept rests still holds true in this book—that of the deficiency of the archive and the need to consider the directions in which these stories could take shape. The erasure and obfuscation of enslaved women's voices in the archive is often deemed an acceptable consequence of the criminality assigned to Black women.

In *Colored Amazons*, historian Kali N. Gross examines the ways that working-class Black women in the North confronted penal and policing regimes as well as public discourses that reinforced the presumption of Black women's criminality. Like the work of Gross, this book examines women's crimes "as a vehicle for gaining insight into the lives of otherwise marginalized black women."[7] In her study of Black women in the Jim Crow South, historian Sarah Haley offers an important analysis of the racial and gendered logics of punishment.[8] This lens reveals that Southern forms of convict leasing, parole, chain gangs, and prisons reinscribed violence and labor exploitation integral to the economic, political, and social development of the South. This book builds on this scholarship to show how late nineteenth-century penal practices were reminiscent of the ways that the state institutionalized the commodification of enslaved women's bodies through the criminal legal proceedings that preceded legal emancipation. Moreover, court records, executive papers, and local newspapers reveal the multilayered contexts in which courts, locals, and the news accounted for the gendered dimensions of enslaved women's lives or applied racialized gender stereotypes to strengthen the case for conviction.

The sources included in the book represent shards that provide limited information and rare archival material that allow for more substantive testimony of enslaved women in criminal cases involving capital charges and sentences that range from execution to whippings and sale outside of Virginia. County clerks documented the women's testimony in imperfect form, with some testimonies recorded and others lost or inaccurately chronicled. A reading of these sources demands an examination of their worlds, the contexts of slavery in Virginia, and the recognition of their decisions and varying capacities to think, feel, and act on their own terms. The auditors' records of transportation and sale illuminate the possibilities for clemency or executive pardon. Many of the cases emerge from county court records that varied in the level of details provided in the trial transcripts. To the extent that cases included relevant details not mentioned in the minute books, I included them in this study but given that many of the transcriptions are similar for the three different sets of sources, with some exceptions, say in a place like Richmond and Prince William County, I focused on highlighting records related to clemency. The bulk of my analysis does not center the *courts*, as legal histories of the enslaved typically do. Ideas about right and wrong manifested on plantations, in households, on streets, in bedrooms, in kitchens, et cetera. Courtrooms are a part of but not central to this panoply of spaces that enslaved women encountered. In fact, the courtroom is the space in which they spend the least amount of time. When I examined the trial transcripts, I focused my search on the voices of the enslaved and the witnesses deposed. The testimonies I quote from appeared in both the trial transcripts (where they exist) and the transportation records and minute books.

The enslaved women's testimonies that exist include opaque recollections of their pasts and their relationships and shed light on the ways that race, gender, and age shaped their experiences of bondage and their subsequent violent resistance. These accounts reveal the excessive violence that made slavery sustainable, but within these Virginia households and estates were women, sisters, daughters, mothers, and aunts, along with their thoughts, desires, abilities, and inner lives on the other side of cruelty. As Walter Johnson notes, slaveholders undoubtedly profited from the human capacities of enslaved people, and any characterizations of the enslaved as dehumanized can be misleading.[9] The shards of testimonies, the actions, and even the silences of the enslaved women in these cases not only underscore Johnson's point, but they also reveal a glimpse of the possibilities for justice, as their actions exposed the violence and imbalance of power that slaveholders relied on.[10] Scholars have examined women's resistance in the form of infrapolitics, rival geographies, and everyday acts of defiance. The historian Stephanie M. H. Camp has given us critical insights into the ways that space and movement became central to the organization of slavery, but also for the creation of rival geographies, a term coined by literary scholar and postcolonial theorist Edward Said and employed by Camp to account for the strategic use of space deployed by the enslaved.[11] In this book, the courts provide one location in which to articulate ideas about right and wrong, but the cabins, yards, mansions, farms, and kitchens also function as spaces in which enslaved women reacted to their experiences in bondage. Countless testimonies from the enslaved that unfolded outside of the courts, many of which historians will likely never recover, and the crimes they stood accused of might offer insight into life in the private domains of Virginia farms and estates. Camp helps us to understand the contours of resistance within households, and the historian Thavolia Glymph shows us the violent power dynamics of the plantation household and misconceptions about the Southern home and its inhabitants. In Glymph's work, plantation mistresses were slaveholders with a vested interest in power, and their homes were not private but rather public and political spaces.[12]

The stories here ebb and flow from these everyday moments to visible and public accounts of refusal that emerge in the criminal record in ways that expose the inner workings of Virginia homes. Rather than bucolic scenes of acquiescence and goodwill, households appear as sites of rigorous and mundane labor, filled with strife, contestation, tension, and violence. Thus, resistance, in the sources collected for this study, appears as a form of retaliation against the abusive liberties legally exercised by slaveholding women and men and by interim white authorities such as overseers and white Virginians who employed enslaved people through hire.[13] If the courts tell us a complete story, then enslaved women committed violent crimes infrequently. But discipline for resistance often occurred beyond the purview of the courts. Even so, judges, lawyers, and citizens debated the circumstances and implications of enslaved women accused of crime. Locals might ask about motivations or question the degree to which a slaveholder or individual adequately disciplined enslaved people in ways that preserved social order. Indeed, white Virginians took slave resistance seriously enough to develop a system of slave laws.[14]

Lawmakers often developed laws in response to the need to adjudicate matters concerning the enslaved in court. In *Slave Law and the Politics of Resistance in the Early Atlantic World*, historian Edward Rugemer shows the relationship between slave resistance and the development of slave law. The efforts of colonial legislatures, many of which comprised slaveholders, attest to the ways that slave resistance shaped the contours of the law and the manner in which the British colonies such as Jamaica and South Carolina responded to social upheaval.[15] In Virginia, the work of building a colony, and eventually a state, coincided with efforts to organize society through the prism of class, race, gender, and age. But not everyone honored these new laws, and the disputes among enslaved women and white Virginians suggest the presence of other values guiding the behavior of the enslaved. Thus, the decisive actions of these women offer evidence of a rival jurisprudence that can be understood as their own methods for refusing the logic of slave law.[16] Whether inspired by exceptional acts of cruelty or the mundanity of everyday toil and tension, enslaved women found ways to make their antislavery attitudes known. From the perspective of the enslaved, the legal and personal meanings of resistance served as moments of retribution that contested the years of wrong inflicted on their lives, minds, and bodies—their own articulations of justice, even as the law categorized these actions as crimes, even if it meant their sale or death.

Virginia legislatures developed a law based on the assumption that the enslaved committed crimes that were impossible for white locals to commit. The colonial legislature of Virginia enacted statutes that specifically regulated and organized the behavior of enslaved and free Black people. Over time, the governing body of the colony, which later became the state legislature, revised and strengthened these edicts in order to protect the political and economic interests of white Virginians. In 1692, the colonial legislature authorized the creation of separate courts to prosecute the crimes of enslaved people, drawing a clear line between the adjudication of crimes committed by enslaved, free Black, and white Virginians.[17] Capital crimes included poisoning, insurrection, rape, and assault with the intent to kill a white person. An enslaved man could be accused of raping a white woman, but the courts did not convict white men for the rape of Black women. Moreover, the degree to which enslaved people were subjected to violence at the hands of white Virginians did not absolve them of conviction or prevent their death or sale beyond the state. Slave law and slave courts, then, placed the crimes of enslaved people within a racial scaffolding for particularly punitive consequences for an offense against men and women slaveholders, slave hirers, overseers, and white residents of the commonwealth.

Unlike white defendants accused of capital crime, courts did not permit enslaved people to issue testimony against a white person, but an enslaved person could testify against another enslaved person. Without testimony, the possible evidence that enslaved defendants possessed was excluded from the case, which resulted in the reification of white testimony unless the court deposed an enslaved witness. In some cases, white and Black witnesses deposed gave testimony in favor of the enslaved defendant, but this occurrence often altered the sentence rather than the conviction. As historian Philip J. Schwarz observes, "The sine qua non of the Old Dominion's criminal justice system was that the general level of judicial punishments for slaves must be more severe than that for whites."[18] The law and the administration of justice reflected an early legal culture that distinguished the capacity for criminality and culpability between enslaved and free Black people and white locals. Some enslaved women accused of murder avoided the death penalty and, instead, received a commuted sentence. But commutation carried different meanings for enslaved people accused of capital crimes.

The cases discussed highlight instances where nineteenth-century jurists explored what they referred to as acts of "leniency," "reprieve," or "mercy" in deliberations over sentencing. According to one historian, between 1801 and

1865, more than twice as many enslaved defendants were transported than those executed.[19] White locals and officials exercised the right to petition the state for executive pardons in Virginia, but the conviction of an enslaved person could not be appealed to a higher court until 1848.[20] The courts did not allow enslaved defendants to testify against white Virginians, and the only method of legal recourse came in the form of executive clemency based on the recommendation or petitions from the courts or local communities. The parameters of clemency differed for white Virginians, who did not face the prospect of being sold into lifelong bondage but served sentences at the state penitentiary or brief terms in the local jail or were absolved of their crimes altogether. When granted "reprieve," enslaved women were jailed and prepared for sale outside of the commonwealth and thus grafted into the growing slave trade. In 1801, the Virginia legislature empowered the executive office to transport condemned enslaved people out of the commonwealth in lieu of execution.[21] The Virginia assembly passed the transportation law on the heels of a conspiracy, known as Gabriel's Conspiracy, a plot to attack white residents in Henrico County, then seize the state armory and Governor James Monroe. Up to seventy-two men were tried for the conspiracy, with twenty-six executed and the remaining acquitted, pardoned, or sold out of state. The commutation of sentences saved the state a little less than half of what it cost to compensate the slaveholders for the executions of those convicted. Commutation savings proved no small matter, since as early as 1705 the then colonial government of Virginia compensated slaveholders for executed enslaved people at full market value.[22]

Officials in Virginia embraced clemency as a possible course of action for a variety of reasons. To begin, the savings to the commonwealth itself appears substantial in Gabriel's Conspiracy, and later collective acts of insurrection that emerged in the first half of the nineteenth century that involved the prospect of compensation on a larger scale made sale and transportation a more sustainable option for the legislature.[23] Clemency also supported the interpretation of Southern slavery as a benevolent institution. Regarding the legal tribunal that tried enslaved people for criminal charges, one historian argues, "Many oyer and terminer justices wished to perceive themselves and to be perceived by other slaveholders, nonslaveholding whites, free blacks, and slaves as benevolent, even as patriarchs."[24] Magistrates and political officials consciously understood that they helped define the formative moment in which American law emerged with the professionalization of the legal discipline.[25] Ever cognizant of the ways that foreign political entities scrutinized the development of American law, they paired a concern with evenhandedness with the adulation for the rule of law, making clemency an important performative gesture politically, especially for courts in the slaveholding South. With growing international criticism of the hypocrisy of a republic committed to both egalitarianism and chattel slavery, jurists and political leaders in Virginia were keenly aware and protective stewards of Southern law. More broadly, the penal reform movement that informed the establishment of the penitentiary in Richmond supported the idea of execution as the least desirable outcome and a last resort.[26] Reform remained in the purview of white convicts, but the slave trade offered the best possible outcome for "reprieve" from the death penalty for the women in this book. This meant the continued profitability of clemency for slave traders, slave owners, pens, and slave markets within and beyond the commonwealth.

Malice and intent determined the type of felonious charge enslaved women faced for capital crime.[27] In early Virginia, when jurists and jurors determined an enslaved woman's capacity for malice, personal encounters and experiences (if any) with that woman, as well as local opinions and attitudes, worked in tandem to shape the interpretations of evidence and, ultimately, the outcome. Furthermore, courts often determined the degree of malice and culpability based on perceptions of Black women that underscored their propensity for crime. But the enslaved women involved in these cases viewed themselves and their worlds differently. Viewing the worlds that enslaved people made through the lens of neighborhoods, the historian Anthony E. Kaye explains that lines of solidarity and conflict were created in both the geographic terrain of neighborhoods and the state of mind that fostered a sense of place. Kaye states, "Creating and re-creating neighborhoods was, among other things, a way for slaves to recalibrate the balance of power in their society. Neighborhoods, then, were a place, a political institution, and a political idea."[28] The violence that came with chattel slavery, the love of kin and community that gave them a sense of belonging, the interiority of their lives, and their own ideas about fairness and injustice shaped the ways they understood their actions. Trials involving enslaved women and capital crimes against white Virginians illuminate competing ideas about the relationship between gender, paternalism, and leniency and, more specifically, the incongruities built into the meaning and the administration of justice in antebellum Virginia. For many enslaved women, transportation as a form of reprieve did not always translate into a benevolent gesture.

Tearing these women from families and communities, forcing them into uncertainty, and causing them to face the persistence of violent labor exploitation meant that the Virginia courts situated the parameters of leniency squarely within the interests of slaveholders and the slave trade. The terror that created volatility in the lives of these women coincided with the rifts they initiated on their own and that ultimately brought them before the criminal court. Indeed, these cases reveal that enslaved women employed their own understandings of justice after years of gendered exploitation and violence. They carried this awareness and knowledge along routes that took them deeper into and even beyond the borders of the American South. Early colonial precedents show that enslaved people convicted and sentenced were often sold to other British colonies, particularly those in the Caribbean. Once transportation became possible through state law in 1801, enslaved people granted reprieve were forced outside of the United States and brought into territories such as Louisiana and Florida, which the Spanish claimed at the time. Slave traders also took enslaved people to Suriname, Cuba, and St. Croix along with other Spanish West Indies colonies. By 1817, enslaved women granted reprieve might be sold to other Southern states such as South Carolina, Georgia, and Louisiana. Slave traders and political leaders often complained of the practice that sent enslaved people convicted of capital crimes in Virginia to other countries or states to which they were sold and where they might bring that same spirit of defiance.[29] For an enslaved woman sentenced to transportation, the record of conviction could inspire harsh treatment from slave traders and new owners concerned about her tractability. Historians refer to the processes of acclimatization and terror as "breaking" enslaved persons in the hope that they arrive to their new destination with a diminished will to resist. One scholar observes, "Slave breaking was a technology of the soul. Buying slaves to break them represented a fantasy of mastery embodied in the public subjugation of another, of private omnipotence transmuted into public reputation. In that way, it was not so different from paternalism."[30] Breaking undoubtedly resulted in terror, and often discouraged enslaved people and onlookers from testing the authority of traders and new owners, but the capacity to resist remained.

Prior to the emergence of scholarship about slave resistance, enslaved women were largely regarded as the least likely to engage in the most visible forms of resistance, despite general knowledge of these incidents among Virginians at the time. The cases that follow show not only that gender did not presuppose violent responses toward white Southerners but also that ideas about gender, race, age, class, and sex influenced local opinion and the possibilities for a commuted sentence. Reports of bondpeople on trial for murder fortified white fears of alleged and actual violent retaliation. Slave laws, local customs, and the grievances of slaveholders changed over time as a result of the actions of the enslaved.[31] Furthermore, Schwarz shows that resistance not only exposed the volatility of slavery but also inspired initiatives to re-orient and adjust laws to counteract the actions of the enslaved. In instances that led to trial, legal historian Ariela Gross observes that the paradox of "double character," or slaves' double identity as human and "property," became increasingly apparent, causing Southerners to contend with the contradictions of slave law.[32] Historian Malick Ghachem refers to this contradiction as "the slave's two bodies," or the tension between the legal fiction of human property and personhood that pervades the liberal themes of Southern law.[33] Schwarz definitively characterized the experiences of enslaved people accused of crimes as "twice condemned" by Southern law and slavery, but here I examine the criminal cases that show the manner in which enslaved women were "thrice condemned" when gender is taken into consideration even with the prospect of clemency.[34] In the cases that follow, the racial, gendered, and sexual conditions of bondage created the contexts in which enslaved women engaged in criminalized resistance.[35]

Legal historians continue to make the case for how local sympathies, contexts, and norms often shaped the outcomes of capital cases. Ariela Gross offers a body of work devoted to understanding the inner workings of racial identity in Southern courts and jurisprudence to show how the courtroom serves as the stage from which these ideas about race and identity are conceptualized, performed, and mapped onto the bodies of Southerners.[36] In *The People and Their Peace*, historian Laura F. Edwards explains the local dynamics and deliberations that played out in important legal cases that bore implications for the stability and overall consensus of local Southern societies.[37] Her groundbreaking study complicates the assumptions we bring to the history of slave law, often shaped by the premise that Southern slave law is all-encompassing and quite literally interpreted. A look at local cases, however, reveals layers of complexity and contingency rooted in experiential encounters and relationships that might shape the legal outcome. This work is critical to the treatment of clemency in this study and helps me think through the role of local petitions and the inclinations toward leniency. Here, the enslaved women faced charges of criminality and defended their reputations in specific local contexts. These cases that appear throughout this book foreground the development of slave law, the significance of race, gender, local opinion, and the advent of Southern jurisprudence concerning justice.

The approach to legal history here marks a departure from freedom suits in that these cases are distinctive because enslaved women did not pursue legal recourse but were instead pulled into the courts to defend themselves.

The legal history of freedom suits, Southern courts, and legal culture provide important insights, however, that apply to this study. Historians such as Loren Schweninger and William Thomas III offer scholarship that shows the ways that enslaved people, and enslaved women in particular, articulated genealogical traditions that positioned them to make freedom claims in Southern courts.[38] Legal histories of enslaved women's claims to the courts, however, remain incredibly important in understanding how courts and jurists approached the unique conditions created to uphold slavery while at times meting out justice and decisions that affirm the claims of enslaved women. These are critical windows into the ways enslaved women maneuvered through the complexity of the law and what might be possible in the way of legal recourse.[39] These studies offer an important intellectual history of enslaved women, their oral traditions, and the manner in which they shaped Southern jurisprudence in freedom suits.[40] In freedom suits, enslaved women demonstrated a sophisticated understanding of not only the law but also the local customs that shaped the perception of their own worthiness of justice. For instance, many of these women might claim white maternal lineage, thus overturning the application of *partus sequitur ventrem*, or others might be known for their high moral character in the context of their labor and social relations within the community.

The legal history of freedom suits shows instances in which enslaved people asserted legal personhood on their terms, using the language of property and liberty to appeal to the legal system. The historian Anne Twitty shows in her study of legal culture in the American Confluence, or the region that includes Missouri, Ohio, and the Mississippi River valleys, that enslaved people "developed a complex understanding of legal procedures and the ways in which statutes and precedents could be used to effect their freedom."[41] In *A Question of Freedom*, William Thomas III shows how Black people employed their own language and ethics in Maryland freedom suits in ways that positioned them to publicly challenge slavery and shape the politics of slavery.[42] Thomas examines the evolution of the use of hearsay evidence and the ways that enslaved people drew on genealogies passed down in Black families to make successful, and at times not so successful, claims to freedom. These claims forced slaveholders to defend their actions in court and prove their rightful ownership of people who claimed they were wrongfully enslaved. In *Black Litigants in the Antebellum American South*, legal historian Kimberly Welch explains that "when suing in court over their right to possess property, protect their families, and assert freedom, black litigants exercised and laid claim to legal personhood—a status both southern law and southern society reserved for white men only."[43] Welch shows that "their litigiousness, more-over, was a form of political engagement. For when black people approached the courts in the service of their own interests, they made claims on the state."[44] This scholarship provides rich insights into how enslaved and free Black people developed legal knowledge and deployed claims to freedom, property, and a range of rights afforded those positioned to access the courts.

Legal historians have examined the legal claims of enslaved and free Black people in antebellum courts, with particular attention to civil suits. This literature offers insights into the ways that Black people developed a legal consciousness that shaped how they approached civil litigation in the courts. Kelly Kennington, a historian of slavery and the antebellum South, refers to legal consciousness to explain the manner in which enslaved people learned about the law and their rights to make certain claims in court. Thus, legal consciousness was informed by the ways that their experiences, their rela-tionships, and the nature of the case influenced their understandings of the law.[45] In *Getting Justice and Getting Even*, anthropologist Sally Engle Merry refers to consciousness as a way "people conceive of the 'natural' and normal way of doing things, their habitual patterns of talk and action, and their com-monsense understanding of the world." Legal consciousness, then, unfolded in the courts as individuals expressed their own understanding of their rights and entitlements.[46] Freedom suits show the ways that enslaved people strate-gically applied their experiences, knowledge, and relationships to make claims in the courts. In *Wicked Flesh*, historian and Black studies scholar Jessica Ma-rie Johnson invites us to think expansively about freedom, offering that "for African women and women of African descent, manumission became one tool among many in the struggle for safety, security, and autonomy. Other practices would need to be cultivated and created to make freedom free."[47] Enslaved women developed epistemologies of freedom, refusal, survival, and existence yet unrealized in society where even legal freedom imposed limits on Black life.

The cases explored here ask: What do enslaved people do when they are deemed unworthy of justice because they are pulled into the criminal justice system for capital offenses? What if the redress they seek is not possible within the legal system as it existed in the nineteenth century? While civil suits al-lowed Black litigants to make claims to property and freedom, what happens when they stand accused of actions that work outside the parameters of the law? Unlike the enslaved people who sued for their freedom or made claims to property, the women and girls in this study likely did not develop a legal strategy for defending the crimes they stood accused of, and there is no evidence that they worked with abolitionists or local attorneys before the alleged acts of murdering masters, poisoning white Virginians, and committing infanticide.[48] What if we seriously considered the battles waged by these women and girls as evidence of a legal system that is insufficient for the justice they seek? Rather than solely emphasizing the repressive elements of the criminal justice system, this study explores the relationship between slave law, gender, and resistance to consider the intellectual possibilities of justice and clemency. This is not, however, a legal history that emphasizes the courts, justices, lawmakers, laws, and legal counsel, but a history of ideas and actions deemed impalpable because of the ways that enslaved women and girls were criminalized.

This study focuses on the alleged crimes and sentencing outcomes of enslaved women to understand the relationship between race and gender, and the possibilities and impossibilities of justice. In *Southern Slavery and the Law, 1619–1860*, the historian Thomas D. Morris provides a foundational study of slave laws to show their origins in English common law and the ways that the actions of the enslaved altered the application of legal rules of property.[49] This study builds on that work by showing how the legal rules of property focused on the protection of property as one particular function of justice, particularly in instances of crime. It reveals how the state legislature accommodated the risks that came with slave resistance by codifying measures to ensure compensation and coverage for any potential losses. This study is also indebted to the work of legal scholar A. Leon Higginbotham Jr. and his work on race and the law to show the correlation between the application of slave law and its ramifications for the economic interests of white Southerners.[50] Along those lines, the work of pioneering Black studies scholar and theorist Cedric J. Robinson offers a frame for understanding the ways that early modern capitalism involved a reconstitution of social hierarchy rooted in violence and subjugation based on formative ideas about race. In *Black Marxism*, Robinson employs the term *racial capitalism* to understand the interrelated processes of creating race in tandem with defining markets and the political configurations of capitalism.[51] This study brings Robinson and Higginbotham in conversation to reveal the interconnectedness of slave law, racial capitalism, and clemency in the radical traditions of enslaved women. Here, the historian Jennifer L. Morgan's groundbreaking study *Reckoning with Slavery* shows this relationship in the sixteenth and seventeenth centuries with an emphasis on the function and meanings of kinship. Kinship became not only a feature of their commodification but also part of the work that enslaved women performed as a rejection of that commodification.

The Black radical tradition, a term coined by Robinson and skillfully deployed by Morgan, offers a grammar for understanding the varied ways in which enslaved women refuted their enslavement and the corresponding exploitation that features prominently in racial capitalism. Morgan's work centers what enslaved women understood about race and their enslavement, asserting that "they knew their own value as kin, as producers, as reproducers, as marketers, as objects of trade, as currency."[52] Morgan asks, "How might the experience of enslaved women have given rise to a Black radical tradition (another of Robinson's core interventions) that was rooted in the intersections between birth and commodification?"[53] Regarding a late nineteenth-century context of racial capitalism, Sarah Haley argues that Black women's convict labor provided for the very material basis for the development of the modern South.[54] Thus, Black women entangled in the Atlantic slave trade all the way to the Southern penal regime of the late nineteenth century reveals a history of gendered racial capitalism. Along the same lines, this work converses with Haley, Robinson, Morgan, and political activist and scholar Angela Davis to explore how criminalized acts of resistance gave shape and meaning to gendered racial capitalism through institutionalized legal interventions that fueled the domestic slave trade through sale and transportation, but also the Black radical tradition of contesting the conditions of slavery.

The incidents and trials in this book provide one of many lenses from which to explore the possibility of transgression in the context of gendered racial capitalism that the women and girls in this book find themselves in. The courts pry into the lives of enslaved women and girls, capturing intimate forms of existence in which they make meaning and they imbue with significance, but also worlds subject to violent and uncertain dynamics that gave the slave South its shape. While ideas are difficult to locate, we can see them in the decision to wield an ax against a rapist, to concoct a "remedy" for a vulnerable mistress, or to escape upon news of war. These decisions offer a response to the ongoing warfare triggered by the Atlantic slave trade. Virginia homes anchored in the commitment to enforcing the subjugation of enslaved people emerged as turbulent households that looked to the courts to restore order and justice.

The experiences of enslaved women accused of capital crime not only reveal the ways they were subjected to a system that exploited their culpability but also tell another story of generations of women who were pivotal actors among their communities of kin. As Davis reminds us, the Black woman, "even as she was suffering under her unique oppression as female, she was thrust by the force of circumstances into the center of the slave community.

She was, therefore, essential to the survival of the community. Not all people have survived enslavement; hence her survival-oriented activities were themselves a form of resistance. Survival, moreover, was the prerequisite of all higher levels of struggle."[55] Embedded in survival-oriented activities lie the ideas and ethics that enslaved women formulated within the conditions of bondage. Jessica Marie Johnson notes, "A life-sustaining definition of blackness emerged out of black women's survival, the survival of their children, the creation of self-sustaining communities across African origins, racial nomenclatures, and the precarity of bondage."[56] Resistance must be reconstituted to include the survival strategies and the corresponding intellectual and emotional labor that enslaved women performed that might be less apparent in the sources and the stories we tell. The historian Vanessa M. Holden invites us to consider the varied forms of resistance and the political implications of such actions even as it might mean the silence of enslaved women.[57] In this book, women's resistance work appears in different forms, both silent and audible, and most prominently in ways that make it onto the pages of court records, receipts, and newspapers. Moreover, these acts of refusal and survival were deeply connected to their relationships with white Southerners, connections forced through the demands of labor, intimacy, and control that came with slavery.[58]

For enslaved women in particular, proximity to white Virginians existed in the contexts of laboring in households, or in the fields under the scrutiny of overseers, or in the intrusions of slaveholders in their intimate lives.[59] Scholars have critically examined conflict between the enslaved and enslavers, and Black women's resistance against white violence and abuse in particular.[60] Ranging from concepts such as the *infrapolitics* of slavery to comprehensive accounts of slave revolts, scholarship about slave resistance elucidates the active and ongoing struggles between enslaved people and white Southerners.[61] Enslaved women committed capital crimes in response to the conditions of bondage they were subjected to, and, in many cases, such responses might serve as a reprisal for grievances that spanned decades and even generations. These cases show how enslaved women served as interlocutors of resistance and the ways that locals formulated disparaging gendered stereotypes of women like them in defense of white Southerners. Many of these stereotypes were also deployed in the contexts of crimes committed among enslaved people. The historian Jeff Forret's study of intraracial violent crimes in Virginia underscores the complexity of behaviors, politics, and motivations at work in instances where enslaved people committed alleged criminal acts against other enslaved persons.[62] Forret takes up the study of intraracial violence comprehensively. I am interested in the conflicts between enslaved people and white Virginians in an effort to understand the racial and gendered contours of criminal law and the varying degrees through which enslaved and free, white and Black, and male and female were able to access the legal technologies of justice. During their trials, however, enslaved women's and girls' grievances received scant consideration even as the justices conducted relatively orderly court proceedings.

The women in these cases were tried before a legal tribunal, and, in many instances, their convictions did not inevitably result in the death penalty.[63] Indeed, lawyers, justices, and locals weighed in on the details of the cases in order to submit their own perspectives and interpretations of justice. When prevailing opinion appeared in favor of a more "lenient" sentence, enslaved women received a commuted sentence that led to their sale and transportation or their confinement in the state penitentiary by the time of the Civil War. White Virginians interpreted these outcomes as a policy of "leniency" or evidence of a local legal culture preoccupied with justice.[64] The variation in sentencing reveals a legal regime that increasingly took extenuating circumstances under consideration but preserved the economic interests of slaveholders and the social and political imperatives of nonslaveholding white Virginians.[65] The Virginia legislature allocated funds to compensate owners for enslaved people sentenced to death; thus, sale and transportation meant that the slaveholder's investment remained secure. Furthermore, sale and transportation allowed white Southerners to remove any persons who posed a threat, while preserving their own liberal convictions about the justness of the law. Hence, commuted sentences were not designed to undermine slavery in Virginia. For Southerners, ideas about justice supported the imperatives of Southern paternalism rather than egalitarian principles of equality. In the cases discussed, the protection of property rights and local opinion of slaveholding and nonslaveholding white Southerners buttressed perceptions of justness and the inviolability of the rule of law.[66]

A particular type of moral cachet came with commuted sentences, and judgments of mercy continued to affirm the presence of slavery in Virginia.[67] With its population of enslaved people the largest in the region, the development of the legal culture of Virginia influenced the politics of slaveholding throughout the American South.[68] According to historians, legal trials and leniency were important demonstrations of evenhandedness to legitimize the Southern legal system. But evenhandedness only went so far in the lives of enslaved women.[69] Race, gender, class, and age determined the degree of protections Black and white Southerners received from the law, and Southerners made connections between the rule of law and the moral demands of even-handedness.[70] In the South, justice was based on the supposition that Southern law was just, but when particularly violent circumstances appealed to the sensibilities of locals, Southerners demonstrated their right to intervene and weigh in on court decisions to request a modified sentence. Moreover, the preservation of social order in Virginia and the justifications for racial slavery made the paternalist motivations for commuting sentences amenable to defending the integrity of Southern law.

Virginia jurisprudence in cases involving the capital convictions of enslaved people and violent disciplinary actions committed against them protected the economic interests of white Southerners.[71] As early as 1669, white slaveholders and overseers were protected from prosecution if they murdered enslaved people as a disciplinary act. By 1788, however, the Virginia legislature adjusted the law to apply manslaughter charges to white people accused of killing slaves they did not own.[72] Financial obligations of the state treasuries, the formation of laws that protected property interests, and the collision of local opinion were just a few of the factors that determined sentencing practices in Virginia.[73] In cases involving murder charges, enslaved persons were denied a trial by jury and thereby tried by justices of the peace and county officials in county courts of oyer and terminer, which operated under a gubernatorial commission.[74] Free Black and white persons charged with capital crimes attended a hearing before a justice of the peace, then approached an "examining court," followed by a jury indictment and a trial. As historian Daniel J. Flanigan points out, "Slave trials required none of these proceedings."[75] They appeared on trial in the court of oyer and terminer, and if convicted, enslaved people were denied the right to appeal to higher courts. The trial record and any supporting materials such as local petitions went to the governor, who held the authority to commute the sentence to transportation in the spirit of mercy or leniency but did not possess power to overturn the conviction. Virginia governors were known to occasionally issue pardons for slaves convicted of capital crimes, but by the nineteenth century the executives increasingly issued them for more serious crimes. According to one study, between 1785 and 1865, 628 enslaved people were executed, and between 1801 and 1865, 983 were transported outside of Virginia.[76] The general perception among white Southerners held that pardons proved a more reasonable sentence than death and demonstrated a degree of moderation that appealed to Virginians.[77] Whether cases ended in execution or transportation, enslaved women's reprisals reverberated through the interracial communities in which their cases were tried.

As much as elites and lawmakers shifted the focus of the law on the property rights of individuals by the mid-nineteenth century, the ethic of communalism remained significant in Virginia counties, particularly among nonslaveholding white Southerners. Edwards argues that "legal localism," or the habit and customs of a specific community, worked in tandem to "keep the peace" or maintain social order.[78] Petitioning provided an avenue for local citizens to weigh in on cases even in instances where they did not serve as witnesses.[79] These petitions reveal opportunities to submit their appraisals of the character and reputations of those involved in the cases under consideration.[80] Petitioning also served an ideological function in which citizens articulated ideas about right and wrong and submitted recommendations for sentencing. The petitions confirm the presence of interracial cooperation in various Virginia counties. As historians Melvin Ely and Kirt von Daacke show in their work on the history of Virginia communities, interactions between enslaved, free Black, and white locals could be rooted in mutual support, economic cooperation, and more social fluidity that transcended racial lines.[81] Not all encounters between enslaved and white Virginians were characterized by inevitable or unresolvable conflict absent of negotiation and mutual interest. The cases explored throughout this book highlight these dimensions to the extent that white locals appealed to the courts for a modified sentence because of their knowledge and interactions with the enslaved women and girls on trial. This study does not deny the presence of interracial cooperation among Virginians, but the cases reveal the racial and gendered contours of the law and how justice existed within their reach in different ways. Thus, interracial cooperation is not evidence of equality among the races and sexes in the slaveholding South. The violent dynamics of power that slavery afforded shaped the conflict between enslaved women and girls and the white adults and children in the cases. The excessive use of violence often inspired locals to petition for a commuted sentence, which in some instances, affirms the presence of ties and bonds across race and gender. As such, the trials might lead to an unpredictable legal sentence. Local justices and the executive office of the state administered executions and occasional pardons with no seemingly consistent guidelines for justice, but through a dynamic process of prioritizing the interests and mores of the locale.[82] In Virginia's courts of oyer and terminer, cases involving enslaved women's violent crimes against white Virginians unfolded in rather unpredictable ways. Even in instances where compelling evidence of particularly brutal circumstances surfaced, clemency offered limited recourse. Clemency made space for the acknowledgment of Southern sensibilities while validating the institution of slavery and the political and economic power wielded by slave owners. These circumstances were scrutinized by magistrates, locals, and witnesses as they deliberated the different categories of crime for which enslaved women were accused.

Virginia lawmakers derived a set of laws that regulated and prosecuted the behaviors of its inhabitants through markers of race, gender, and class. Class appears to be a more meaningful legal distinction during the colonial era, whereas race and gender appear increasingly more significant in organizing the social, and thus the political and economic, lives of Virginians by the nineteenth century. The book is organized by a gradually advancing chronology that maps out enslaved women's relationships to Virginia courts from the colonial era to the end of the American Civil War. While the emphasis of the book rests on that which constitutes a criminal offense throughout the nineteenth century, as chapter 1 shows, the dynamics of colonization and the ideology of race shaped early Virginia legal culture in important ways. The commodification of slave labor and the biopolitics of racial slavery meant that leaders within the colony determined the degree to which enslaved women could access legal justice. This book is as much a study of the legal contexts and outcomes of enslaved women's capital crimes as it is an intellectual history of competing ways of understanding the meanings of enslaved women's transgressions.

The remainder of the book focuses on possible capital crimes, as decisions and sentencing were often determined by degrees of severity alleged in the cases. Chapter 2 examines cases that involve enslaved women charged for poisoning. Deemed a particularly pernicious offense, poisoning exposed the vulnerability of slaveholders who employed cooks in their kitchen cellars, a responsibility typically designated to an enslaved woman. Poisoning was a crime relatively difficult to furnish with evidence, as some poisonous substances also served medicinal purposes, and many doctors failed to make firm conclusions about the cause of illness or death. In the early nineteenth century, countless Virginians were prone to deadly diseases, but in inexplicable circumstances someone needed to take the blame, and it was often enslaved women serving in white Virginians' homes who were charged with foul play. Poisoning raised local concerns about the intimacy of women's domestic labor and the possibilities of enslaved women's retribution for grievances. Convictions for poisoning might lead to execution or a commuted sentence of sale and transportation further south. Poisoning reminded white Southerners that fantasies of trust and compliance often obscured the realities of stifling tensions.

In rare instances, conflict among enslaved women and white Southerners exploded in public, bringing the terror of slavery to the surface of slave society. In chapter 3, I examine records of enslaved women charged with the murder of white Virginians. These records capture in more detail the depositions of enslaved women and their explanations of their motivations. Cases involving the murder of a white person set off a firestorm of local and legal concerns about Black women's capacities for violence and whether or not the gallows appropriately served the demands of justice. Such cases offer a poignant window into years of terror, violence, and sexual exploitation and sparked local responses to the gendered dynamics of these deadly altercations. In these cases, Black and white Virginians deliberated ideas about right and wrong and articulated their own conceptualizations of justice in the early nineteenth century. Life and death remained at stake in considerations of how enslaved women and white Southerners conceptualized and acted on their understandings of justice.

Chapter 4 examines the corporeal experiences and decisions of enslaved women and girls that unfolded in cases of infanticide, which appeared throughout the antebellum dockets of Virginia.[83] Enslaved women accused of infanticide issued a powerful indictment of the justness of slavery that stoked the moral responses of white Northerners but also Southerners who petitioned for executive pardon. In some instances, infanticide cases also appear incredibly complex as jurists and legal experts attempt to account for factors such as malnutrition and brutal working conditions to determine whether or not enslaved women were motivated by protecting their children from a life of bondage or to account for conditions that critically determined the infant mortality rates among slave populations. Commuted sentences appeared rather consistently, depending on the nature of testimony, evidence, and circumstances that informed each case. These cases, however, reminded Southerners that the prospect of fertility control remained within the corporeal purview of enslaved women to make decisions about their reproductive lives.

The preceding chapters show how slave societies responded legally to the actions of enslaved women and girls in the form of court decisions, slave laws, and legislative measures designed to ensure the regulation of their behavior instead of slave behavior and the protection of the economic interests of slaveholders. The actions of the enslaved, however, underscore the ongoing combustible conditions in which enslavers attempted to control Black Virginians. Chapter 5 examines the realities of insurgency through antebellum manifestations of insurrection, theft, escape, attempted murder, and arson as strategies of revolt leading up to the Confederacy's own rebellion.[84] Theft in the form of escape appears as a legal crime and an expression of enslaved people's rituals of taking what they believe they earned in an arrangement where they could collect little to nothing for their labor. These cases reveal not only local reactions and legal responses but also the kinds of material goods that enslaved people valued and desired or even needed in times of scarcity triggered by the war. Indeed, enslaved women went even further by escaping, committing an act of theft that severely affected the economic futures of slaveholders. Local white Virginians viewed theft differently and appealed to the courts for punishments that might include whipping or sale outside of the state. But with the realities of war, slaveholders found very little recourse in the courts at a time when the Confederacy demanded their presence and resources on the war front. Enslaved women also committed acts of arson during the war, using the opportunity of distracted slaveholders to initiate their own assault on the Confederate effort. Arson proved difficult to verify, with many instances lacking sufficient evidence and some resulting in a mishap or mistake. War might shift the motives for enslaved women, as resistance could lead to life-threatening consequences or to favorable conditions that they could experience on taking advantage of wartime instability.

Enslaved women accused of arson during the Civil War complicated matters depending on whether their cases appeared under the wartime jurisdiction of Virginia, a member of the Confederate States of America, or the newly formed state of West Virginia. In addition to the legal complexity of wartime crime, these cases reveal enslaved women's resistance under a Confederate legal regime that inflated the commercial value of enslaved people and protected the property interests of Southerners through a sharp departure from execution. Thus, what might be interpreted as an increase in clemency really signaled the desperate financial conditions of the Confederate States of America. Richmond served as the capital of the Confederacy but was also a hub of sabotage brought on by enslaved people in the city. The Union war marked new efforts to dismantle slave laws that Virginia legislatures worked to codify and fully integrate in the early years of the commonwealth.

Historians of slavery in Virginia, and this study is no exception, typically consult the comprehensive compilation of early Virginia laws assembled by William Waller Hening, an early nineteenth-century legal scholar. Hening's *Statutes at Large* begins with a preface that underscores the historical significance of recording the laws of Virginia and what the laws might reveal about society. Hening writes, "Homer has interwoven a few historical facts, with a strange mixture of Grecian mythology. His heroes were all allied to the Gods, and the celestial beings in every conflict, had their feelings enlisted on the side of their respective descendants." Homer, the great historian of the Trojan War, and Livy, "one of the best of the Roman historians," like many historians of antiquity, introduce their work with "legendary tales" from which to remember their ancestors. But Hening argues that these tales of old can only reveal so much about a people. He offers, "Indeed, until we come to the laws of a nation, it is impossible to form a correct idea of its civil polity, or of the state of society."[85] Indeed, Thomas Jefferson recounts in his *Notes on the State of Virginia* the great lineage of philosophers and historians like Homer who have interrogated the moral degradation of slavery and law in society. The issue of right and wrong might imbue the legal virtue of property, "but the slaves of which Homer speaks were whites," he reminds us.[86] He affirms that the enslavement of Africans, however, "is not their condition then, but nature, which has produced the distinction" of race, and the degree to which race is gendered in the formation of slave law worked in tandem with pseudo-scientific theories of the "natural" correlation between Black bodies, bondage, and criminality. This study of enslaved women's articulations of justice renders not only a new reading of the history of Virginia law but also a history about a conflict of ideas and how these ideas were violently expressed. As the book will document, enslaved women and white Southerners fought continually over ideas about slavery, crime, and justice.

The records mined for this study do not always yield specific articulations of enslaved women's ideas in the ways that the records reveal the ideas of prominent political thinkers of their time. But the *actions* of enslaved women and girls, whether they appear in physical, chemical, corporeal, violent, or secretive expressions, tell us something about the intellectual and emotional work that enslaved women performed for themselves and their kin. This history of enslaved women and capital crime in early Virginia not only illuminates their unique experiences and relationship to early legal culture but also inspires important questions about the ongoing connections they forged between race, gender, and the American criminal justice system. It also reframes what constitutes intellectual history and considers the possibilities of how our methodologies might breathe new life toward an intellectual history of enslaved women. The stories of these women offer insights about what early Virginia can tell us about the demands of justice over time, and who plays a role in articulating such demands, even as explicit explanations might fail to appear in the written records and, instead, emerge in a set of responses.

Throughout this study, I question: What is clemency or justice in a society organized by slavery and gendered racial capitalism? In what ways did enslaved women dispute the basis and parameters of justice in the slaveholding

South? How did these women contribute to a Black radical tradition? This is a complicated story to tell, but one with which we must grapple. Resistance was not a romanticized escape for these women and girls, as they paid dearly for their actions. The experiences of enslaved women and girls offer a window into the range of perspectives on justice that expose the imbalances of power that appeared from the very beginning. In taking seriously their violent encounters, we might more fully consider slavery, criminal justice, and its reverberations.

CHAPTER ONE

Virginian Luxuries

But the growth of this country in the sixteenth, seventeenth, and eighteenth
centuries, resting heavily on the availability of free labor, is complicated and
exceptional. Exceptional because of its length and its chattel nature; complex
because of its intricate relationship to the cultural, economic, and intellectual
development of the nation.

—Toni Morrison, *The Source of Self-Regard*

In the beginning decades of the nineteenth century, an unidentified artist
mixed the ochre color palette that featured prominently in a mysterious rendering of life in Virginia. The painting revealed the strokes of oil paint to
capture the flesh of subjects in the portrait. The painter manipulated this ad-
mixture to create contrasts from light to dark hues of the flesh, from deep
ebony to chalky ivory tones. Historians know little of the provenance of such
a painting that featured the portrait of a distinguished gentleman, presumably a planter on the brink of gentility in Virginia, and, on the back, a shocking scene of what is titled *Virginian Luxuries*.[1] Two scenes appear on the back
of the canvas, one of a slaveholder wielding a whip aimed at a featureless
enslaved man and the other of the slaveholder grasping an enslaved woman
(also featureless) by the hips and face as though they were kissing. The enslaved woman's arm seems entangled in his as though to assume consent.
These parallel images offer a glimpse into the gendered and sexual dynamics
of slavery in early Virginia. The law codified such interactions, rendering the
social concepts of patriarchy and later concepts of true womanhood an impossibility for the enslaved. Instead, a different set of characteristics, ideas, and
values concerning African-descended Virginians shaped how they configured in the broader organization of Virginia society.

The provenance of *Virginian Luxuries* and even the motivations of the
painter might lead to a range of conclusions, including that of antislavery sentiment or nineteenth-century pornographic art, or perhaps the artist did not
possess any antislavery sentiment, but found the scenes of slavery appalling,
nonetheless. But the late seventeenth century marked the emergence of a
planter class with aspirations for the material comforts associated with the
gentry. Indeed, fine art allowed for expressions of social standing, and as

the historian Richard L. Bushman reminds us, "People justified the purchase of luxury items as a means of raising themselves to a higher plane."[2] Art signaled one's status in more ways than one. The consumption of luxury goods not only affirmed a particular financial reality, but with art, in particular, an observer might also bear witness to the cultivation of ideas and tastes. In this case, the painting shows a duality both physically and figuratively between the politeness associated with patronizing fine art and the indulgence in the unruly passions of desire, sex, and violence.[3] Moreover, as the literature and postcolonial studies scholar Simon Gikandi reminds us in his *Slavery and the Culture of Taste*, "It is not an exaggeration to say that in many human societies, in all geographical areas of the world, there has been an intimate connection between a sense of cultural achievement and superiority and the practice of domination."[4] Ideas of taste and politeness in this instance are not separate from the possession of power or the ideology of race. The materiality of refinement in Virginia emerged in tandem with the sustained flow of African labor and hinged on the codification of such forms of labor that ensured unlimited access to the productive capacities of enslaved people. While historians lack clarity on the origins of *Virginian Luxuries*, it is striking for what it tells us about popular understandings of the dynamics of gender, sexuality, and power on plantation estates that employed the labor of the enslaved. Such scenes of race and gendered expressions of domination that appear in *Virginian Luxuries* find their origins in the design of colonial slave law. The origins of slave law were firmly rooted in the colonial structure of governance dictated by the mandates and aspirations of empire.

The laws of colonial Virginia supported the economic aspirations of colonists seeking to transform the Chesapeake into a viable enterprise, justified the theft of Native lands, and allowed for the importation and implementation of African slave labor. William Waller Hening, a prominent attorney and chronicler of Virginia laws, offered that, as in every emerging state, the statutes reflect efforts to creates laws "to promote the increase of population, supply the wants of the people, improve the agriculture and staple commodities of the country, provide for the due administration of justice, and guard against the incursions of the aboriginal inhabitants."[5] Indeed, the English regarded the sovereignty and equality of Native peoples an impossibility, even as the English viewed the prospect of their assimilation and religious conversion as obtainable. They might be proselytized or serve as temporary diplomatic allies at best, particularly during conflicts with competing Native nations, but as legal historian Christopher Tomlins explains, "Even if the existence of indigenous sovereigns and governments were acknowledged, in other words,

Virginian Luxuries, ca. 1825 (back of canvas, unidentified artist, probably New England, oil on canvas). The Colonial Williamsburg Foundation (museum purchase).

what rights did they actually possess?"[6] Colonists created property regimes that affirmed their entitlement to Native land; the indentures of Natives, émigrés, and Africans; and the perpetual bondage of African-descended people born into slavery. Native nations resisted these policies and manipulated them when opportunities surfaced, and indentured servants and enslaved people cooperated to undermine this regime, but these efforts continued to fuel the proliferation of statutes to protect colonial interest in property over time. Access to land, the protection of property, and the delineation of policies that made settlement in Virginia a sustainable venture meant that the laws, as Hening put it, "had an obvious tendency to increase the population, and promote the improvement of the country, by rendering the *persons* of many of the inhabitants free from restraint, and by securing to every man the *fruits of his labour*."[7] These fruits were not just material, but rooted in expressions of social and sexual power. The protection of the laws, then, remained in the purview and reach of

Anglo-Americans, and Native and African peoples forced to labor for colonists found limited access to legal recourse. Thus, governing authorities of the colonies did not frame justice or even civic identity in terms of inclusivity. English empire and enterprise were at the heart of colonial law.

In 1606, King James granted the Virginia Company a charter to colonize Virginia, and it did not take long for the impact of English settlement to appear in the landscape and demographics of the Chesapeake. The futile search for ores of gold coincided with their reliance on the Algonquians who dominated the region. By 1616, colonists followed John Rolfe's lead and focused their energies on cultivating a strand of tobacco developed in the Caribbean and popularized throughout Europe.[8] At the same time, Bermuda became the first British colony in the western North Atlantic Ocean to directly import African labor.[9] When the first Africans arrived in the Chesapeake in 1619, they did not arrive as a result of the demand for the importation of enslaved people, but as a result of the pilfering and harassment that occurred between European empires. As historian Philip D. Morgan states, in the initial decades of the colony, "most Chesapeake settlers do not seem to have conceived of African slaves as the solution to their labor scarcity."[10] Hoping to replicate Bermuda's relative agricultural success, the humid conditions of Virginia offered the ideal environment for growing tobacco and led to the recurring depletion of soil and the increased demand for land. A few years later, colonists enjoyed every incentive for producing the crop, with access to profits ranging anywhere between five and ten times the initial costs of planting a crop and the headright system that granted land for those with the means to cover their transportation to North America, as well as the travel costs associated with bringing in more laborers. Based on this system, those who settled in Virginia received fifty acres along with an additional fifty acres for every additional person or laborer they brought to the colony.[11] Two decades later, Virginia became the leading supplier of tobacco in Europe, which meant that colonists made greater demands on the land. Consequently, this led to heightened tensions and eventually persistent violent conflict with Native peoples. Colonists brought with them not only their aspirations but also deadly diseases and violence that led to a significant decline in the Native population.[12] From the arrival of the colonists to 1669, the Algonquian population declined from 24,000 to 2,000, while the English population doubled.[13] The devastating impact on Native nations and the expansive exploitation of land in the Chesapeake marked only the beginning of colonial encroachment.[14] Distinctions made between Natives, Europeans, and Africans and, furthermore, the status of freedom framed the bounds of civic identity within the British empire.[15]

Lawmakers were attentive to ethnic distinctions in the creation of colonial law even as these demarcations appeared less fixed in early jurisprudence.

Racial lines were relatively fluid, and gender and class status remained an important configuration of colonial social relations during the first half of the seventeenth century.[16] As early as 1643, the colonial assembly in Virginia began to grapple with the gendered and ethnic distinctions between inhabitants. As scholars have shown, so much of Anglo-Virginian identity hinged on clear demarcations of class, gender, and eventually race.[17] Historian Kathleen Brown observes that "in Virginia, discourses of gender and race became integral to the planter class's practice of power as well as to its ability to communicate its own authority."[18] Historians argue that race appeared less prominently initially, but ideas about the productive capacity of enslaved women were embedded in the early tax laws.[19] In 1643, lawmakers determined which individuals were "tithable" in order to support the militia and arms supply of the colonies. In England, taxes were assessed based on the property owned in a given household, which the law viewed as a unit of production. Early conditions of colonial life in Virginia meant that households appeared less prominently than individually driven units of production because of the gender disparity of the population and the dependence on servants and enslaved people for labor.[20] The constant threat of conflict with Native nations also exacerbated the demand for tax revenue to support the military needs of the colony. Initially, Virginia imposed a tax on men beginning at the age of sixteen, as they were distinguished as the productive laborers who performed work associated with agricultural revenue and possibly military service. Despite the fact that English women performed agricultural labor as well, they remained exempt from taxation. Enslaved men and women, however, became "tithables" at the age of sixteen. As Brown has argued, this tax law associated enslaved women with the gendered labor performed by men.[21] West African societies viewed the agricultural labor of enslaved women as highly valuable to their gendered identity, but the English reconstituted the meaning of their skilled labor to disassociate them from the tenets of English womanhood reserved for Anglo-Virginian women. African-descended women navigated life in colonial Virginia with a sense of the legal distinctions between indentured servitude, freedom, and lifelong bondage.

Colonial law codified slavery as a distinctly African condition, implicating the reproductive futures of enslaved women. In 1662, the Virginia legislature proposed and enacted a law that stated that enslaved women served "according to the condition of the mother."[22] Largely known as *partus sequitur ventrem*, the measure emerged from questions concerning "whether children got by any Englishman upon a negro woman should be slave or free." Clarification of the matter revealed an unspoken truth in the chambers of the grand assembly—that of interracial sex, and rape. These matters were of critical importance in a society where no assembly desired to care for orphans. If not orphans, then, enslaved children became quite the opposite of a financial burden. They became the key to sustaining the financial momentum that came with economic mobility in a burgeoning plantocracy. *Partus sequitur ventrem* supplied generations of laborers over the course of two centuries, but the historian Jennifer L. Morgan argues that "enslaved women's maternal possibilities became a crucial vehicle by which racial meaning was concretized."[23] The effects of this measure shaped the maternal lives of enslaved women and sexual dynamics on plantations and in urban households in the South and spilled over into the lives of African-descended people if they became free. The racial meanings tied to slavery made Blackness synonymous with slavery. Scholars have recognized this phenomenon, but these legal developments must be viewed in relation to the reproductive lives of enslaved women. Law was no mere abstract concept but the very lifeline of economic sustainability and social power for early Virginians.

The aspirations of the British empire relied on the economic viability of the colonies. A decade into the seventeenth century, John Rolfe experimented with the prospect of growing tobacco. When Rolfe tried the tobacco native to the Chesapeake, he found it robust in flavor yet bitter to the taste. Having collected some seeds from Trinidad and Caracas, Venezuela, Rolfe experimented with *Nicotiana tabacum* seeds to cultivate a crop of tobacco as close to the brand of tobacco grown by the Spanish, which at that point had dominated European markets.[24] By 1618, the demand for tobacco from Virginia doubled.[25] This imported plant that Rolfe poked, pried, and cured set in motion a shift in the flow of people and the processing of land. To begin, the headright system ensured fifty acres of land for the costs of transporting more settlers across the Atlantic to the Chesapeake shores.[26] Acres along the James River were planted with seeds to be cultivated by indentured servants working toward the promise of social mobility beyond anything they could imagine in Europe. As layers of soil nourished one crop after the next, the soil rapidly declined, leading many settlers to encroach on lands claimed by Natives.[27]

Algonquian-speaking Natives raided the budding plantations, but the lure of tobacco proved impermeable as the colonists witnessed yet another successful crop. These harvests, and subsequent sales abroad, provided much needed capital to support the labor force that the crop demanded. A decline in white labor led to the increased purchase of African slaves to populate the tobacco fields in efforts to expand the capacity to grow and sell tobacco.[28] Seeds taken from Latin America and the Caribbean took root in the Chesapeake, breeding new demands of empire and facilitating a similar journey taken by the earliest Africans to arrive in North America. These colonial objectives hinged on the extraction of Native land and the labor of enslaved people who increasingly populated the North American colonies through the transatlantic slave trade. Without the labor of these African-descended peoples, the prosperity of the British colonies was deemed implausible. The colonists understood this, and according to their logic, the legal authorization to compel enslaved people to labor on planter terms made the governance of colonies in North America a malleable enterprise often without English precedent.[29] While English legal traditions shaped colonial law, many officials deliberated legal matters with responses specific to the conditions of slavery and warfare in the colonies. The reproductive labor of enslaved women became essential to the logic of inherited slavery.

The enactment of the 1662 *partus sequitur ventrem* law underscores the manner in which the Virginia House of Burgesses adapted English legal traditions to colonial conditions. The burgesses considered this concept based on Henry Swinburne's *A Brief Treatise of Testaments and Last Wills* (1590) to determine who possessed the legal capacity to make wills.[30] As Thomas D. Morris reveals in his analysis of this legal matter, Swinburne applied civil law to release a child from inheriting the legal burdens of the father "as a principle of freedom, not slavery."[31] Some scholars argue that the phrase is derived from legal matters concerning bastardy, with slaveholders standing in as the lawful guardians in the absence of any legal recognition of slave marriages. These considerations, while tethered to what English law may permit with regard to the inherited condition of an enslaved person, lead some to simply conclude that the law was created out of uncertainty about the property entitlements of a slaveholder.[32] The result is a law that not only made slavery possible through the bodies of enslaved women but also codified their bodies "as a location of pleasure, production, and procreation as well as a site of exploitation, alienation, loss, and shame," as argued by the historian Brenda E. Stevenson.[33] This legal concept is illustrated in the everyday interactions and relationships forged and forced within a society that foreclosed the possibility of enslaved women's ownership of their bodies and manual and reproductive labor. The legal codification of the reproductive labor of enslaved women in colonial law made a sexually based determination of slave status to constitute slavery as a "natural condition" of African-descended women and their children. The colonial period marked an era of unprecedented legal authority granted to burgesses who often held an interest in the outcomes of cases under consideration. The racial and gendered fluidity of the colony's earliest stages shifted toward further distinctions. The changing tides of colonial law reflected the responses of colonial lawmakers to the threat posed by alliances made among colonists, Natives, and Africans.

English colonization ignited new dimensions of warfare and violence in the region, a place of contestation that served as the homelands of Native polities, the site of captivity for Africans, and competition among European empires. The volatility of the landscape made colonists increasingly aware of the capacity for insurrection, among the business interests represented by the English, but also among the class of servants who labored in the colony. In 1639, the burgesses passed a statute that declared, "All persons except Negroes are to be provided with arms and ammunition or be fined at the pleasure of the governor and council."[34] While the status of African-descended people did not quite align with the "chattel principle" that defined their legal status in later years, the ambiguity of the servant class showed signs of increasing clarity. The distinction along Native, African, and European lines became important features of the legal tapestry designed by the Virginia legislature. For them, conditions on the ground warranted these developments.

In 1676, Nathaniel Bacon led a rebellion of free and indentured inhabitants of Virginia that underscored the threat of class conflict that united men across racial lines. A multiethnic collaboration between discontented Englishmen and African men, the rebellion signaled the possibility of disorder and mayhem for a colony struggling to clarify social distinctions. The historian Ira Berlin observes that "throughout the seventeenth century, black and white ran away together, joined in petty conspiracies, and, upon occasion, stood shoulder-to-shoulder against the weighty champions of established authority."[35] The decline in tobacco prices, exorbitant taxes, and heightened anxieties about neighboring Native groups led Bacon on a rampage of accusations against them and demands that colonial governor William Berkeley tighten restrictions on Native groups within the vicinity. Berkeley refused, which inspired Bacon to mobilize nearly 500 disgruntled men, who torched Jamestown.[36] Bacon's movement of the common man included men of European and African descent, as well as some Native allies whom the group terrorized not long after relying on their assistance.[37] The event, however, did not mark one of racial harmony. It became increasingly clear that the rebellion served an accumulation of grievances expressed by free Anglo-Virginians. The historian Edmund S. Morgan notes that "discontent with upper-class leadership would be vented in racial hatred, in a pattern that statesmen and politicians of a later age would have found familiar."[38] Before Charles II made attempts to intervene in the rebellion, disease killed Bacon, and, without their leader, the rebels ended their assault, with many faced with execution.[39] Berkeley stood by his censure of the affair, and yet Bacon's rebellion served as a cautionary tale for colonial governors and lawmakers to be wary of the potential for multiethnic and class revolution and made painstaking efforts to cement the bonds between elite and aspiring planters. This common thread gave the local and state consensus concerning justice its shape. As Morgan notes, the liberty of such men ultimately meant the exclusion and persistent bondage of African-descended people and the displacement of Native peoples. Bacon's rebellion birthed the lessons of white supremacy as political necessity in order to ensure the longevity of race-based slavery and economic mobility.[40]

Throughout the colonial era, conflict between multiethnic servants and English proprietors led to the enactment of laws that protected the economic interests of free colonists. This meant that to ensure the security of their landholdings and authority, the law became a tool through which to define the social parameters of servitude or lifelong bondage. In 1669, the Virginia legislature attended to the enslaved in particular. Bacon's rebellion already established the possible threat of blurred lines between the English, Natives, and people of African descent. Even as society became increasingly structured around the limited terms of servitude for European migrants, and perpetual bondage for African-descended people, the law gave the colonists invigorated power over the enslaved. In 1669, the burgesses passed "An Act about the casuall killing of slaves" to address the potential for deadly violence as a form of discipline between slaveholders and the enslaved. The statute states, "Be it enacted and declared by this grand assembly, if any slave resist his master . . . and by the extremity of the correction should chance to die, that his death shall not be accompted Felony, but the master (or that other person appointed by the master to punish him) be acquit from molestation, since it cannot be presumed that propensed malice (which alone makes murther Felony) should induce any man to destroy his own estate."[41] The 1669 statute made a clear distinction of the power that slaveholders exercised over the enslaved. The implications for this law can be seen in the countless murders and unrecorded deaths of enslaved people at the hands of owners who possessed the legal right to discipline their human property to the point of death. Malice appears nearly an impossibility since the legislature could hardly imagine a slaveholder destroying "his [or her] own estate." By the next century, the burgesses made a provision for deadly losses by offering compensation for enslaved people executed for offenses.

By the end of the seventeenth century, Parliament dissolved the mono-poly on the slave trade driven by the Royal African Company and colonists increasingly invested in the importation of African slave labor.[42] The empha-sis on African labor meant that the investment of the planter went a long way compared to the truncated terms of servitude associated with indentured ser-vants. The shift was notable in the demographic transformations of the popu-lation of Virginia, which included thousands of Africans by 1700 and growth by the tens of thousands in the mid-eighteenth century.[43] After importations reached a peak rate of increase, much of the expansion of the enslaved popu-lation occurred through the reproductive labor of enslaved women.[44] Ac-cording to one estimate, by the mid-1700s there were two children for every enslaved woman, and they produced "enough children to more than replace adults of the previous generation."[45] These children appeared in an array of hues, leading to pejoratively applied categories like mulatto, quadroon, and octoroon to account for the varied shades of enslaved people in Virginia.[46] The reproductive labor of enslaved women illumines the complexity of their sexual lives, lives marked by force, and also the possibilities of desire and pleasure.

Enslaved women's sexuality might be shaped by the power dynamics evi-dent in *Virginian Luxuries* or by enslaved women and their male counterparts with whom they shared cabins or made painstaking efforts to meet between neighboring plantations. The colonial era began with iterations of fluidity in intimate relationships forged across class and ethnicity. Whereas Africans who arrived as enslaved laborers in the early and mid-seventeenth century worked alongside indentured servants and many eventually secured their freedom after a term of servitude, the generations of Africans arriving in large numbers coincided with the enactment of laws that placed more parameters on life for African-descended inhabitants of the colony.[47] Bacon's rebellion loomed prominently in the memory of colonial leaders, and the increase in the African population reminded them of the possibilities for interethnic and intra-ethnic rebellion. It became essential for Europeans to unite across class, and efforts to make slavery and servitude a distinctly African experience were underway.

Thousands of captives regularly arrived on the shores of the Chesapeake as more planters possessed the means to make long-term investments in en-slaved people. Many of these first arrivals had already survived the transatlan-tic voyage from West Africa to the Americas. These people came from the colonies chartered by the Portuguese, French, Dutch, and Spanish having brought with them their knowledge of the culture, religious practices, laws, and social norms of these imperial outposts.[48] This knowledge shaped the manner in which they navigated life in the Chesapeake, a place that still allowed for a relatively fluid dynamic between slavery and indentured servitude and the possibilities of freedom. As historians have shown, in the early seventeenth century many of the colonial laws were not so strict as to prevent free Black men from owning property, bearing arms, testifying in court and even voting.[49] These "charter generations" or Atlantic creoles, as historians have referred to them, leveraged opportunities to baptize their children, purchase property, and even own enslaved people. Most of these Afro-Virginians arrived from other port cities in the Atlantic and crossed imperial boundaries, bringing with them languages and customs from West African, Spanish, Portuguese, Dutch, and French cultures.[50] By the mid-eighteenth century, Africans made up nearly half of the population of Virginia, and the ties between elite and common planters were solidified by colonial laws that made distinctions between European, Native, and African.

The transatlantic cultural encounters of enslaved women in Virginia shaped their legal understandings and strategies. For instance, Mary Aggie, an enslaved woman, at the age of twenty-one petitioned the General Court for her freedom. Aggie worked at a tavern owned by Anne Marot Sullivant, a slave owner who employed the labor of at least four enslaved women charged with the cooking, cleaning, washing, serving, and general upkeep of the establishment. These women served at the pleasure of Sullivant and her husband, as well as guests of the tavern. In addition to the labor she supplied, Aggie likely encountered a number of guests and boarders with whom she interacted. These interactions could potentially subject her to a number of abuses, but they also might furnish important insights and information that she applied to her experience in colonial Virginia. The petition and superior court records have not survived, so we cannot ascertain a complete account of Aggie's claims to freedom. Governor William Gooch, however, found her testimony compelling as she expressed her unwavering faith in a Christian God. Her religious conversion, spurred by the theological underpinnings of the British empire and its colonial charters, made available access to participation in the religious culture of Virginia. While Aggie did not successfully attain her freedom, her testimony and expressions of faith were compelling enough to later inspire Gooch to make the "benefit of the clergy," which made mercy or pardon a possibility for enslaved and free Black Virginians accused of crimes. Appeals for reprieve and the decision to make clemency a possibility worked synchronously with the imperatives of empire and the paternalism that gave such power dynamics their shape. Indeed, as legal historian Michelle McKinley argues, "Nowhere or at any point did the discourse of mercy undermine social hierarchy."[51] This measure would be put to the test when Aggie stood before the courts, not for her freedom, but for accusations of theft.

In 1730, Aggie stood accused of stealing several household items from her mistress and pleaded not guilty before the court of oyer and terminer in York County.[52] On learning of her arrest, Gooch remembered Aggie as the woman who compellingly articulated her commitment to the Christian faith, but these previous pronouncements failed to work in favor of her innocence. The court found her guilty, and Aggie faced the prospect of execution, as was the custom for felonious theft. Gooch argued that "as a christian, she was Intitled to the benefit of the Clergy," and with the added layer of possibility and complexity thrown into the matter, the justices were split evenly on the decision, causing Gooch to appeal to the General Court, the superior court of Virginia.[53] Bringing the matter before the superior court opened up the possibility for precedent, as rights to the benefit of clergy did not extend to the enslaved. The benefit of the clergy allowed for commuted sentences for first-time convicted felons who professed their Christian faith. The General Court failed to reach a consensus, and Gooch took the case to the solicitor and attorney general of England for consideration. Officials in England did not find any legal measures that outlawed the possibility of issuing the benefit of the clergy, making more promising the prospects for clemency. Aggie's case mobilized support from Gooch, who facilitated the effort to establish legislation that allowed for people to invoke the benefit of the clergy regardless of race.[54] These theological undercurrents that shaped the possibility of mercy also informed how African-descended women like Aggie acted on established and locally recognized ideas of fairness and evenhandedness. Even as many contemporaries might view the Church of England as proscriptive, there were fundamental rights associated with Christianity that African-descended people appropriated for legal ends. Enslaved women searched for any possible path of recourse, as their reproductive futures and an increasingly secularized law became the lifeline lawmakers relied on to sustain slavery in the British colonies.

The period in which Virginia was restored to a Crown colony set in motion an era in which lawmakers made an effort to stabilize more flexible social dynamics into fixed categories of bondage and freedom, and race and caste. This period marked the institution of *partus sequitur ventrem*. Moreover, in the same law that codified enslaved women's access to the "benefit of the clergy" in response to Mary Aggie's case in "An Act for settling some doubts," burgesses clarified the role of testimony from Native and African-descended witnesses.[55] The law observed, "And whereas negros, mulattos, and Indians, have lately been frequently allowed to give testimony as lawful witnesses in the general court, and other courts of this colony, when they have professed themselves to be christians, and been able to give some account of the principles of the christian religion," attesting to the fluidity of inclusion and possibilities of civic participation on the basis of professed faith in Christianity.[56] The calculating spirit of the age, and the emerging discourse of race, led lawmakers to assert, "But forasmuch as they are people of such base and corrupt natures, that the credit of their testimony cannot be certainly depended upon, and some juries have altogether rejected their evidence, and others have given full credit thereto: For preventing the mischiefs that may possibly happen by admitting such precarious evidence."[57] The "base and corrupt natures" that presumably clouded the judgment of Native and African-descended people codified distinctions among inhabitants of the colonies that determined their capacity for innocence.

The development of colonial law began haphazardly, almost as a response to colonial conditions but with much emphasis on English common law. By the eighteenth century, however, as evident in other English colonies, such as Barbados, Jamaica, and South Carolina, much of the revised codes reflected the responses of colonial governments to the possible threats of Natives, Africans, and indentured servants.[58] The "Act for settling some doubts" concluded that "no negro, mulatto, or Indian, either a slave or free, shall hereafter be admitted in any court of this colony, to be sworn as a witness, or give evidence in any cause whatsoever, except upon the trial of a slave, for a capital offence."[59] The absence of testimony from Natives and free and enslaved African-descended people foreclosed the possibility of white culpability in conflicts involving Anglo-Virginians, unless their white peers testified against them. The legal hierarchy created by these laws dictated who participated in legal processes as legitimate purveyors of information.

In 1692, the Virginia House of Burgesses passed "an act for more speedy prosecution of negroes and other slaves for capital offences" to immediately attend to the case under consideration rather than wait for the regularly scheduled sitting of the court that tried free men and women in the commonwealth.[60] This act supported the "more effectual punishing conspiracies and insurrections" and led to the establishment of a separate trial process that began with the immediate imprisonment of the enslaved person charged and to the prosecution of the case under a separate process that replaced a trial by jury with a panel of four or more justices of the peace. Prior to 1765, these justices were appointed by the governor, but for fear of offering commissions

based on the inclinations of the executive office, these justices afterward
needed to be formally trained in the law, and by the time the colony became a
state, the Constitution of 1776 allowed for the governor to appoint justices
with the advice of the Privy Council. These justices tried the cases and issued
judgments and sentences on capital cases involving enslaved people in courts
of oyer and terminer. On learning of a capital offense alleged against an enslaved person, the sheriff held him or her in the county jail until trial. The
conditions of jails varied in the different counties throughout Virginia, but
jails typically involved a two-story structure that served as the residence of
the jailer and his family as well as prisoners awaiting trial.[61] The first state
penitentiary did not appear until 1804, and most matters concerning convicts
were handled at the local or county level.

Once the sheriff secured the enslaved person in jail, officials commissioned a court of oyer and terminer to gather evidence and testimony and
determine the outcome of the case. These ad hoc county courts, typically
composed of at least five justices of the peace, often included slaveholders
and, until 1865, expanded in function to consider cases of enslaved defendants facing felonies.[62] While enslaved people could not issue a testimony
against an Anglo-Virginian, the court allowed for a confession or plea and for
the owner of the enslaved person to offer a defense for the alleged crime.[63]
While the procedures encouraged a "speedy trial," these matters could take
months to resolve, especially if white locals submitted a petition in support of
a revised sentence.[64] The trial proceedings were a matter not only of order
but also of the beginning of justice. The law and trial proceedings outlined
the rights, albeit limited rights, that enslaved people possessed when charged
with capital offenses. As historians have shown, English common law made
possible some semblance of due process for the enslaved, but this changed as
criminal legal proceedings increasingly functioned under the authority of
slaveholders appointed as justices of the peace in the form of panels that replaced the function of juries.[65] The possibility for witnesses and slaveholders
to attest to their character might overturn a deadly sentence to that of whipping, sale outside of the colony, or dismembering. Burgesses designed this
law "for the better government of Negros, Mulattos, and Indians, bond or
free."[66] What became clear is that the law presumed the inability of the enslaved to self-govern, making provision for the protection of the rights of
white Virginians to issue various forms of correction, even if said punishment
led to death. Up until 1723, enslaved people could not testify in capital cases
unless they issued a confession, but this rule changed to allow for enslaved

witnesses to provide evidence in cases involving enslaved people charged for crimes. Enslaved witnesses might have a direct relationship to the enslaved person on trial or might have been present during the incident under investigation. As the following chapters show, these relationships between enslaved defendants and witnesses might offer evidence of kinship and alliances built over time or fraught dynamics filled with conflict and tension. Most criminal cases were not decided on the basis of enslaved witness testimony alone but included depositions of white witnesses as well. Acquittals were rare but made more available to those accused of committing noncapital crimes.

During the first decades of the eighteenth century, Virginia burgesses passed statutes that authorized the discipline of enslaved people, with the issue of "dismemberment," which gave a glimpse into the range of "corrective" measures they were subjected to.[67] Lawmakers addressed the issue of escape or going at large, whether for shorter periods or more permanently, by "dismembering." For these offenses, the county courts were permitted "to order and direct every such slave to be punished, by dismembering, or any other way, not touching the life as the said county court shall think fit."[68] The statute offered that, "if any slave shall happen to die by means of such dismembering, by order of the county court, or for by reason of any stroke or blow given, during his or her correction; by his or her owner, for any offence by such slave committed, or for or by reason of any accidental blow whatsoever, given by such owner; no person concerned in such dismembering correction, or accidental homicide, shall undergo any prosecution or punishment for the same."[69] The only exception to this rule required proof of malice. What rights might a slaveholder possess to ensure the protection of his or her investment or inspire future compliance if the enslaved person were caught and reprimanded? The latter remained a more complicated dilemma, but the burgesses pointedly accounted for the possibility of recovering financial losses incurred as a result of discipline. Part of retaining that investment in human property appeared in the calculus of dismembering without "touching the life." The statutes provided that "all and every owner or owners of such slave or slaves, shall and may bring his or her action, for recovery of damages for such slave or slaves so killed or dying, as if this act had never been made."[70] If the enslaved person subjected to these punitive measures died, the court would rely on the presence of a white person to contest the homicide of the enslaved defendant. Thus, contestations about the deadly punishment of enslaved people accused of the offense occurred only in the rarest of instances. As the statute clarifies, homicide that resulted from efforts to dismember can be understood as "accidental." Stipulations about the discipline of fugitives were not created without provocation, and the laws remained in practice as the colony shifted to a state in the new republic.

The decisions of the burgesses in the nearly first two centuries of the Virginia colony established legal traditions that Virginians brought to the revolutionary cause. While the colonial legislative bodies wielded a significant degree of power and flexibility in responding to the interests and demands of colonists, they were less prominent politically at the heart of the empire. By the late eighteenth century, England boasted global dimensions of imperial power, and North America remained one of many colonial outposts, albeit one of tremendous value. Virginia joined the chorus of colonial cries of bondage and lambasted the Crown and Parliament for abuses of power. Revolutionary rhetoric used the language of slavery to emphasize the vulnerability of colonists. Liberty was slavery's opposite, and the patriots intended to secure it for themselves. These ideals were not lost on the enslaved; indeed, liberty germinated fervently in the minds of enslaved and free Black Virginians.[71] We understand this in their efforts to flee the homes of slaveholders during the Revolutionary War and efforts prior to and after the war to probe and act on the possibilities of liberty. The new republic, however, would become one of liberty for property-holding white men and one of slavery for African-descended people. The Commonwealth of Virginia deployed a secularized set of rights determined by state legislators that introduced a legal culture that worked in the interests of the yeomanry and planter aristocracy. Laws of a free nation worked in tandem with the maintenance of racial slavery.

The legal culture of Virginia did not take shape within the exclusive domain of the burgesses, but after the Revolutionary War political figures like Thomas Jefferson, former governor, founder, and president, made connections between the emergence of epistemologies about race and the development of the law. In the only book published by the statesman, Jefferson's *Notes on the State of Virginia* included a series of queries intended to offer a comprehensive overview of the history, culture, and physical attributes of the commonwealth. Most notably, in between the mundane details of the flora and fauna found within the crevices of the Blue Ridge Mountains lies query 14, aptly titled "Laws." In this distillation of environmental and human ecosystems, Jefferson not only delineates the legal processes that gave the commonwealth a more systematized portrayal but also spends a great deal of space devoted to explaining the distinctions between the races. Throughout most of the query, enslaved people appear as mere property, chattels to be entailed and tithed for transactional purposes, recipients of the fruits of civilization and the oversight of Anglo-American men. Jefferson's account offers his own interpretation of the "substantive" differences of both moral and scientifically oriented attributes, but he aims to hone the reader's understandings of matters not just of race but of beauty.

For Jefferson, matters of beauty require an analysis of the bodies and features of women. "The first difference that strikes us is that of colour," he begins. "Is it not the foundation of a greater or less share of beauty in the two races?"[72] His fixation on the appearance and appeal of women shows the gendered dimensions of theories about racial science. To begin with color is to point out the phenotypical distinction between the races to advance a broader, but unsubstantiated, argument about the biological differences between the races. "Are not the fine mixtures of red and white, the expressions of every passion by greater or less suffusions of colour in the one, preferable to that eternal monotony, which reigns in the countenances, that immoveable veil of black which covers all the emotions of the other race?"[73] he posits. If one does not find color alone compelling enough to be convinced of the incompatibility of the races, then he offers: "Add to these, flowing hair, a more elegant symmetry of form, their own judgement in favour of the whites, declared by their preference of them, as uniformly as is the preference of the Oranootan for the black women over his own species." These aesthetic and sexualized contexts in which he measures the integrity of each race factor into how women of African descent configured into the laws, even if in contradictory ways. Enslaved women, men, and their offspring can be enslaved, but also sexually available to white men, betraying his own theory of superiority in more ways than one. But why beauty? Jefferson asserts, "The circumstance of superior beauty, is thought worthy of attention in the propagation of our horses, dogs, and other domestic animals; why not in that of man?"[74] *Notes on the State of Virginia* proposes a system of classification that not only includes the species of plants and animals but also imposes a theory of racial hierarchy to help readers understand the logic of Virginia law—it codified what planters and legislators already began to put into practice, even as they made efforts to prohibit American involvement in the transatlantic slave trade. Beauty involved matters concerning Virginian luxuries and tastes. The corporeal qualities of enslaved women did not warrant the designation of racial equal, but the reproductive lives of these women could be exploited to advance the economic interests of slaveholders. The intellectual argument for the inferiority of Black women corresponded with the ideological underpinnings of race that gave Southern law its distinctive shape.

The law determined the degree to which enslaved people possessed rights, and it also organized life and labor in the commonwealth, showing the manner in which racial theories configured in the application of the law. This, of course, shaped the contours of everyday life for enslaved women in Virginia, even as they confounded this logic. Advancing more theories of African-descended people, Jefferson offers: "They seem to require less sleep. A black, after hard labour through the day, will be induced by the slightest amusements to sit up till midnight, or later, though knowing he must be out with the first dawn of the morning."[75] These ideas, proposed without the context of violence as a compelling motivator for work, also assume that enslaved people possessed no desires to create lives apart from slave owners. This broader assumption that Africans were best suited to build the enterprises of white Virginians undergirds popular perceptions and expectations of the Black work ethic that bear consequences well into the twentieth century. To pick up on their lives from where they left off the night before because slave-holders monopolized the majority of their time in the hours of daylight meant that the enslaved treasured moments for themselves, privacy, and interactions with one another apart from the surveillance of planters and overseers. These theories were conveniently grounded in the absence of the context of forced bondage, or any ideas formulated by the enslaved. What follows is the ways in which race props up the fantasy of contented and compliant enslaved people. But the lives of the enslaved involved much more complex strategies of survival and belonging.

The manner in which Africans forged ties of kin and community speaks to the formation of multiethnic connections, not only in the contexts of the diversity of Natives and Europeans but also with respect to the various West African and Atlantic origins of Africans in Virginia. The historian Michael Gomez explains how Virginia's population included enslaved people taken from the Bight of Biafra and high levels of Akan speakers from the Gold Coast.[76] Ibo and Akan cultures shared characteristics that might have informed reconstituted bonds of kin. For instance, Gomez explains that "both had established a high regard for women, reflected by such evidence as the veneration and popularity of the earth mothers Asase Yaa and Ala, the perfection of gender balance represented in the name of the high god Chineke, the matriliny of the Akan and some of the Igbo, and the freedom with which Igbo women engaged in commercial and civic enterprise."[77] Evidence of African cultural formations that precede the Middle Passage remind us that enslaved women brought epistemologies that grounded their sense of self and their values to the colony. Colonial life and collective survival meant the possibility of multiethnic ties, but the law soon proscribed the nature of these interactions. In 1723, Virginia lawmakers outlawed "meetings of negroes, or other slaves" unless they met in the contexts of church services held on Sundays or deemed lawful by local authorities.[78] Not only did the law limit the nature of gatherings among the enslaved, but the law also circumscribed collective interactions across different legal and ethnic categories. The law forbade any "white person, free negro, mulatto, or Indian" from keeping company with enslaved people in gatherings, a form of unlawful assembly. Any violators of this law faced a fine of fifteen shillings or 150 pounds of tobacco to pay the informant.[79] Any enslaved person who entered another plantation without the consent of his or her owner, authorized "the master, owner, or overseer of any such plantation or quarter, to correct and give such slave or slaves ten lashes, well laid on, on his or her bare back."[80] The premise of this law was based on the idea that the bodies of the enslaved required collective governance, with flexibility built into who might administer "correction." Ideas about the capacity of the enslaved for self-governance were rooted in emerging theories about the intellectual facility of Africans.

Ideas about the mental capabilities of African-descended people worked in tandem with the logic of slave law in Virginia. The propensity for reason proved one's capacity and potential for virtue. Jefferson inferred, "Comparing them by their faculties of memory, reason, and imagination, it appears to me, that in memory they are equal to the whites; in reason much inferior, as I think one could scarcely be found capable of tracing and comprehending the investigations of Euclid; and that in imagination they are dull, tasteless, and anomalous."[81] If reason can be based on the mastery of European concepts made available in formal education, then perhaps the critique of the enslaved and their ability to facilitate reason points to the manner in which they are prohibited from institutions of formal learning. But this does not factor into Jefferson's analysis, and, indeed, it is not because he lacks any interactions with intelligent African-descended peoples who have mastered the epistemologies of the Western world. Benjamin Banneker, a self-taught mathematician, astronomer, and surveyor, is one of many people who embody the contemporary contradiction in this argument. Moreover, the African poetess Phillis Wheatley built a body of world-renowned poetry that ultimately hit a nerve, as Jefferson noted: "Religion indeed has produced a Phyllis Whately; but it could not produce a poet. The compositions published under her name are below the dignity of criticism."[82] The query set out to make clear the impossibility of African-descended people's capacity for reason, intellect, and imagination. Leaders in the early republic subscribed to the connections between the capacity for reason and that of virtue and independence.[83] These were the tenets that qualified one for civic equality in the new nation, but such principles did not translate apart from race in this case.

Without accounting for the power and design of Virginia law, the phenotypical and intellectual attributes of a particular race became the exclusionary basis of liberty. "This unfortunate difference of colour, and perhaps of faculty, is a powerful obstacle to the emancipation of these people," Jefferson concludes.[84] Drawing his own conclusions about the correlation between skin color and intellect, Jefferson tethered the prospect of liberty for African-descended people to late eighteenth-century constructions of race. These ideas involved a combination of biological theories and phenotypical classifications that established a hierarchy of the races along a scale of gradation that relegated Native peoples inferior but perhaps assimilable and African-descended people as particularly inferior. He was neither alone nor solely responsible for such ideas since an entire field of craniology and racial classification was underway.[85] While these theories were not grounded in substantive evidence, much of this perception of the races paved the way for an American logic of slavery and thus slave law. These ideas proposed in Jefferson's *Notes on the State of Virginia*, along with many studies of race to follow, became the basis on which slave law was expanded.

Well before Jefferson penned his *Notes on the State of Virginia*, these ideas were embedded in the everyday legal interactions of colonial inhabitants. Jefferson's *Notes*, then, established his reputation as a leading intellectual of his time; it marked a demonstration of his knowledge of the theories and European epistemologies of what rendered an orderly society. Even as he embraced racist ideas about African-descended people, the reality of bondage and the contradiction it posed to the premise of the revolution did not sit well with him. In his *Notes on the State of Virginia*, Jefferson outlined his thoughts on the problem of slavery and believed that new restrictions on the transatlantic slave trade could facilitate a reduction in the reliance on slave labor. In 1783, Jefferson proposed a revision to the Constitution for Virginia that prohibited the introduction of any new enslaved people and declared enslaved people born after December 31, 1800, free, but Virginia maintained the provisions of the 1776 Constitution, which did not outlaw slavery or accommodate gradual abolition.[86] Congress eventually made the importation of enslaved people illegal after 1808, but this development fueled the domestic slave market and coincided with the development of statutes that became the laws that specifically governed the lives of the enslaved. Enslaved women, men, and children were excluded from the promises of liberty and egalitarianism that inspired the revolution. But this fact did not deter them from embracing their own ideas and desires for freedom. Even as they were governed by the new government and laws of the commonwealth, enslaved women operated on terms outside the parameters of slave codes and within a different set of principles, even if it meant their death.

In 1793, Daphney, an enslaved woman living in James City, appeared on trial for the murder of Joel Gathright, the overseer who supervised and enforced the work she performed. The court decided to postpone her execution, for reasons not mentioned in the record. The reasons for postponing the execution might have been that Daphney appeared with child or perhaps locals or witnesses offered new evidence or requests for reprieve on her behalf. We know that she waited from July 16, 1793, until the first Friday of August that same year to learn of her fate on the gallows.[87] Based on testimony, Daphney faced execution because she decided to help another woman, Nelly, fight off the repeated blows inflicted on her by Gathright. The women began to whip the overseer, changing the tide of the conflict by overpowering him through their collective force. Daphney's intervention and their joint effort to fight him off conveyed a sense of outrage and intolerance for his unchecked violence. Overseers possessed the right to enforce the demands of laboring on a plantation and performed the disciplinary work that many planters avoided. Enslavers and their overseers disciplined enslaved women regardless of whether they were pregnant. Nothing in the record confirmed that the court postponed Daphney's execution because of pregnancy, but Nelly appeared well into her third trimester and advanced in pregnancy during the time of her beating. When Daphney caught sight of Nelly, with a swollen belly trying to protect her child in utero from one blow after the next, she quickly came to her aid, and perhaps once the overseer fell to the ground, they wanted to ensure he would remain there. What flashed in their minds as they fought off and soon overcame this man who surveilled their every move each day? Did they recall similar scenes that inflicted their memory of life on the estate? After they fought Gathright off of Nelly, both women fled into town in search of Champion Travis, their enslaver. They did not attempt to escape entirely, but likely called on the authority of the slaveholder in order to make an appeal of their innocence. Locals knew that matters between demanding overseers and enslaved people escalated with relative ease after bouts of brewing tensions. Daphney sought to protect not only Nelly but her child as well—an action that also served Travis's financial interests. But Daphney likely did not risk her life to protect the coffers of a slaveholder. On their way to town, they ran into the local miller, who urged them to continue making their way to Travis, but just before they continued, Daphney asked whether a woman could be executed for the murder of a man. Here, she called on the gender norms that demanded honor and civility among men, especially in their encounters with women, and pregnant women in particular. But did late eighteenth-century Virginia begin to view enslaved women on these gendered terms? The racial and gendered lines of slavery seem to suggest that the courts might not view the incident this way. With no response recorded from the miller, the women made their way to Travis and eventually stood trial in their own defense.[88] Knowledge of Nelly's advanced pregnancy during the beating seemed to appeal to the locals who petitioned the court for her reprieve. And perhaps Daphney's instincts to stop the assault on the pregnant woman also made the jurists think twice before sending her to the gallows. Ultimately, their fate remained tethered to the fact of Gathright's death. If overseers, often below the class standing of planters, could not rely on the court to protect them from the retaliation of the enslaved, then on what basis of legal protection could they perform their duties with confidence and security? Daphney's and Nelly's execution reassured the men of Gathright's class that all remained in order in Virginia. Daphney operated under a set of values that slave law did not allow for. To watch a pregnant woman receive a merciless beating violated principles that Daphney observed about right and wrong. But these guiding norms that led her to defend Nelly thrust her into a criminal justice system that prioritized the demands for obedience and the protection of the white parties involved and normalized the abuse of enslaved women, pregnant or not. Lawmakers designed statutes that responded to the constant threat of a growing enslaved population.

The incidents that implicated enslaved women and girls in violent crimes reminded Virginians of the regular threat of turmoil that came with forcefully subjugating people and the impact that violence created in the dynamics of the home. In 1798, York County commenced trial proceedings in a case involving "Polly a girl." The age of an enslaved person designated as "girl" or "boy" could be wide ranging, but during the late eighteenth century, the court used these terms infrequently, despite the general use of search terms to connote demeaning and infantilizing characterizations of the enslaved. Witnesses described Polly as wielding "a certain pair of fire tongs," along with a "knife made of iron and steel," which she allegedly brandished with her right hand. According to witnesses, she used these weapons to inflict damage on the breast, neck, and head of William Hughes, which led to his immediate death. The court sentenced Polly to execution, which took place on March 23, 1798. Catherine Miles claimed $200 for Polly's life, a girl whose life met an early end amid the violent turmoil of slavery. Unlike Polly's case, some records illuminate the incident in isolation of the days, weeks, and years leading up to the clash between enslaved people and those authorized to dictate the terms of their lives and labor.[89]

In the summer of 1798, Milly reached her limit when she lashed out at members of the Robe family in Monongalia County. According to testimony, Milly made a number of attempts on the life of those who enslaved her. That summer, the court tried Milly for burning a barn belonging to David Robe and violently assaulting his brother, William Robe Jr., the man who owned her. In addition to burning the barn, she also stood accused of taking a hammer and bludgeoning William Robe Jr.'s head and attempting to administer poisonous medicine. What were the dynamics within the household that drove Milly to the multiple measures to end Robe's life and her term on their estate? Descendants of the Robe family believed that he suffered from mental illness. According to the Robe family, he "went entirely insane" after leaving the homestead to try his hand at working a plot of land. Members of the family pondered the possibility that lightning struck him and left him forever changed. The volatile behavior brought on by Robe's mental health might have made for impossible working conditions for Milly. What were the dimensions of his behavior that the family might not have been aware of, but that Milly understood more directly? Milly appealed to the court to postpone her execution, as she believed herself to be in the early stages of pregnancy. Why did she believe herself to be pregnant and by whom? Or was this a ploy to buy some time? The court summoned a group of twelve women to examine the veracity of her claims. As we will see in later chapters, by the antebellum era the court typically appointed a medical expert or examiner for this task, but in the early years of the republic, rural county courts might call their own local sources, such as midwives and women who assisted with pregnancies and deliveries, for information needed. The record is not clear about the relationship between Milly and the twelve women. It is likely that she knew some of the women and that some might be seen as allies and others as enemies made throughout her time on the Robe farm. The women discounted Milly's claims of pregnancy, and the court proceeded with her execution. Milly went to great lengths to wreak havoc on the Robe family with the burning of the barn, the physical assault, and the attempted poisoning of William Robe Jr. Women like Milly sent signals throughout the commonwealth that confirmed the discord and incongruity of the arrangements of power.[90]

Capital crimes, particularly those that ended in death, informed the manner in which power manifested in slave societies. The act of infanticide conveys one of the ways the reproductive labor of enslaved women posed a complex set of considerations that enslaved women deliberated. In 1799, the King and Queen County court of oyer and terminer met to decide the fate of Amey, an enslaved women accused of murdering her two children, Isabell and Harrison. Amey labored on the homestead belonging to John Gresham, a bricklayer of the same county. According to records, Amey used an ax made of iron to inflict the mortal wounds that ended the children's lives. One enslaved man, Phil, and two men of the Gresham clan and another neighboring witness offered testimony that implicated Amey in the act. On June 15, 1799, Amey died on the gallows, valued at seventy pounds which the auditor of public accounts disbursed to John Gresham.[91] The record makes it impossible to understand the motivations of infanticide, but we can infer from the contexts of slavery itself that some women drew a line in the face of lifelong bondage. The meanings behind such cases cannot be adequately determined within the framework of America's early legal culture. The court deemed her a criminal, and the act inhumane even, and yet Amey held her reasons close. Amey's case is the first of many involving infanticides in this book, and yet this case precedes the more well-known cases of the antebellum period. Historians typically regard the late eighteenth century as a golden age of sorts, one in which the revolutionary spirit of the era inspired a number of manumissions and successful freedom suits. Amey's story is one that we tell less frequently, in which countless enslaved people remain in the throes of lifelong bondage and the promise of liberty remains increasingly beyond their reach. Perhaps alongside the golden age, we might also consider a moment in time where enslaved people enacted the consequences of a repressive system by doing the unbelievable and even the reprehensible. But reprehensible to whom? The enslaved possessed their own social economy of right and wrong. This is not to say that infanticide resonated with all enslaved people, but to make possible alternative frames to a legal system committed to slavery and the protection of the property interests of slaveholders. In other words, we can dismiss Amey's actions as a confirmation of her criminality, or we can consider the varied meanings and motivations of a mother impounded in bondage. What appears criminal in the record illumines an entire world of enslaved women taking risks and making decisions that confound both historian and reader. We are confounded because these actions give a limited, yet unequivocally foreboding, sense of the devastation that slavery wrought on the lives of enslaved people. Thus, it is no surprise that they made decisions that led to their own peril. Indeed, enslaved women contemplated other possibilities than the everyday realities that shaped their lives. Some even discovered ways to plot escapes from Virginia plantations, even as they faced the possible risk of unlimited disciplinary measures.

During the winter of 1797, Temp escaped from the homestead belonging to James Houslin in Henrico County. Houslin had purchased Temp less than a year prior to her escape. He described her as five feet, five inches tall, "well made," but with "a down look" and "very artful." Perhaps he viewed Temp as "artful" because the escape caught him by surprise? If someone discovered her, they might notice the blue petticoat and jacket she wore or the scar on the right side of her face. The scar alone tells a story that we will never be apprised of, but perhaps it might reveal insights about how violence and conflict appeared in her interactions with slaveholders.[92] The advertisement noted that she was thirty years old, which tells us that she was old enough to have forged some important ties of her own that probably shaped the course of her plans to leave. Did she escape to loved ones, or did slaveholders catch her somehow? The advertisements of enslaved women on the run tell only part of the story.

In 1799, an enslaved woman escaped from Goochland County, where she had worked for several years after Edward Jennings purchased her from Richmond. Jennings explained in an advertisement that Creasy "generally call[ed] herself Nancy White," and he described her as "of a light complexion, round full faced, and very likely—about twenty years old." In addition to introducing herself as Nancy White, anyone who interacted with her might take notice of the cotton petticoat made of Indian cotton along with the gown and felt hat she wore.[93] Unsure about her whereabouts, Jennings assumed that Nancy might be headed to Richmond, Manchester, or even Petersburg, where she maintained "connexions or acquaintances." These "connexions" were the networks that Nancy likely forged over the course of her experiences in bondage throughout Virginia. Prior to her sale in Richmond, she probably lived in Petersburg or Manchester, where she made acquaintances or developed ties that constitute beloved kin. These relational ties informed the direction in which many of these women took flight, but they also reveal a tapestry of interactions that gave them a sense of belonging.

In August 1799, Thomas Walker reported that Biddy, an enslaved woman he owned, escaped from Fredericksburg. Located close to Alexandria and the Maryland border, Fredericksburg offered some proximity to locales with a higher concentration of free African Americans than the rural counties further south and west. But Walker suspected that Biddy planned to head in the opposite direction, toward Richmond, where, he said, "she is pretty well known in that place."[94] Biddy lived in Fredericksburg because her owner,

Walker, hired her out to William James. Walker actually lived in Richmond, where Biddy likely lived before hire arrangements forced her to Fredericksburg. Richmond served as the place in which she made acquaintances throughout the city, which gave her a reputation and network that might assist with her escape. It was not uncommon for slaveholders to hire out enslaved women, as many residents were in need of additional labor, particularly that of enslaved women who cooked, cleaned, washed, and nursed. Moreover, Biddy likely went to Richmond to reconnect with someone particularly significant in her circle—her husband. Biddy's husband worked as a rope maker in the city, likely bringing in a handsome source of revenue for his owner. Perhaps they plotted and dreamed that someday they might be in a position to secure those earnings from their labors for themselves. But these dreams were crimes in the eyes of the law. We do not know what happened to Biddy, but many fugitive women were caught in their attempts to reconnect with kin.

Enslaved people caught, sold, and confined in preparation for transportation spent time in the local county jail. Slave traders and local sheriffs ensured that the time of sale and forced travel toward new owners included heightened security and surveillance of human property. During the winter months, Nancy arrived in a jail in Nansemond County likely in preparation for a long journey, since a local sale did not necessitate a long stay within local facilities. On Christmas day of 1806, a day of merriment and repose for many Virginians, she did what many strategically did during the holidays—she broke out of jail. That year, officials remained baffled in their search for the girl whom her owner referred to as Dinah, but to no avail. Two years later, they discovered that Dinah went by the name Nancy, and, in the winter of 1808, officials arrested her in Surry County and sold her.[95] Nancy had traveled over forty miles and absconded for an extended period of time. Who kept her secrets? Who fed her? These experiences of intraregional fugitivity remind us of the limits of what we can know about the lives of enslaved women and girls. We know only that Nancy took steps that the sheriff and the court did not anticipate. Did she always want to be called Nancy? Or did her naming occur as a matter of survival? Her time away, however, came to an end when officials learned of her whereabouts, and on September 27, 1809, the court confirmed disbursement of funds to the sheriff for her transportation. Slaveholders took every possible measure to return fugitive women and girls to their worlds. They proved much too valuable to let slip away. Enslaved women fueled the aspirations of early Virginians in ways that proved too lucrative to surrender to the ideals of universal liberty.

Lucy Parke Byrd (Mrs. William Byrd II, 1685–1716), England, ca. 1716. A portrait of a woman associated with Virginia's gentry alongside an enslaved person in the background. These portraits included enslaved people as a display of wealth. Virginia Museum of History and Culture (2018.41).

Luxury is a concept defined by extravagance, and luxuries gradually abounded over the course of the seventeenth and especially the eighteenth centuries in Virginia. Luxury constitutes that which brings ease, comfort, and even pleasure—an ostentatious display of position and power. The consumer revolution and the Revolutionary War shifted the reach of the aspirations of white Virginians, but no other phenomenon like the transatlantic slave trade made such social mobility possible. In North America, this evolution occurred on the basis of the legal status of enslaved women and their progeny. Planters in Virginia enjoyed the luxury that the labor of the enslaved and indentured servants provided, which freed them up to do the work of crafting the legal scaffolding that protected their interest in this form of labor exploitation. Ease came with the option to stay clear of the fields and kitchens where servants toiled, and pleasure gushed from access to abundance, and even violence and sex without blame. Luxury allowed for liberty to be expressed on terms that worked for the European men who arrived with the determination to seize land and labor based on laws they crafted in order to affirm their authorization to do so. This process did not manifest without the commodification of enslaved women's sexual and reproductive lives. Laws governing the lives of enslaved women accounted for the numerous ways the enslaved challenged lifelong bondage. The mundane and backbreaking labor that pulled on the physical and intellectual capacities of the enslaved might have led to a series of disruptions that broke up the facade of efficiency and disturbed fantasies of submission.

CHAPTER TWO

Poison

I hereby certify, that at a court of oyer and terminer held at the courthouse for the county of Princess Anne on the 6th day of September 1803 Charity a negro woman slave belonging to Thomas Lawson, was condemned to be hanged on Friday the 7th day of the next month for administering medicine for the purpose of destroying the said Thomas Lawson and his white family, and that the said Charity was valued to fifty pounds, and the clerk ordered to certify the same accordingly.

—Auditor of public accounts

In 1803, the court of oyer and terminer of Princess Anne County accused Charity of poisoning the Lawson family with the intent to *destroy* them. The court made clear that this case involved an enslaved woman, marked by race and identified by her gender, in contrast to Lawson and his *white* family. These racial and gendered lines drawn to explain the guilt attributed to Charity, "a negro woman slave," show indications of how criminal boundaries were drawn.[1] The intimacy demanded of serving in a household protected by a new white slaveholding republic created challenges that the young nation made painstaking efforts to address through the law. Poison created a problem for white families regardless of whether they owned enslaved people, hired them, or occupied the higher ranks of Virginia society. Incidents involving poison reveal the inner workings of a knowledge war, one in which enslaved women tapped into a pharmacopoeia filled with various intellectual and incorporeal dimensions. Virginia's lawmakers conveyed their own understandings and concerns about the threat of poison to slaveholders and their families.

Colonel David Mason of Sussex County held a seat in the Virginia House of Burgesses from 1758 to 1776. He was a vocal participant in the Virginia conventions and was a state senator in 1776 after serving as a colonel of the Fifteenth Virginia Regiment.[2] In the 1790s, he petitioned the court, alleging that two enslaved people confined to his estate attempted to poison him.[3] He accused them of attempted murder, and the court ruled against them, sentencing them to death by execution and furnishing Mason with the funds that accounted for their value. It was not ironic that he served on the governing

body that enacted and preserved the laws necessary to ensure that slaveholders were fully compensated for any loss that came with the execution or imprisonment of enslaved people found guilty by the court. Between 1705 and
1723, Virginia enacted laws that banned the testimony of enslaved people
charged with capital crimes, denied them a trial by jury of peers, and denied
the possibility of slaveholders' culpability if they killed enslaved people they
owned.[4] The emergence of legal measures designed to outlaw the transgressive behavior of enslaved people signaled the ongoing tensions that shaped
life on plantation estates and in households. Slaveholders exercised influence
and discretion in the creation of legislative measures that governed slavery in
the new nation. Lawmakers designed slave laws to inspire and enforce obedience to slaveholders. The law worked to counter renewed efforts to resist,
which corresponded with the acute sense of vulnerability that slaveholders
hoped to stave off with a carefully conceived code that applied to the enslaved
alone. Criminal slave law did not always discourage crime, but Virginia law
ensured that the authority to discipline and punish could be liberally granted
to slaveholders. It is in this context of early lawmaking that enslaved women
and girls in Virginia appeared before the courts for the crime of poisoning.
The laws functioned within a landscape that looked different from the one
that enslaved people experienced during the seventeenth century. Virginia
underwent critical transformation.

By the late eighteenth century, Virginia boasted a successful regional economy largely based on the labor of enslaved people who cultivated crops ranging from tobacco and later wheat. In this agricultural staple economy, led by
an emerging gentry of revolutionary-era planters, enslaved women and girls
met the demands of backbreaking labor in and out of the expansive and rolling hills of Virginia. As a state that boasted many vocal and influential political voices, it was no surprise that Virginia also became the leading state in
matters of slave law. To trace the legal parameters of life as an enslaved girl,
one must begin in 1662. Her labor and eventually her reproductive capacities
were accounted for in the law that made slavery inheritable through any sexual encounters she experienced.[5] But her life also meant interactions with
elders and kin who shared knowledge about strategies for survival and healing. In the late seventeenth century, enslaved women and girls would need to
learn how to survive the law that circumscribed their lives and futures. It is
within the context of the legal proscriptions of slave law that we notice the
ways that lawmakers authorized the violent realities that enslaved women
and girls confronted in a slave society. Poison, in this chapter, appears both
figuratively and literally, both bearing meanings with physical and life-altering

This 1853 sketch captures Black people in Lynchburg dancing and playing music. The women are adorned with jewelry and headpieces. Sketches like these were used to capture caricatures of Black people but can also provide evidence of merriment, joy, and connection. Lewis Miller, *Sketchbook of Landscapes in the State of Virginia* (1853–1867). The Colonial Williamsburg Foundation (gift of Dr. and Mrs. Richard M. Kain in memory of George Hay Kain).

ramifications. The figurative poison signals the slave law that gave Virginia slave society its shape and tenor. The noxious concoction of laws that permitted reproductive exploitation, authorized rape, and unbridled force to compel enslaved women and girls to bear the weight of economic prosperity and social hierarchy coursed through the veins of the early republic and spilled out into the courtrooms, trials, and public debates of Virginia's burgeoning legal culture. At the turn of the century, slave laws poisoned the possibilities of a truly egalitarian republic, and as enslaved women and girls appeared before the court, they made more visible the profound contradictions that such laws imposed. Enslaved women and girls encountered that poisonous root and dictated different terms of justice, even at their peril. This chapter offers an examination of how the actions of enslaved women and girls made a statute against poisoning a necessity for slaveholders. What follows is both an understanding of how lawmakers shaped Virginia slave law and an intellectual history of how enslaved women and girls deployed their knowledge of poisonous botanicals and substances.

Evidence of enslaved women accused of poisoning appears in the Virginia court dockets in the eighteenth century, revealing not only the persistent threat of resistance but also stores of knowledge about the power of herbs and plants.[6] Poison tapped into the deepest fears of white Virginians who relied on the goodwill of enslaved women to make their meals, fetch their medicines, tend to the most private aspects of their daily lives, and nurse and care for their children. During the mid-eighteenth century, more cases of poisoning were prosecuted than any other criminal offense adjudicated in the slave courts.[7] In 1723, the General Assembly passed an act condemning insurrections to respond to "negroes [who] under pretence of practising physic, ha[d] prepared and exhibited poisonous medicines, by which many persons ha[d] been murdered." The laws against poisoning emerged from suspicions and allegations of enslaved people who gave polluted substances to local Virginians. In 1748, the burgesses passed a revised version of the act specifying the "negroes, mulattoes, and Indians" to whom the law applied.[8] The law implied the possible exchange of medicinal and botanical knowledge among African-descended and Indigenous people in the commonwealth. When Europeans ventured into the West African coasts and the Americas, their presence and the forced migration of Africans meant the convergence of multiple avenues of learning shaped by the presence of Africans, Atlantic Creoles, and Native Americans.

The eighteenth-century Atlantic world contained a range of healing and medicinal remedies with origins in African and Indigenous knowledge and healing practices.[9] The historian James H. Sweet observes that "Africans possessed knowledge of plants and other substances that were often unknown to European pharmacists, let alone slave masters."[10] Knowledge traveled with the enslaved throughout the Atlantic, and they applied understandings of healing to everyday ailments, life-threatening illnesses, complications, and even resistance. Enslaved women and girls created orally transmitted databases of knowledge about herbs, plants, and tinctures that healed, purged, nourished, and even initiated death. Some women, like many men throughout the Atlantic world, grew in stature among communities of the enslaved as healers and midwives, or, as Sweet refers to them, *public intellectuals* who possessed both spiritual and intellectual powers to heal.[11] Historian Mary Hicks explains that "Black healers in colonial slave societies acted as the preeminent intellectuals and social leaders of their communities, dispensing usable knowledge in perilous contexts and commanding mysterious powers formidable enough to transform the human body."[12] These healers were the stewards of the health and well-being of the enslaved community, particularly in the typical instance in which the methods of European medicine proved ineffective, undesirable, or simply unavailable. Even when such medical attention became available, enslaved people held their own suspicions of the medical methods and practices administered to the enslaved. Many slaveholders also came to rely on the expertise of the enslaved in lieu of a call to the nearest doctor.[13]

Enslaved women and girls in Virginia acquired knowledge of plants, herbs, and healing methods through the instructions of other enslaved people, notably enslaved women, but also men.[14] In the eighteenth century, this knowledge might reflect syncretic forms that involved both Indigenous and African epistemologies of botanical properties and techniques for healing. Many of these plants were gathered over a long span of time when enslaved women and girls managed to find moments to venture out into nearby forests and meadowlands where they foraged and collected plants. Additionally, the demands of subsistence, hunting, gardening, and concocting meant that the enslaved gained knowledge of the land, the soil, and its different properties. Planters both relied on the healing work of enslaved women and dismissed their knowledge as inferior. The historian Sharla Fett argues that the enslaved maintained relational understandings of health and proposes alternative definitions of medical authority as we examine this history.[15] The tension between the exploitation of enslaved women's health work and the rejection of African and African American healing knowledge is rooted in both the racial and gendered social position of enslaved women as healers. Over time, the healing and health work for the enslaved was largely done by enslaved women,

Mary Anna Randolph Custis (later Mrs. Robert E. Lee), *Enslaved Girl*, 1830 (Arlington County, Virginia; watercolor, pencil, and ink on wove paper). The Colonial Williamsburg Foundation (museum purchase).

and eventually, Virginians regardless of legal status and race relied on their knowledge and experience.[16] The intellectual and spiritual basis of their work, however, has largely been overlooked or dismissed by Anglo-Americans and American institutions. Fett offers that "defining skill in relation to collective need, spiritual revelation, and teaching from older generations, enslaved African Americans left much richer descriptions of the content and meaning of slave women's health work."[17] Enslaved people valued the knowledge that healing work demanded, and enslaved women's epistemologies of healing through plants, remedies, and methods persist even today. Enslaved women used this knowledge to heal and also for the purposes of refusal.

The slaveholding class of Virginia considered poisoning a most pernicious offense that violated the presumptions of trust that made enslaved women's labors in kitchens, chambers, and nurseries plausible. Even when evidence appeared scant at best, cases involving enslaved women and girls might land at a judgment of guilt. Many of the most powerful plants might simultaneously provide promising prospects for health and in other instances lead to deadly outcomes. Plant remedies involved a number of side effects or outcomes depending on preexisting conditions and the reactions of the body, but these possibilities did not always factor in the details of the court trials. With no legal right to testimony or a trial by peers, it was the word of white Virginians against an enslaved woman. The gendered division of labor, and the trust that laboring in the intimate environs of the household implied, meant that women and girls often faced accusations of poisoning. As antislavery sentiment proliferated throughout the nation, paranoia concerning the threat of intimate resistance appeared in the local news and in accusations of poisoning. In the early 1840s, Virginia legislators passed a law against poisoning with greater description of the forms in which poison and medicinal substances became criminalized.[18] Often the slave codes illuminated the various dimensions of enslaved women's resistance, marking both a preemptive and reactive response to what unfolded in Virginia households.

The General Assembly passed a law in the 1840s prescribing the kinds of punishment to be administered to enslaved, free, and "mulatto" Virginians.[19] This law offers one of many examples of the ways race defined the boundaries of crime and punishment. The law stipulated that any enslaved, free, or mulatto person who administered, or attempted to administer, or caused to be taken "any medicine, deadly poison, or other noxious and destructive substance, or thing, with intent thereby to murder," faced the death penalty.[20] Colonial law stipulated that those accused of poisoning could be sentenced to death by poison.[21] Unlike in the colonial era, revised laws stipulated that enslaved or free women could not avail themselves of the benefit of clergy.[22] Additionally, any effort to sell, or attempt to sell, or prepare or administer "except by direction of their master or mistress" any medicines of any kind became a misdemeanor category of crime punishable with stripes or any "discipline" administered by the slaveholder. In addition to any act involving poison to create harm or providing substances with medicinal properties outside of the discretion of the slaveholder, the law criminalized any instance where enslaved or free Black Virginians used substances to initiate the abortion of any pregnant woman. In cases involving free Black people, the defendant faced a term of at least five years in prison at the penitentiary, and enslaved persons received thirty-nine lashes for the first offense and the death penalty for the second offense. The notion of the absolute power and control of enslaved women as property could be checked at any moment with the decision to grind glass into invisible minerals or carefully place arsenic droplets into a stew. These possibilities were not lost on slaveholders, giving provender to an appetite for violence as a means and measure of power over the enslaved in these Virginia homesteads.

In the first decades of the nineteenth century, plantations looked different from the colonial estates that produced record amounts of tobacco, and Virginia showed signs of change. The western region of Virginia became the home of farmers engaged in diversified agriculture that appeared less dependent on slave labor. In the east, cities such as Fredericksburg, Richmond, and Petersburg supported businessmen, manufacturing enterprises, and artisans. Eastern Virginia was a region where planters commanded estates with large slaveholdings and smaller farms rented or hired the labor of enslaved people, revealing varied but consistent use of slave labor. Eastern Virginians, many who boasted long lineages in the region, emerged as powerful voices in Virginia politics. The antebellum decades signaled a departure, from the view that the problem of slavery plagued Southerners to dismissing the idea that slavery posed any problem at all. Agricultural production appeared more diversified, and slaveholders owned more enslaved people than they necessarily employed on their own properties. Slaveholders addressed this surplus in enslaved labor by renting or "hiring out" the labor of enslaved people to households short of help. Even as a portion of white Virginians did not own enslaved people, many employed them as hires to support the labor demands of their households. The hiring-out system blurred the lines between slaveholder, hires, and overseers, all typically, but not exclusively, white. Virginians who hired enslaved people learned the approaches to management and supervision that slaveholders defined, with the expectation that hires performed the

Joseph Hutchins Colton, *Colton's Virginia*, ca. 1855 (map mounted on paper).
Library of Congress Geography and Map Division.

labor and behaved within the social bounds of slavery. These arrangements often sparked tensions, as the hiring-out system placed enslaved women and girls in close proximity to unfamiliar households and men and women who possessed temporary authority over their lives. These tensions played out in violent ways, and the dockets that reveal accusations of poisoning illuminate this dynamic.

In 1806, the Charlotte County court held a trial in a case involving Fanny, a woman who attempted to poison Thomas Goode, the son of Philip Goode, the man who owned her. If the testimonies bear any truth, Fanny planned an elaborate scheme to ensure that Thomas Goode ingested the poison she prepared for him. Three enslaved witnesses, two men and one woman, gave testimony after barely surviving beatings they received from Goode, who suspected a plot to kill him. Jacob, the first witness, testified that Fanny instructed him to place some black pigment on his face to "make his master love him." Then she gave him a small "whitish root" to be mixed with water and offered to Goode. When he approached Goode, the "black stuff" fell out of his pocket and caught Goode's eye. Jacob immediately disposed of both substances. The second witness, Andrew, explained that Fanny approached him with "a small root of whitish color," which she told him to give to Goode. Andrew kept the root for two weeks, before Goode searched him on learning of the root in Jacob's possession. Next, the court heard testimony from Rina, an enslaved woman who testified that Fanny gave her some "black stuff" to pour over Goode's daily serving of milk. Fanny promised that the root would "kill a man quickly." Why did these three enslaved people agree to help Fanny administer poison to Goode in particular? These were calculated risks. Such risks involved weighing the deadly and violent consequences but also marked decisions that speak to the social economy of the enslaved. Fanny concocted black and white substances, colors that contain spiritual meanings of life and death. She called on knowledge and beliefs about the power of roots and maintained a reputation among the enslaved that convinced them to participate.[23]

The cooperation of the enslaved people involved was a testament to Fanny's significance among the people she interacted with, but also to their collective perception of Goode. In each of their testimonies, the enslaved people deposed explained that Goode whipped Fanny's husband and that he treated him, along with her children, badly. But why did this matter to Jacob, Andrew, and Rina? It is quite possible that they shared a collective sensibility about Fanny's grievances, but perhaps her experiences looked much like their own. For them, Goode violated tenets of the social economy of right and wrong that they observed. Why might Fanny tell Jacob that the substance would make Goode "love him"? Goode discovered the roots on Jacob's person while beating him for another matter, unrelated to Fanny's plot. Any account of their individual encounters with Goode prior to the incident did not appear in the record, but the information that does exist reveals that the enslaved people viewed him in the context of his history of violence. On learning of the plot to poison him, Goode explained to the court that he whipped each of them for their possession of Fanny's root. The possibility that the root might "kill a man quickly" offered a result that Jacob, Andrew, and Rina agreed to help manifest. In fact, Goode ingested the root that Rina mixed in with his milk, which, he explained, made him feel sick, but did not result in his death. He recovered from the effects of the root, administered his own forms of punishment for the enslaved witnesses, then proceeded to have Fanny imprisoned. Goode owned Jacob, Andrew, and Rina, but his father claimed

Fanny, and perhaps their involvement reflected the fact that she resided on another estate and her family lived on Goode's farm. Although Rina administered the concoction, Goode understood Fanny to be the mastermind behind the plan. The court ordered her execution and paid his father, Philip Goode, £100.[24]

Accusations of enslaved women attempting to harm their mistresses also appeared throughout the court docket, even as incidents of mistresses abusing enslaved people became a fact of everyday life in the South. In 1818, Isabella Mitchell of Louisa County accused Delphy of attempting to poison her with the intent to end her life. Thomas Mitchell claimed ownership of Delphy, but the record indicates that she attempted to poison Isabella Mitchell alone as opposed to the entire family, as such cases appear in later years. Scholarship about the history of women slaveholders reveals the contours of conflict between enslaved women and the mistresses of slave-owning households.[25] White women served as supervisors of the labor and responsibilities associated with the domestic upkeep of white homes, which meant the presence of ongoing tension and violence that often escalated to circumstances that Delphy arrived at in Louisa County. The court found her guilty, and the sheriff executed her on the gallows located in the county seat on August 10, 1818.[26] The court issued the Mitchells payment of $200 as her assessed value.

The ruptures created by poison signal moments when slaveholders and those temporarily hiring enslaved people were reminded that, at any given moment, their lives might hang on a mere thread. In the winter of 1822, Hannah, an enslaved woman claimed by Hannibal Bush Washington of Fairfax County, awaited her trial for the charge of attempted murder.[27] The crime for which she stood accused was waged not against Washington, however, but the Seale family of the same county. Hannah served the family of three, likely as a hire or an enslaved person loaned to another party. The Seales accused Hannah of placing arsenic in their food and thus threatening the life of the entire family.[28] That there are no concrete details about her life poses a challenge to understanding whether or not Hannah committed the crime she stood accused of or if matters unfolded differently than presented by the white witnesses deposed. Seale accused Hannah of administering arsenic in a plot to kill him and the members of his family, but under what circumstances might Hannah have been compelled to add arsenic to their meal? We will never know. These conceivable incidents of refusal were learned through generations of bondage, of assessing what power women like Hannah could retain under such circumstances. The court eventually authorized her sale and transportation outside of the commonwealth and paid Washington $50, an abbreviated sum of the $350 the courts designated as her value. Virginians who hired enslaved labor did not necessarily feel obligated to restrain themselves from acts of cruelty, but enslaved people might also use such incidents of resistance to register their frustration or rejection of the arrangements forced on them.

In the early winter of 1823, Mariah, described as a young "mulatto girl slave," could be found laboring in the home of Paschall and Mary Townes.[29] The Towneses claimed ownership of her, and she was one of a few enslaved people forced to work for the couple for life. They were married in December 1816 and were quite possibly anticipating another anniversary with meals prepared for them and family who lived nearby.[30] Enslaved women prepared those meals, a task that Mariah likely assisted with. From the 1780s to well into the 1820s, members of the Townes clan could be found in the marriage and property registers of Amelia County, a place that attracted planters and aspiring slaveholders alike. The county boasted rolling hills and ridges tucked between the Blue Ridge Mountains and the coastal plains. Located in the Virginia Piedmont, the county bordered alongside the Appomattox River, creating unique conditions for the growth of diverse plant life. Most of the local economy relied on slave labor, and enslaved women and girls might be found foraging throughout the vicinity of the plantation households they served. As was the custom in Virginia, members of the family dropped in unannounced to visit with their relatives, and, in these instances, Mariah would have waited on them, or perhaps due to her age, she even played with the young children in the family as companions before her duties became more rigidly confined to household chores and the daily tasks of cooking, cleaning, serving, and tending to other white members of the household closer to her age. This bucolic scene of life in the Townes family fell apart in late November 1823.

On November 26, Mariah served a dinner for the Townes family, along with guests Ishain C. Booker and John Booker, after which everyone appeared ill and disoriented. According to the testimony of those present and the records of the court, Mariah fed the family "medicine," deemed poisonous depending on the amount and preparation involved in administering the substance. Given that the substance is not specified, it is difficult to determine culpability. What is clear is that the "medicine" in the food fit the typical sketch of substances used for therapeutic purposes, a concoction that could either lead to healthful results or make conditions worse. In this case, the depositions revealed that Mariah confessed to accessing vials from Paschall Townes's office and using an emetic known as calomel, or mercurous chloride.

Prescribed in large doses in the eighteenth century, calomel was typically used by people in the nineteenth century to relieve constipation and initiate bowel movements. John Booker, deposed as a witness, testified that he found the substance at the bottom of the cream pots after the Towneses finished breakfast.[31]

The courts did not accept the testimony of enslaved defendants testifying against white people unless they issued a confession of the crime, so it would be impossible to know Mariah's side of the story unless she volunteered such a disclosure or the court allowed for it in a deposition. The court described her as a young girl, without specifications about her actual age. In the nineteenth century, referring to an enslaved person as a "girl" might invoke infantilizing meanings associated with someone who is older or simply suggest a person of younger age. Either on her own volition or on the advice of legal counsel or her owners, Mariah pleaded not guilty. By 1823, the Virginia legislature required that slaveholders pay for the legal fees associated with assigning legal counsel to enslaved people charged with capital crimes.[32] Scholars have argued that Southern courts were generous with their considerations of the procedural rights of the enslaved.[33] This measure to assign legal counsel to enslaved defendants gave the appearance of putting equitable measures in place; however, we know very little of what form such counsel took in these matters. For instance, how might legal counsel advise Mariah in this instance? What were the factors under consideration, and what was possible with a plea of "not guilty"? If Mariah was not legally permitted to offer her testimony, then how could guilt be determined? In addition to counsel, what of the county sheriffs charged with serving as escorts from the moment the charges were issued to the final verdict that might involve death on the gallows or transportation further south? In 1818, legislators discovered that public authorities were using an "engine of torture," or finger screws, to extract "voluntary" confessions.[34] The structure of the courts incentivized using one's voice only through the admission of guilt. But Mariah pleaded not guilty, even as she admitted to the Towneses that she put the medicine in their breakfast, attesting to the ways that enslaved women used what limited oath-making and truth-telling possibilities were at their disposal. What does it mean for Mariah to plead "not guilty" and yet admit to the act? Mariah informed Mary Townes that she "meant no harm." This admission is not one of guilt, but one that made clear that Mariah did not believe her action to be worthy of the sentences that came with the capital crimes of the enslaved. The court, however, affirmed her guilt. Valuing Mariah at $350, the court sentenced her to death. She received a commuted sentence, and the court sold her out of the state. We will never know her side of the story, an incredible frustration for historians who seek to understand the lives of the enslaved. But this is also by design. Perhaps it was her younger age or inconsistencies in the evidence that informed the decision to commute her sentence, but as an enslaved woman or girl moving beyond state lines and away from people and places she knew, transportation and sale to another owner did not promise the kind of reprieve that the legal gesture might insinuate. The removal of the testimonies of the enslaved, especially in instances where their lives depended on it, shines a light on a legal culture designed to protect ideas about enslaved people's capacity for truth, oath making, and criminal activity.

As young girls matured into women, the gendered divisions of labor that demanded their skills as cooks and house servants made them targets of accusations of poisoning.[35] Enslaved women's experiences with slavery and exposure to forms of resistance disrupted the power dynamics in the intimate environs of the plantation household. On December 22, 1828, two enslaved women, Susan, otherwise known as Suckey, and Kesiah, whom locals knew as Kelsie, received instructions to prepare breakfast early for the Garthwright family. The owner, Samuel Garthwright, woke up to the smell of fresh coffee on the brisk morning in which he planned to travel to Petersburg. Garthwright and his wife Elizabeth enjoyed their breakfast, and after three cups of coffee, he hastily left for Woodson's Ferry. Just as he prepared to board the ferry, he suddenly felt "very sick and vomited after which he felt better," but soon "he again fell very sick," with "his eye sight considerably affected." One man in the area "attempted to bleed him," but not long afterward Garthwright became blind. Even with his sight obstructed, he attempted to resume travel in order to return home, but he hardly remained balanced on the saddle and fell off his horse. Medical professionals called on in instances like these were often baffled by the rapid decline triggered by the condition of the patient. Some doctors relied on local healers just to gain an adequate sense of the possible substances or plants at their disposal in the area and to rule out different causes. Philip Grayson, a neighbor, approached Garthwright and notified him that his wife and child experienced similar symptoms. He later learned that Kelsie also became sick after his wife Elizabeth complained about the coffee and made her drink it—"which she done reluctantly." On questioning, Kelsie confessed that the coffee contained "James Town Weed," also known as the devil's snare, a poisonous, fibrous root that can trigger a number of harmful reactions. Several enslaved witnesses were deposed for the case.[36]

The witnesses recounted their versions of the incident and responded to questions about their interactions with Suckey and Kelsie. One enslaved girl named Viney testified that "Suckey sent her to get the seed, that she went and got a hand full of the seed of the James Town weed and gave them to Suckey." Viney asked Suckey what she planned to do with the root, and she replied that she intended to make a medicinal concoction for herself. Another enslaved witness recalled that "he heard Kesiah say the next morning to her mother that it was not her that put the seed in the water," but that Suckey in fact put it in the coffee. An enslaved woman named Silvey testified that she saw Viney give Suckey the poison, and when she asked Suckey about her intentions, she replied that "she would not tell." These deposing sessions strained existing relations among enslaved people, who reacted in a variety of ways to accusations of poisoning.[37] Some might have been frustrated or overwhelmed by the fact that the onus of the truth now rested on their testimony, and others might have offered their perspective willingly or hesitatingly depending on the person posing the questions. These incidents disrupted the daily rhythms of life and labor, and in an effort to stave off any thought of replicating the act, slaveholders often uttered threats that sent ripples of fear among enslaved communities. After consideration of the evidence and depositions, Suckey and Kelsie were charged with the intent to kill and murder their owner and his wife and sentenced to death by execution. Suckey died prior to the scheduled execution, and the cause of death remains unclear, but given the circumstances and conditions of the penitentiary, she faced limited, if any, options. A range of possibilities might explain her death, including illness, abuse, or mistreatment in prison or suicide. But according to Viney, Suckey intended to use the root to make a remedy for herself. Perhaps she battled an illness that did not appear in the records or that she decided not to disclose? If Suckey attempted to heal herself and failed to do so, prison only made matters worse. The court scheduled Kelsie's execution for early spring, but during her detainment at the state penitentiary, she received word that the governor revised her sentence from death to sale and transportation. Kelsie likely received a commuted sentence because the testimony primarily implicated Suckey.[38] These cases came across the desk of the governor, who made recommendations for commuted sentences of enslaved people accused of capital crimes.

In 1829, William Branch Giles served the second of three one-year terms as governor of Virginia. He championed a diluted governorship modeled after George Mason, who supported limited political authority for governors. Despite this view, the executive office allowed for a certain degree of discretion and gave Giles the authority to make important decisions with implications for Virginia law. Trained at Princeton University, then the College of New

Jersey, and the College of William and Mary, Giles studied and practiced law in Petersburg, Virginia. Like most Virginians, Giles viewed slavery as a nuisance both politically and socially for the young nation, yet still relied on enslaved labor. In line with the thinking of Thomas Jefferson and James Madison, Giles believed that the close of the transatlantic slave trade and the expansion of slavery to other states initiated the diffusion of slavery.[39] This "diffusion" thesis emphasized the gradual thinning of the slave population but did not account for the insatiable demand for and dependence on slaves to cultivate these expanded lands. Transportation outside of the commonwealth fueled the demand of the slave market, albeit with enslaved people viewed as undesirable for their criminal record, but profitable nonetheless. The population of enslaved people remained robust even as those accused of crimes might be sentenced to sale and transportation outside of the commonwealth.

Cases that involved enslaved women who faced charges of murder or attempted murder show that sentences varied among courts that tried the same charge and conviction. In Amelia County, Annie, an enslaved woman documented as the property of Marten Green, the infant son of William Green, and Nanny, claimed by Edward James, appeared before the court for "plotting and conspiring to kill" Matthew Allen and his wife. Annie, a person to whom a white infant became legally entitled, served as the cook. William Green, Marten Green's guardian, likely hired Annie to the Allens, a testament to the ways that young white Virginians of means began to accumulate revenue and wealth before they even understood such concepts. Hired cooks prepared food throughout the day and managed the organization of the kitchen and the execution of meal service. Annie articulated a set of conditions that worked best for the labor she performed. Matthew Allen noted that Annie kept people out of the kitchen unless they prepared or served meals. Annie's children typically played around the kitchen, an exception she made to her rule about who could enter the kitchen. This small, yet significant, gesture allowed her valued moments with her children. But on this particular day, Annie strictly enforced her policy, and witnesses noticed that, on this day, she did not permit her children to enter the kitchen. Once Annie prepared and served the food, Allen consumed a mouthful and, on chewing, discovered something between his teeth. Ignoring the strange mix of textures uncharacteristic of the greens Annie prepared, he tried another mouthful and experienced the same sensation. He glanced at his plate and "found amongst the greens small pieces of glass."[40]

As the Allens quickly approached the kitchen to question the presence of broken glass in their meal, Annie took the plate of greens and approached the window, where she threw the greens out. As the pot liquor quickly soaked into the soil, Matthew Allen interrogated Annie, and she explained that she mixed in chemicals typically used as dye, which in many instances might be harmless if used as a form of food coloring. Allen expressed his disbelief and sought to get to the bottom of the matter. Something shifted in Annie. Her tone went from defiance and defensive to hesitant. She confessed that "her object was to quit lying," and she admitted that she mixed in both glass and hair she secured from "an old negro woman Nanny." Elderly enslaved women offered wisdom and strategy in seasons of conflict. Nanny knew the repercussions of being involved in volatile matters, but she drew from experience and stores of knowledge about concoctions and their powers to alter the circumstances of an enslaved person's life. Nanny stored the sights, sensations, and wisdom from years of living through the labile and turbulent realities of bondage. As an elderly enslaved woman, Nanny ranked higher in the social world of the enslaved. She embodied a database of knowledge and power that transcended the habit and legal customs of slavery.

The court deposed enslaved people who resided among the Allens. Lovelace, an enslaved woman called on to testify, indicated that Annie disclosed her plans to "do as old Nanny told her," as there was no doctor on earth who could "cure" Matthew Allen. What did Allen need to be "cured" of? What illness befell him that required old Nanny's powers? The problems in the household became somewhat clearer in the testimony. According to Lovelace, "Annie went to see Nanny before the stuff was put in the victuals" prior to the departure of Rebecca Mann, one of the guests who stayed in the Allens' home. Lovelace explained that "Miss Becky was staying at her masters and Annie said she would not put anything in the victuals whilst she was there as her Miss Becky had not injured her and she did not want to hurt her." Mann left an impression significant enough to convince Annie that she should be spared of what she planned to inflict on the Allens. According to Lovelace, Annie declared that "she would not stay with Mr. Allen" and disclosed her plans a few days after she suffered an unforgettable beating at his hands. Where would she go? Or where did she plan to send Allen? Annie made her declarations not only to her but to others with whom she shared her plans and motivations.[41]

The court records did not consistently include the testimony of the enslaved, but when such sources did appear, the contexts of household dynamics became more discernible. The court deposed Peter, an enslaved man who explained that Annie shared the details of her plan and instructed him to hide the glass and hair in exchange for valuable goods she planned to secure for him. She told him that "the stuff was prepared by old Nanny," but "she did not want to bring her in" on the plan. In exchange for her valued knowledge and resources, Annie made clear that she did not plan to disclose the fact that Nanny assisted her. Peter explained that Annie intended to blame Lovelace, because "she had before that run away and she had borne that character before," but that day she remained some distance away from the house and kitchen. Peter's account reveals that for the enslaved women, including Lovelace, the household became unbearable enough to warrant an escape attempt. The court called in a medical expert to confirm the details of the concoction. Doctor Chappell, who examined the plate of food, confirmed that hair and glass were present and that the combination "if taken intentionally would produce disease and death." William Green, listed as Marten Green's guardian, appeared surprised by the news that Annie attempted to poison Allen and his wife. Green stated that he "would rely on her as soon as any negro" and that he considered her "a negro of good character." If Green's statement is to be believed, then what compelled Annie to poison the Allens? The beating that inspired her to seek out Nanny to find a way to "cure" Matthew Allen provides a small clue of why Annie mixed in pieces of glass and hair in the pot of greens. In July 1829, the court determined her guilt, but recommended clemency and set her value at $275, to be paid to her owner. The justices likely suspected the volatile dynamics of life under the authority of the Allens, but the governor did not approve the request for clemency, and Annie was executed on October 20, 1829. The court dropped the charges against Nanny, who never appeared on trial. Perhaps locals dismissed "old negro Nanny" as an elderly woman with diminishing faculties. But in the social economy of the enslaved, she held an important position. Enslaved people sought such women and gleaned from the insights of women like Nanny.[42]

The social hierarchies of Virginia did not shield the elite from the vulnerability and embarrassment caused by enslaved people's alleged crimes. In March 1829, King and Queen County held a court of oyer and terminer to try the case of Peggy, who stood accused of attempted murder. The Knapp family hired Peggy out from Lawrence Muse, who lived in the northern neck, worked as the deputy collector of the port of Tappahannock, and led a mercantile business with his cousin under the firm name John Muse & Co. In addition to possessing a retail license for the northern neck and Richmond, he served as a member of the Virginia legislature in 1808.[43] In this case, not only did he hold a place of political importance in Virginia society, but he also served as an owner and hirer of enslaved people. According to court records, Peggy served Joseph Knapp's wife and daughter a healthy dose of arsenic.

The context in which she administered the substance remains unclear, but the Knapps remained convinced that she served arsenic "with an ill intent and attended by bad consequences." Reactions to arsenic might range from acute toxicity to death. Knapp's wife and daughter survived the ingested substance, and Peggy received a commuted sentence to sale and transportation. The conditions of Peggy's hire and the precise details of the incident make the case difficult to decipher.[44] Vague or insufficient evidence and the possibilities of resistance appear regularly throughout the record in instances absent of a confession, but the accusations against Peggy dragged Muse's name through the county courts, and news of the incident was not lost on those who considered hiring enslaved people from him in the future.

Enslaved women accused of poisoning often administered substances that Virginians used for medicinal purposes as well. Another enslaved woman named Susan appeared before the court in Prince Edward County, for attempted murder charges. According to testimony, Susan, also a cook, prepared a dinner of cabbage and bacon for Judith Brightwell. The meal revealed remnants of poke root, an herb with medicinal properties that increased in toxicity over time and typically led to poisoning. Grown near meadows and swamps, poke root helped fight off infection, reduce inflammation, and assist with constipation, but, in this instance, it made Brightwell ill.[45] The court found Susan guilty and sentenced her to sale and transportation at the value of $600.[46] The outcomes of these cases might point to the kind of evidence found in the food they prepared. Broken glass sends a clearer signal of harm than roots that might be used for either healing or harmful purposes. Other factors present include the general reputation of these women among locals and whether the incident marked one of many alleged offenses.

These cases reveal a sense of dynamic conflict present within the households that enslaved women labored in, making the kitchens, cellars, and dining rooms sites in which they administered substances that might subdue, deter, or cancel out completely the frustrations and cruelties they experienced in bondage. Southerners typically employed enslaved women as cooks, a well-known feature of the gendered organization of household labor that made enslaved women the primary suspects for incidents that involved poisoning. Decisions were often determined by testimony, evidence, and local opinion, but the records did not consistently explain these variations or the reasons behind a change in sentence.[47] Some cases, however, appeared on the docket in greater detail.

On October 5, 1832, Fanny, an enslaved woman, waited in jail in Prince Edward County as the sheriff prepared for her execution.[48] Fanny arrived at the jail in August and, since then, waited to learn of the date scheduled by the justices of the peace to end her life, and also end her lifelong term of bondage. Earlier that August, her owner, Henry Davison, accused Fanny of murdering Orford, an enslaved man whom he also claimed as his property. According to court records, Fanny prepared medicine for Orford that ultimately ended in his death. In the absence of her testimony, there are a number of factors to consider in this case. On Virginia plantations, it was not uncommon for enslaved women in particular to serve as healers and midwives entrusted with the task of assisting an ailing enslaved person or even a white person. Many medicines or substances with healing properties also contained poisonous qualities that made their administration as remedies an exact science. It would not have been uncommon for Davison or Orford to request Fanny's services if Orford appeared ill or struggled with deadly symptoms. The record, however, only supports her attempt to administer the medicine as an act of murder, since no other explanation from Fanny appeared without the admission of guilt. Thus, the courts recorded that Fanny feloniously poisoned Orford that August of 1832. What is most clear is that Davison received the compensation in damages on October 19, just shy of two weeks following Fanny's death. There was limited incentive to account for Fanny's possible innocence, which illuminates some of the possible risks and liabilities associated with being a healer or administering remedies. Davison navigated a system that paid for his losses whether Fanny possessed murderous motivations or not. Motivations and culpability appeared difficult to prove even if most cases assumed the guilt of Black women.

In addition to the work of cooking, the duties associated with nursing and supervising young children put enslaved women and girls in close proximity to white children they were expected to care for. In 1834, the Bedford County court met for a trial involving Nelly, an enslaved woman who labored in the household of Forest Wheat. Part of Nelly's duties, like those of many enslaved women, involved caring for children, and, in this case, she nursed Wheat's son, Joseph H. Wheat. According to Forest Wheat, on May 12, 1834, Joseph died from poison that Nelly administered. The sheriff of Bedford County swiftly performed her execution on October 23, 1834.[49] As Joseph's nurse, did Nelly administer a substance that nineteenth-century Americans used for sick or inconsolable children? Incidents involving enslaved women who served as nurses underscore the heightened sense of responsibility and trust that such work demanded. Cases involving the poisoning of infants certainly implicated enslaved women and girls charged with the care of white infants.

In the stifling heat of August 1849, Brunswick County locals heard rumor of two enslaved women who attempted to poison the six-month-old infant belonging to Mansfield Noble. As a capital crime, poisoning was often treated as attempted murder, which foreclosed any opportunities that the two enslaved women, Eliza and Roberta, might have to offer in terms of testimony in their defense.[50] What we do understand is that both women pleaded not guilty, and their pleas serve as the only recorded evidence of their defense. On October 3, 1843, Mansfield Noble married Mary W. Poyner and immediately started having children, including their third in 1849, a boy they named John. Mansfield worked as a tailor, earning roughly $1,000 annually in a household that included two apprenticed tailors as well as an enslaved woman named Fanny. Eliza and Roberta were not permanent residents of the Noble compound, but most likely were hired out to him by their owner, Nancy Griffin. The case begs the question of the different circumstances that might have led to the accusations against them.

One might read the case record as it is written. The records show that Eliza and Roberta appeared guilty of poisoning the infant child belonging to Mansfield Noble, but they pleaded not guilty to such claims. Why might two enslaved women contrive a plan to poison an infant? Perhaps John grew ill, as was common among infants during the nineteenth century. Multiple enslaved women with knowledge of infant care, nursing, and healing were called on when someone fell ill. Some enslaved women healers trained other young, enslaved women, who provided support on calls to assist with the sick.[51] Might the "poison" be an attempt to help heal the child in the humid summer months of rural Virginia? We also do not know the kind of power dynamics that shaped Eliza's and Roberta's interactions with Mary or Mansfield Noble or the other inhabitants of the household. Working conditions shaped by tensions, violence, and frustration might characterize their experiences as hires in the Noble household. Each of these considerations demands that we do something that the legal record shows little evidence of—question the presumption of criminality and culpability typically assigned to Black women. Neither considerations of execution nor clemency makes space for exoneration. Guilt and culpability remain, even if the sentence varies. With the word of Mansfield Noble against theirs, the decision was made before Eliza or Roberta could speak. On October 12, 1849, the two women were executed, and Griffin received a total of $550 in compensation for her loss.[52] Cases involving enslaved people accused of poisoning might appear in the broader politics of the state, especially if public opinion diverged from the decisions of the executive office. These cases inspired debate about the state of slavery in Virginia.

By the late 1840s, the argument against slavery gained momentum and the spotlight focused on the South and the territories that the United States might acquire further west. Some white Americans, while not convinced of equality between the races, began to see slavery as a stain on the nation, a force so strong as to poison the integrity of the republic. One publication called for the boycott of goods produced by enslaved labor, a growing movement of politicized consumption that critiqued the support for "sugar, cotton and rice poisoned with slavery."[53] For those who failed to resist the temptation to support goods produced by enslaved labor, the publication declared, "It is time for them to learn and remember, that there is poison in it; the poison of the masters' tyranny and of the sufferings of the slave."[54] Political discourse that emphasized the need to purge the states of this poison did not manifest in the northern reaches of the nation alone. In newspapers circulated throughout the commonwealth, Virginians read of abolitionist speeches delivered throughout the country that raised concerns about the powerful chokehold slavery maintained throughout the region. One such account published in the *Richmond Daily Whig* included an excerpt reprinted from the *Cincinnati Atlas*, arguing, "[Political leaders need to] call upon Virginia to throw off the nightmare of Slavery, which now holds her spell-bound, and she would rouse her latent energies at once, and would be able to compete with the Free Labor of the North, which she can now only gaze at with envy."[55] The Virginia press responded to these mounting critiques with praise for what it believed Virginia stood for, offering, "Would that they could appreciate and understand the greatness of the motives by which she is animated, and the intelligence which prompts her acts."[56] For the author of one particular editorial, these acts, or laws and customs of the oldest state in the Union, prompted admiration rather than criticism. The writer went further, stating, "She stands to-day, as she has ever stood, the model commonwealth— the guiding star of the republic, rebuking on the one hand the imbecility which surrenders up liberty, and on the other the base and selfish haggling which sacrifices it for a price."[57] Virginia, its laws, slavery, and way of life were all beyond reproach. Any acquiescence to the political demands of abolitionists appeared equivalent to surrendering the freedom of Virginians to Northern tyranny.

The heated political tensions that emerged between the states shaped the election and term of Joseph Johnson, who ran for the executive office of the commonwealth and in 1852 became the first popularly elected governor of Virginia and the first to represent the counties west of the Appalachian Mountains. That same year, Johnson's name appeared embroiled in an anti-Whig campaign that involved Phillis, a young, enslaved girl accused of poisoning an infant, the son of Patrick and Anne Butler. Phillis made headlines after the hustings court determined that she "maliciously administered poison," specifically morphine, to the infant. Morphine can be traced to the opium poppy plant, which nineteenth-century healers and doctors administered for pain relief, but also to assist with insomnia and for the purposes of calming crying children.[58] Despite an understanding of its toxic properties, most scholarly publications from the sixteenth to the mid-nineteenth century promoted its use to calm crying children, wean infants from nursing, and soothe the aches and pains of teething.[59] The local news covered the case, arguing that although her actions were deemed "an uncommon atrocity," "she [was] not hung, but [was] 'humanely condemned to transportation'" by a court primarily composed of Whigs.[60] The court found her guilty, and primarily "in consideration of her age commuted her punishment from death to transportation." These insights offer a window into the limited demands of justice in cases involving enslaved girls. "Humane" treatment might be possible in instances where age introduced a moral dilemma into the calculations of criminal prosecutions of enslaved adolescents. According to this logic, Phillis seemed too young to die but not too young to be sold further south. This manner of thinking creates little space for imagining the inhumane conditions that gave the domestic slave trade its form and reputation; however, in the legal culture of Virginia, transportation translated into a lighter sentence to pay compared to death. Phillis might have developed a different interpretation of this logic. But we do not know what she thought, because her name remained buried in the contentious politics of the 1850s. One writer commenting on the case observed, "Poisoning has always been regarded as a crime of singular enormity, for it is a deliberate act, necessarily implying malice."[61] Malice, as opposed to perhaps accidental poisoning through accepted methods for soothing infants, emerged as the only lens through which locals might view Phillis's actions. But the story is much more complicated if the context of Phillis's life is under consideration. The emphasis on the "humane" sentence signaled an important political gesture during a decade shaped by tensions over slavery. Phillis's story appeared less visible as Virginia politics stewed over the political implications of slave law.

Firebrand politics played out in the news and a case that otherwise might go unnoticed served to prove the point of Virginia Democrats who feared the influence of the Whigs presiding over the hustings court. The article pointed out that the Whig press, specifically the *Richmond Whig*, launched a number of political diatribes against the legal discretion exercised by the previous Democratic governor, John Buchanan Floyd, who preceded Johnson's administration. "Far be it from our intention to follow the example of the Whig press and attempt to make political capital by assailing this Whig Court for what it believed to be a conscientious discharge of public duty," the editors maintained.[62] According to one opinion, locals in Richmond were outraged at the idea that the Whig press could launch an assault against the governor, who previously commuted the sentence of Jordan Hatcher, a seventeen-year-old enslaved hire, but withhold criticism in the instance where Whig justices commuted the sentence of an enslaved girl accused of poisoning with the intent to murder an "infant." What appeared as a set of political contradictions also reveals the different manner in which people read the alleged crimes of enslaved people.

The same year Phillis faced attempted murder charges, Hatcher found himself in a tussle in the Walker and Harris tobacco factory in Richmond. He worked as a "stemmer," cleaning stems by removing the midribs from tobacco leaves.[63] William P. Jackson, the overseer who scrutinized Hatcher's work, "found fault with a bundle of tobacco stems" he processed, stating that this was one of many instances in which Hatcher produced unsatisfactory work. According to a petition of citizens and some witnesses, "the boy begged his forgiveness and promised to endeavor to do better for the future."[64] This, too, proved an unsatisfactory response in Jackson's mind. Jackson immediately started whipping Hatcher until he caught the cowhide, and Jackson ordered him to the stove nearby. Jackson resumed the whipping, when Hatcher seized the whip. Jackson kicked him, until Hatcher picked up an iron poker and struck Jackson on the forehead. According to witnesses, "the boy dropped the poker and left the room immediately," and "the boy did not attempt to repeat the blow, although he might easily have done so, as no one attempted to prevent him, many being present at the time."[65] The hustings court allowed for several enslaved men to be deposed, not for the purposes of speaking against Jackson, but to confirm that Hatcher struck the fatal blow. Robert Jones, Daniel Walthall, Alonzo Heath, and William Barkus were all enslaved men hired at the tobacco factory who confirmed the same story that supported Hatcher's culpability. Barkus specifically verified that Jackson whipped Hatcher even as he promised to improve the quality of his work output. All four of the enslaved men were faced with the precarious task of telling their account without giving testimony against Jackson or any white party involved that might jeopardize their hire arrangement at the factory or cause trouble with their owners. Jackson chased after Hatcher, but he escaped. Later, a physician came to examine Jackson and found him sitting up and functioning as normal. The same physician reappeared the next morning and discovered Jackson "laboring under a compression of the brain."[66] Other physicians were called on to examine him and concluded that the skull was fractured and the brain wounded. Jackson survived only a few hours after the medical examination, and Hatcher was arraigned to answer to murder charges.

The court found Hatcher guilty for the murder of Jackson, which led a significant number of "respectable citizens" to prepare a petition in support of a commuted sentence of sale and transportation.[67] According to the petitioners, the fatal wound inflicted on Jackson's head certainly came from Hatcher's attempt to fend off the overseer, but the facts of the case "tend to establish that the blow was struck under circumstances tending greatly to aggravate the boy, without premeditation and with no design to kill." They determined that no evidence of "malignant, willful or deliberate purpose developed by the proofs to commit murder" appeared in the testimony. While they found the conviction to adhere to "the strict letter of the law," they believed Hatcher's case represented "one of those cases upon which a sound discretion would induce the exercise of some degree of executive clemency." The petitioners emphasized the nature of such provocations that "aggravate" and spark a gut reaction. The circumstances that led a young man to counter what appeared to be an unreasonable, but broadly accepted, attack seemed to resonate with the men who signed the petition. They read no intent to kill on Hatcher's part, and the demands of justice, as they understood it, made executive clemency an amenable response to the case. Governor Johnson commuted Hatcher's sentence and authorized that he be sold for $600 to compensate Mrs. P. O. Godsey, his owner.

Governor Johnson gained popularity as a Democrat who appealed to a broad base of white Virginians, including established planters of the eastern regions of the state as well as Virginians west of the Appalachians who relied less on slave labor. As a slaveholder who lived in the state's western region, he held the kind of profile that appealed to planters in the eastern regions where slavery dominated, while also maintaining credibility among western voters who thought that eastern politicians were overrepresented in state politics. Johnson ran against George W. Summers, a Whig, who appeared too light-handed on the issue of slavery. Summers expressed support for the Virginia colonization society, which promoted the removal of enslaved and free Black Virginians as opposed to their full inclusion in Virginia society after manumission.[68]

The election of 1851 went decisively to Johnson because Summers appeared too weak in his support for slavery. But Johnson's decision to grant Hatcher clemency points to the complexities of antebellum Virginia politics. One article noted, "As we suspected, the Whig press have been entirely silent—raising not even a whisper of complaint against the action of the Whig Court."[69] The origins of this critique from the Whig faction stemmed from the election of 1851 when Democrats villainized Summers as an abolitionist. One article in the *Staunton Spectator* offered, "The whole affair seems like a just visitation upon the Democratic party, for the course they pursued during the Gubernatorial canvass."[70] They fired on, stating, "To defeat Summers—one of the safest men in the State—they called him Abolitionist and everything else that was calculated to prejudice the popular mind against him."[71] Citizens published a resolution in the news condemning what they viewed as "a flagrant abuse of the pardoning power, and a dangerous precedent if not at once sternly rebuked by the public voice."[72] But as scholars have shown, the article is misleading in that this was not primarily a partisan issue.[73] While citizens organized a petition to make the case for a commuted sentence and others countered with a petition against clemency, thousands of locals flocked to city hall and later the governor's residence to protest Johnson's decision, but they were less concerned with the critiques of the Whigs and mostly galvanized by the possible threat to their own position in the hierarchy of Virginia society.

Hatcher, an enslaved person, received a commuted sentence after having caused the death of a working-class white man.[74] One historian notes that "the judicial system could serve an important function in reasserting the primacy of race, yet when slaves routinely escaped punishment as a result of executive clemency and in the property interests of individual slaveholders, white racial solidarity was potentially compromised."[75] Overseers in tobacco factories ranked well below the status of elite Virginia planters. Countless immigrants from Germany and Ireland made their way to the urban centers of Virginia and competed with hired enslaved men for jobs in such factories.[76] The men accused of mob violence and threatening the property and home of the governor were associated with the working classes and saw the precarity of their own position in Virginia. Furthermore, men and women who lived in Richmond also protested largely out of concern for a possible insurrection in an already expanding enslaved and free Black population in Richmond. According to the historian William A. Link, between 1840 and 1860, the enslaved population of Richmond grew by 56 percent.[77] But what of the case and the actual enslaved girl implicated in the legal matters under scrutiny?

In Phillis's case, one news report argued: "Gov. Johnson is a Democrat and for commuting the punishment of Jordan Hatcher he is to be hunted down, with the miserable view of making a little party capital. Will these Whig journals show themselves equally willing to rebuke their fellow Whigs for doing a similar act?"[78] The issue of clemency reveals the intricacies of antebellum politics and the impact of the actions of enslaved Virginians. Phillis and Hatcher became central to the political debate without ever being centered in what their experiences might tell us about the inconsistencies of the law and its implications for their futures.

Some reports described Phillis as a malicious murderer. Age fluctuated in meaning in court cases, but jurists and locals considered numerical determinations largely shaped by race, gender, and slavery. For instance, the Butlers' child being characterized as an "infant," and the act viewed as an "uncommon atrocity," overshadows the fact that the little boy was five years old. While he appeared young, he certainly did not fit the description of an infant. The hustings court did not confirm Phillis's age but deemed sale and transportation a more evenhanded measure given her young age. In the Butlers' testimony, they viewed her as anything but a child, only a murderer. Despite the court viewing her in the context of adolescence, Patrick Butler explained that "Phillis had lately become so insolent and abusive towards his wife, that he had to whip her two or three times, and finally sent her to jail for correction, about a week since."[79] The Butlers sensed in Phillis an air of defiance, and something set them off to make them engage in one violent act after the next to reinforce their sense of power over her. They had lost control. Their authority hung by a thread, to the point that Butler sent her to the local jail, a concession or last resort that few planters found desirable even if they understood its potential effectiveness. To send a young enslaved girl to jail implied that something was broken in the private domain of discipline and punishment that Southerners prided themselves on maintaining, even in the face of the most ardent resistance waged by enslaved people. In this case, something about the girl triggered the family, and perhaps because someone else owned her and the Butlers hired her out, the Butlers felt limited in their efforts to discipline her. But the series of beatings and the nights she spent in jail, subjected to various forms of violence inflicted by strangers, suggest otherwise.[80]

Local jails imprisoned enslaved people to temporarily confine them before they were sold and also when owners "wished to punish" enslaved people who exhibited defiant behavior.[81] In the vicinity of the Butlers' home, one such jail became known as "one of the prominent and characteristic features of the capital of Virginia," the capital that also housed the court that tried Phillis's case. The establishment appeared in one account detailing the story of Anthony Burns, a fugitive enslaved man who escaped to the North only to be returned to the South and confined in the jail. The author described Burns's experience and concluded that "the torture which he suffered, in consequence, was excruciating."[82] One description offers that "it was a large brick structure, three stories in height," and "the whole was enclosed by a high, close fence, the top of which was thickly set with iron spikes." These were the jails that forced enslaved girls and women into concubinage or prepared them for sale further south to work as field laborers, domestic servants, or prostitutes.[83] Those confined in this prison might hear the cries of the enslaved being subjected to the cruelest forms of torture. According to testimony, Phillis returned from the jail "unusually sullen, treating the little boy in particular—whom she had always appeared to dislike—in a harsh manner."[84] What caused her to be "unusually sullen"? What did she see, hear, smell, or experience during her confinement in the jail? Phillis, a young girl deprived of the childhood afforded the Butler child, witnessed and lived through much more than what might be expected for a child to bear. But this was slavery. And age did not shield enslaved girls from the realities of exploitation and violence. Some attributed "her antipathy towards him" as an outcome of "his often playfully teasing her."[85] We lack the details of what "playfully teasing" actually meant or what kind of behavior and language the Butlers permitted their son to use with Phillis. Her enslavers did not allow space for her or any enslaved person to be "aggravated" or provoked. Indeed, countless white boys and girls were socialized to understand their relationship to other enslaved children in the context of mastery regardless of possible affections shared between them.[86] Perhaps the demands of childcare became too much to bear or her interactions with Patrick or Anne Butler made dynamics in the house fraught with tension. The household, as a place of intimacy and a space in which power is expressed and made manifest in the interactions between enslaved and free, remained, in this case, a place of fragility.[87]

Tensions intensified in the Butler home and left Phillis vexed by her daily interactions with members of the household. According to the Butlers, Anne fell ill, and the doctor ordered a morphine solution for her to take to address her symptoms. She left the vial on the fireplace mantel and later that evening discovered that the vial had been emptied. She remembered that her son went to bed in "good health the night previous," but he came down the stairs in the morning quite ill, convulsing and foaming at the mouth. The doctor returned to the house to examine the boy and concluded that the child suffered from poisoning, likely the result of narcotics, namely, the morphine solution he prescribed to treat Anne's symptoms. The doctor "applied the proper restoratives," and along with another doctor whom he called on, he "succeeded in clearing off from the stomach of the child, the poison" and in "rescuing him from his death struggle."[88] According to the boy, he asked Phillis for a drink of water and she gave him one that tasted sour.

An expert called in to analyze the condition of the child concluded that the boy took the equivalent of two grains of opium, or fifty drops of laudanum. From the testimony of white witnesses, "it was found that Phillis had carefully cleaned the tumbler and spoon" to "hide her guilt" and that the "previous good health of the boy and her antipathy towards him" must then "prove the culpability of Phillis and her murderous intent."[89] The family wanted to make an example of her and made that clear: "It is to be hoped that Phillis will receive the fullest measure of punishment for her fiendish offence, prescribed by law."[90] And in case the "spirit of the age" should arrest the officials charged with administering justice, they warned, "Let there be no more *commutations* to invite to rebellion and murder our population."[91] The "spirit of the age" that made abolitionism a formidable foe worried locals about the prospects for Southern justice. While the testimony implicated Phillis's culpability, it reveals a household rife with conflict, tension, and unchecked violence.

Phillis appeared almost as an afterthought until writers found an opportune moment to incite fear. One editorial raged on, stating, "The conduct of these Justices is even worse than that of the Governor, for in this case murder was willful and premeditated; and if nurses, for poisoning children, are only to undergo the punishment of transportation, (which is in most instances a pleasure rather than a punishment,) whose child is not in danger?"[92] "What parent can feel secure when youth and the spirit of the age are to triumph over laws, justice and humanity?" the writer added. The fearmongering shifted to resolve when the author of the article offered, "In my opinion (and I trust I am not alone in this opinion) the good of society demands a more rigid execution of the laws," which he or she signed anonymously as "JUSTICE."[93] For this Southerner, justice meant legal protections for white Virginians alone. For countless state locals, transportation inched much closer to injustice than they were comfortable with. Fear remained at the heart of this critique of clemency. Working-class white Virginians and white owners and renters of enslaved people believed the political tensions created by abolition warranted harsh sentencing to convey to the enslaved that resistance would not be tolerated. But beyond the political fervor, the resistance or even suspicion and allegations of foul play hit the nerve of a society dependent on slavery and its corresponding hierarchies. The Committee of the Courts of Justice in the House of Delegates reported of enslaved people, "[They] know that they are often transported for murder, arson, poisoning, burglary, robbery, larceny, and indeed almost every crime."[94] The committee interpreted transportation as a favorable outcome that enslaved people exploited, and it concluded that "the power of the Courts to transport should be taken away."[95] Evenhandedness and the legal use of clemency through sale and transportation did not satiate the appetite for execution and more violent means of punishment in a society growing increasingly anxious about the unraveling of the racial order in the commonwealth. Even as these debates raised a sense of alarm and concern, the looming threat of poisoning and the use of clemency remained a feature of future criminal court dockets.

In the spring of 1854, the infant belonging to Mr. and Mrs. William Jennings of Caroline County appeared ill, pale, and strangled.[96] The clothing on the seven-month-old showed traces of laudanum, and on the mantelpiece in the room was an ounce phial of laudanum. Just before Mrs. Jennings took note of her infant's condition, she instructed Sally, an enslaved girl hired out to her, to make her way upstairs to care for the child. The details of her instruction do not appear in the records, but, as mentioned earlier, parents and healers used laudanum to calm and soothe infants. Mrs. Jennings apparently went to the yard to wash out some clothing and returned to the nursery to discover her child struggling for air. The physician J. Dove Jr. examined the child and confirmed that someone administered laudanum to the infant. Officials arrested Sally, and as she made her way to the local jail, the child died. Very little evidence appeared to establish motive, but the court found Sally responsible for the child's demise.

As the political climate intensified in the South, locals made known their suspicions of the enslaved within the intimate environs of their homes, nurseries, and kitchens. In 1855, Martha, an enslaved woman accused of poisoning her mistress, Mrs. John Tully, was acquitted.[97] Martha's case also lacked sufficient evidence, and Mrs. Tully likely fell ill for reasons that were unexplainable or due to other medical issues. False accusations of poison and rebellion, however, were not uncommon. In Norfolk, Nancy, an enslaved woman charged with attempted poisoning, was acquitted and her owner required to pay a bond of $1,000 or sell Nancy for that amount.[98] Some cases appeared with very little evidence beyond the hysteria and paranoia of slaveholders. Editorials that put slaveholders on notice of the possibility of insurrection and the influence of abolitionist agitators appeared in Virginia newspapers. One such article cautioned slaveholders that outsiders from the abolitionist camp came to the state to "tamper with our slaves" and that there might well be a "well digested plan of rebellion among the slaves."[99] Rather than conceiving of the possibility that enslaved people might conjure up these ideas independent of abolitionists, the writer charged that outsiders were "laboring to incite discontent among the slaves, to poison their minds by false and seditious words, and by artfully contrived persuasives to excite revolt and lead to the murder of slave owners."[100] Informants alleged that they received this information from enslaved people who "cheerfully answered" their queries, but suspicion of Northerners who came to the South abounded throughout the antebellum decades. Leaders of the South vigorously defended slavery, Southern law, and their way of life. Any "outsiders" making their way to local communities caused some Virginians to question the motives of these Northerners. The writer concluded, "It is to be regretted that all such worthies were not lodged in jail, or soundly flogged by the very negroes whose destruction they were contriving." The article encouraged locals to pursue every measure necessary to ensure that biracial incendiary activity was prevented in the state. One editorial argued, "Are not the Abolitionists bent on our ruin? Are not their emissaries even now all through the South, inspiring our quiet slaves to poison and kill, to introduce anarchy and horrors?"[101] Suspicions of poison became the default explanation for someone who had suddenly fallen ill after ingesting food, drink, or medicine from an enslaved woman.

In the winter of 1858, Lucy, an enslaved woman laboring on the estate of Gilbert and Araminta Moxley, began preparing food as a part of her regular responsibilities. Everyday Lucy performed a series of tasks that ranged from cooking, cleaning, and serving, duties associated with her role in the maintenance of the Moxley household. Enslaved women working on the estates of Virginia planters made beds, dressed slaveholders and their families, nursed children, cleaned, dusted, ironed, and made preparations necessary for the daily upkeep of the households. On this particular day in December, Lucy performed her usual chores and mapped out her plan for executing tasks, but according to the court, something else probed the depths of her mind that day. She walked through the house and into the kitchen with a vial of arsenic in her pocket. No court accounts reveal a dispute, but these documents included scant details that might not reveal that working in the household involved the dynamics of force and refusal. On finishing their meal, the family grew ill, but it was Araminta Moxley, the mistress of the estate, who met her end after she consumed the food Lucy prepared. The court found Lucy guilty of murder and sentenced her to execution. Moxley's heirs received payment for Lucy's death to compensate them for the loss of labor and property.[102]

In August 1860, the court condemned Amelia to sale and transportation further south for attempted murder through poisoning. Enslaved in Amherst County, Virginia, the record leaves comparatively scant details concerning the circumstances, evidence, and any witnesses deposed in the case.[103] Several reasons accounted for a commuted sentence. To begin, the white victims involved may have lacked the confidence of the justices for matters of reputation or the absence of witnesses or sufficient evidence. The absence of sufficient evidence, however, never became a barrier to the death penalty in cases involving enslaved women and capital crime. Many of these deliberations were shaped by the justices themselves and locals who weighed in on the cases. The interpretations and opinions of legal administrators, witnesses, and locals factored into the administration of clemency. Another consideration might land at general concerns about the financial costs associated with compensation. By 1860, many enslaved women accused of capital crimes were sold further south, making the legal system a conduit of the domestic slave trade and releasing the commonwealth of the burden of compensation on behalf of Virginia slaveholders. The labor of enslaved people proved even more vital to the survival of the state as legislators, split by region, decided to join the Confederate States of America and secede from the Union.

War, however, did not stave off the threat of poison. The sheriff in Richmond detained Eliza, an enslaved woman accused of poisoning Augusts Kuper, but acquitted her on account of insufficient evidence.[104] Amid the turmoil of war, and given the vulnerable position of the Confederate capital, such matters might appear to be logistically challenging to address legally. In another case, the accusers could not clearly identify the person responsible for administering poison to Charles W. Fallan and a Miss Williams of Richmond. They suspected that enslaved people were the cause of the poisoning, but they also appeared on the mend. What they could not recover, however, were the "four horses, two mules, twenty hogs, and a number of sheep" that died, also as a result of poisoning.[105] The party responsible sought the life of the slaveholders and all of their valuable livestock, illuminating the fatal scope of poisoning as a form of wartime resistance.

Right at the height of conflict, as the war intensified around Richmond, Amanda, an enslaved woman who served the Clarke household, continued with her usual duties as the war raged on. In 1864, the four Clarke children were attending a school run by Miss Maria Allen. In the mornings, Amanda ensured that the young pupils received some breakfast, and while they went to school Amanda made preparations for meals and tended to the cleaning and maintenance of the house. One morning, Amanda made some short-cakes and gave one to Betty, one of Clarke's daughters. Betty took the cake to school and divided it to share with her siblings. According to Allen, the pupils immediately fell ill and suffered from "violent vomiting and pain in the head and the stomach."[106] Allen tried a number of remedies but to no avail. Sus-pecting that the shortcakes might be laced with arsenic, two doctors called in to examine them administered some medicines that counteract the effects of arsenic consumption and managed to alleviate some of the symptoms. The children showed signs of improvement the next morning, when an officer came to the house to examine them. The officer brought some flour and pa-pers of powders to determine the substance used in the shortcakes. In one of the samples, he discovered zinc sulfate. Modern usage of zinc sulfate aids in zinc deficiency, but during the nineteenth century, people used the inorganic compound as a violent emetic. The officer concluded that none of the baked goods Amanda prepared included arsenic, but instead they showed traces of zinc sulphate, which contained poisonous properties and appeared as a white powder similar to baking soda. A doctor prescribed Amanda the zinc sulfate just a few months prior to the incident, but the doctor testified that he con-sidered it not a poison "but a very active emetic." Amanda's counsel argued that while she "doubtless put into the dough the sulphate of zinc," she mis-took the compound for baking soda, "they both being alike in appearance."[107] Initially, the judge did not appear fully convinced that Amanda made a mistake. The court pursued further examination of the case, but eventually ac-quitted Amanda of the charges.[108] As acquittals for poisoning appeared most frequently during the war, enslaved women and girls suspected of the crime returned to the conditions of slave labor until the Confederacy surrendered.

The lines between healing and poisoning remained as blurred as the reasons for clemency and the death penalty for enslaved women and girls accused of the crime of poisoning. Healing, poisoning, clemency, and death all bore varied meanings and appeared as mutable terms in the emerging medical and legal pro-fessions. Enslaved women, however, developed their own ideas and meanings associated with healing and resistance. In most of the cases discussed in this chapter, motive or culpability appeared difficult to determine. What remains clear is that enslaved women developed and maintained their own knowledge of the healing and toxic properties of plant-based remedies, and, depending on the case, they administered these concoctions for a number of possible reasons.

These epistemologies of healing and toxicity were transferred through gen-erations, particularly among women and girls, and were to be administered wisely and, at times, strategically. Women and girls foraged in the surrounding environs, exchanging knowledge and information about how different plants might be transformed into remedies. On the other side of healing, cruelty and violence emerged in the intimate quarters of slaveholding households, prompting enslaved women and girls to contemplate the alternative uses of that which might also heal. These considerations of refusal and defiance offer evidence of how enslaved women manifested retribution even if it meant their demise. These intimate ruptures spilled out into the public in the form of political tensions where abolitionists increasingly vocalized their opposition to the "poison" of slavery. The realities of enslaved women's resistance, and the political movement against slavery, led to a decreasing sense of security. Virginians demanded that state leaders remain consistent in their commitments to make an example of those who undermined this need for security. As long as owners and renters relied on the labor of the enslaved, poison remained an ongoing threat to the possibilities of domestic tranquility.

CHAPTER THREE

Murder

He was a hard master. He would not give us enough meat to eat. He would not
allow any of us to go from home, nor give us any of the privileges which other
people's servants have. He told us we should stay at home during the Christmas
holydays & work. We concluded to get rid of him.

—Nelly's testimony

During the Christmas holiday of 1856, Prince William County local G. A.
Hutchison stumbled upon a fire that consumed the home of George E.
Green. As he approached the burning house, to his horror, he discovered
what he described as the "charred spine & pelvis of an adult." Hutchison proceeded to walk down the path leading from the house to the barn, where he
found traces of blood smeared along the road and the slats that lined the gate.
Scenes of blood, broken gates, and a split latch to the entrance gave indication that a struggle occurred prior to the fire. But the bloodstained hatchet
that survived the fire confirmed suspicions of a potential "scuffle." Nelly, an
enslaved woman, and her children, Betsy and James, and her grandchildren,
Elias and Ellen, were jailed and charged with the murder of their owner,
Green. The court identified Nelly as the ringleader.[1]

Virginia locals took a collective interest in the court proceedings involving the murder trials of white Southerners and the enslaved women who bore
the weight of the accusations against them.[2] By the mid-nineteenth century
Virginia lawmakers protected the property rights of individuals, but an ethic
of communalism also remained significant at the county level, particularly
among nonslaveholding white Southerners who intervened in highly publicized cases. Historians show that "legal localism," or the habit and customs of
a specific community, worked in tandem to "keep the peace," or maintain social order.[3] Petitioning provided an avenue for local citizens to weigh in on
trials even in instances where they did not serve as witnesses.[4] These petitions reveal opportunities to submit their appraisals of the character and reputations of those involved in the cases under consideration.[5] Petitioning also
served an ideological function in which citizens articulated ideas about right
and wrong and submitted recommendations for sentencing. Furthermore, local justices and the executive office of the state administered executions and

occasional pardons with no seemingly consistent guidelines for justice, but through a dynamic process of measuring their own decisions against the interests and mores of the locale.[6] In Virginia's courts of oyer and terminer, cases involving enslaved women's violent crimes against white Virginians unfolded in rather unpredictable ways. In Nelly's case, ideas about Black women's deviant behavior and considerations of age guided the debate about culpability as locals scrutinized the three generations of enslaved people tried for the death of Green.

According to Nelly's testimony, the group confronted Green in his home, when Nelly reached for an ax and struck him. Green attempted to escape, but the others pursued him with shovels, axes, and slats from the fencing. Among networks of kin based on trust and loyalty, enslaved people shared knowledge about plots of resistance, but some also inadvertently became involved.[7] Afterward, Betsy, James, Elias, and Ellen tied up Green's body and dragged it back to the house, where they set the dwelling on fire.[8] When Nelly was asked about her motivations for the murder, she offered the following statement: "He was a hard master. He would not give us enough meat to eat. He would not allow any of us to go from home, nor give us any of the privileges which other people's servants have. He told us we should stay at home during the Christmas holydays & work. We concluded to get rid of him."[9] As scholars have shown, withholding the modicum of privileges some enslaved people received marked one of numerous grievances that inspired slave resistance.[10] According to Nelly, Green violated what historians refer to as the paternalist ethic described as the mutual obligations between master and slave that allowed for the "privileges" that she referred to.[11] These privileges, however, do not suggest that Nelly or any other enslaved women were compelled by Southern paternalism. Indeed, Nelly told the examiner, a doctor Ewell, that they were "tired of living with him," meaning that perhaps Green made a habit of making life particularly difficult for enslaved people on his plantation and that her resolve to continue to survive such suffering had worn thin. James stated, "He was hard upon us & we could [do] nothing to please him."[12] Despite the fact that the bondpeople on Ewell's homestead described Green's difficult personality, the focus of local debate emphasized community perceptions of the enslaved defendants, and Nelly in particular. The court found Nelly, Betsy, James, Elias, and Ellen guilty of murder and sentenced them to death. On the morning of the execution day, Nelly, Betsy, and James, the elder members of the enslaved family, died by hanging. Petitions appeared on behalf of Elias and Ellen to keep them from the gallows.

The court records identified Nelly as the ringleader of the group, but she meant more than that to those she called kin; she was the matriarch, the grandmother to Elias and Ellen, and the mother of Betsy and James, the glue that held the family together for generations. Betsy and James were treated as accomplices in the record, and Nelly vocalized her personal dissent, noting her exhaustion from years of serving a "hard master."[13] Locals offered neither gendered critiques of Green and his failed paternalism nor even an account of Nelly's experiences with a slave owner who lacked the evenhandedness that Southerners referred to when they defended slavery as a "positive good." She survived decades of enslavement, bore children, helped rear her grandchildren, all while enduring the harsh conditions of life on Green's plantation, and yet the debate placed the moral burden on Nelly. Years of devotion and survival, not to mention the reproductive profit she produced for the Green family, were reduced to descriptions of Nelly as a corrupting and evil influence. Elias and Ellen, twins around the age of fourteen, allegedly participated in the struggle to bring Green to his demise. Petitioners, however, were unconvinced that their participation warranted the death penalty. Their reservations explicitly probed the question of whether the twins willfully assisted with the homicide or fell under the pressures of their grandmother.

The petition shows that members of the local community disagreed about the appropriateness of the death penalty in this particular case. Concerns about the age of the defendants appeared in letters sent to Governor Henry A. Wise, to whom petitioners appealed for pardon on behalf of the siblings. One resident, Luther Lynn, offered that it was "usual for parent slaves to exact obedience from their young children and to correct them," suggesting that they had limited, if any, say in their participation in the act if parents were involved.[14] Locals who questioned the culpability of the twins simultaneously reinforced a scathing critique of enslaved mothers and grandmothers as the purveyors of violent crime. Similarly, Thomas B. Baless of Snow Hill, Maryland, noted, "Some who attended the trial and heard the evidence are impressed with a strong conviction that the two children might have been instigated by their seniors."[15] To underscore the moral tone of his letter, the former Presbyterian minister cautioned the governor, saying, "Acts of mercy are the acts which guide our own exit from the World."[16] But even the moral suasion of onlookers met with equally passionate conviction in arguments for Elias's and Ellen's executions.

The petitions received in the governor's office represented different ideas about race, gender, and age. J. B. Grayson, a Prince William County resident, argued that all of the convicted slaves "went most deliberately to work" and further noted that "the woman Ellen [was] of large size for a woman, and very well developed physically—probably as well developed as she ever would be."[17] Grayson shifted the conversation to direct attention to the development of Ellen's body as an indicator of maturity and to probe her capacity for culpability. Ellen's perceived physical, and even sexual, maturity coincided with typical assumptions that shaped slaveholder exploitation of the sexual and reproductive aspects of pubescent girls' bodies.[18] This racial and gendered calculation of the bodies of enslaved children rendered the innocence and adolescence attributed to white children beyond their reach as they faced charges and forms of sentencing assigned to adults. Moreover, Elias was smaller in stature, but Grayson asserted that he was "admitted by all to be the most intelligent of the set." He concluded that physical maturity and mental acuity superseded moral arguments that focused on their age.[19] Thus, the intellectual propensity to formulate both an attitude of malice and the physical possibility to act on those motives colored perceptions of Ellen's and Elias's involvement. According to Grayson, only those who claimed residence in Prince William County offered the most reliable perspective on the matter. Writing as "a citizen in the immediate neighborhood and of this most fiendish murder," Grayson argued that petitioners such as W. E. Gaskins and others in favor of transportation were primarily residents of neighboring counties: "[They have] no more right to petition your Excellency in regard to this our own County business, than I have to advise that you do not allow your overseer in Accomack to whip one of your negroes there, who disobeyed him."[20] The decision, however, fell in favor of dissent when Governor Wise issued a statement commuting the sentences to transportation.[21]

Ellen and Elias escaped the gallows but remained in bondage without the elders who raised them and perhaps offered daily examples of generational resistance and their own ideas about justice when they were alive.[22] Wise declared, "The three oldest were executed, which I deem all sufficient for public justice and example."[23] The latter part of Wise's statement reveals that these gestures held a notable degree of symbolic value. The imperative to make an example of one or a few suspects appeared in earlier approaches to the punishment of slave rebellions, but this statement also offers an example of how commuted sentences inferred the symbolic meanings of balance and moderation.[24] Issued only in sporadic instances, the power and logic behind "mercy," as it appears in the records, remained elusive, as every case resulted in an uncertain and yet still violent outcome. According to the historian Wilma King, slaveholders determined that enslaved girls and boys reached adulthood at the age of sixteen, when they became full hands, or even younger for girls, when they began menarche.[25] King also notes that white males were considered adults between the ages of eighteen and twenty-one. In other cases, enslaved people could be treated as adults as early as fourteen.[26] These ideas shaped the gendered calculus that determined the innocence or culpability of enslaved girls.

Age was also a consideration in the case of Caroline, an enslaved girl from Fauquier County.[27] On May 21, 1832, the court tried Caroline for the attempted murder of a white infant named Maria Catharine Smith, likely a child she attended to due to her own young age.[28] Caroline pleaded not guilty to the charge, but the court ordered her execution. Although she received a death sentence, the court included in its records a recommendation of sale and transportation, and the governor subsequently commuted Caroline's sentence. In Monroe County, however, Rebecca, another enslaved girl on trial for murder, did not receive a commuted sentence. She appeared in court for the murder of a four-year-old white girl named Adeline. Perhaps the fact that Maria survived and Caroline was tried for attempted murder factored into the change in her sentence, but Rebecca, despite the fact that she was considered young, was convicted of the charge and executed.[29] From an early age, enslaved children discovered the dynamics of power that made slavery possible, but throughout the generations they also discovered ways to wield their own power, even if it cost them their lives.[30]

In Fluvanna County, the court tried Judy, an enslaved woman, for the murder of a white woman named Sarah Branson, the wife of Stephen Branson. Judy pleaded not guilty, but the testimony of both white and free Black witnesses supported a guilty conviction. The treasury department of the state issued payment of $250 to her owner, Mildred Ware, for her execution.[31] These deliberations took into account the overall reputations of enslaved women, and both white and Black witnesses testified of her guilt. The manner in which the law remained hostile toward enslaved and free Black Virginians offers some insights into whether these testimonies were autonomously issued. Did the free Black witnesses truly find guilt in Judy, or were there unspoken factors that motivated them to comply with arguments affirming her guilt?[32] Free Black witnesses certainly used their voices in court for strategic purposes, and not all testimony was shaped by the possibility of intimidation or blind support, for that matter. The details of the case are scant at best, and Judy eventually gave a confession admitting that she killed Sarah Branson. The arrangements made by Ware brought Judy into the Branson household, with unfamiliar, and perhaps volatile, dynamics that led to Branson's death.[33]

Murder cases involving the death of white Southerners and the enslaved people accused of the crime brought to light the violence inflicted and at times exchanged between white women and enslaved women.

In Charlotte County, the court heard a case involving Pat, an enslaved woman who stood accused of murdering Martha Fariss, the wife of John Fariss, who claimed ownership of Pat. The court determined Pat's value at $250 and sentenced her to death. The sheriff performed her execution a month later, and the auditor disbursed the funds to John Fariss.[34] The courts were as much sites of deliberations over justice as they were financial institutions that shaped the direction of transactions for the property claims of Southerners and slaveholders. In Southampton County, the court tried a case involving Nelly, an enslaved woman accused of murdering Sally Shields, the wife of John Shields, the man who legally owned Nelly.[35] Witnesses, including Sally Shields's son, explained that they noticed Shields was missing, and, as they searched for her, Nelly went for a wash and did not plan to return until she finished. When Shields failed to return, the witnesses grew anxious and began a more earnest search. They discovered a bloody frock, coat, and handkerchief under Nelly's bed. As they circled the premises, they eventually found Shields's lifeless and bruised body. According to one witness, Nelly confessed and admitted that she "killed her mistress." The court delayed her execution after she reported a pregnancy. She spent a number of months in jail, and without mention of whether or not she gave birth to a child, she died by execution on March 17, 1828.[36]

The court did not need evidence of actual murder to end the life of an enslaved woman charged with attempting to murder. In Southampton County, the court tried Mary for "maliciously assaulting and beating" Elizabeth Pond, the wife of Henry Pond, who owned Mary. According to witnesses, which included Elizabeth Pond, Mary not only violently beat her but also intended to kill her. The historian Thavolia Glymph explains that "a kind of warring intimacy characterized many of the conflicts between mistresses and slave women in the household."[37] The court decided the outcome of the case based on the testimony of two white witnesses, one of them Pond herself. In instances of physical rebuttals, most slaveholders opted to inflict their own disciplinary measures, a testament to the power that Pond wielded and one that she downplayed in instances when postured as the victim of Mary's violence. Unlike in cases involving conflicts between enslaved people and those who temporarily hired them, Henry and Elizabeth Pond owned Mary. So why submit the case to court, especially if Elizabeth Pond survived the alleged beating? Both the Ponds and Mary knew that if she inflicted a severe beating, they held the power to end her life. In this case, her life ended on the gallows as instructed by the court. The couple received remittance for her execution.[38]

Conflict unfolded in instances where enslaved women took a decisive stance against inconveniences, unfairness, or limits they communicated with slaveholders and overseers. Phoebe, an enslaved woman in Rappahannock County, went to great lengths to guard the spaces she claimed as her own. Like many enslaved women in the South, Phoebe slept in the cellar of the homestead belonging to her owner, which, depending on the structure, stood attached or separate from the main house. Her owner, Carter Lumpkin, and Phoebe quarreled frequently, and the dynamic tended to escalate rather quickly. On one occasion, they quarreled over a matter, and when Lumpkin struck her, she threw him on the ground. She used her strength in ways that she knew could land her on the gallows and that sent a clear message of her limits. One incident brought her to court and ultimately to her death. One day, Lumpkin barged through the cellar to get potatoes. Apparently, Phoebe placed her bed in the path to the potatoes, and when Lumpkin instructed her to move her bed, she refused. He stormed off but, according to his wife Frances, returned at midnight to retrieve the potatoes. Frances "heard him at the house of the prisoner after midnight and there appeared to be considerable noise as if the prisoner and deceased were quarreling." The following morning, Lumpkin's body lay on the ground outside the house.

Witnesses discovered clothes and a hoe soaked in blood just outside of Phoebe's dwelling. Why did Lumpkin wait until midnight to make another attempt to retrieve the potatoes? Did Phoebe make a habit of withholding stored provisions, or was this about food at all? The record does not provide details beyond limited testimony, but the witnesses explain a volatile dynamic in which Phoebe refused Lumpkin's attempts at wielding power over her, even if it meant her own demise. According to witnesses, Phoebe "was very disobedient to her master and frequently ran away." Others noted that she possessed "one of the most violent tempers of any negro." Lumpkin whipped her in the past, but at a certain point Phoebe resolved to prevent it from ever happening again. Phoebe grew accustomed to conveying her own imperatives and limits in ways that demanded a stop to beatings and any requests she deemed unreasonable.[39]

While the cases of enslaved women accused of murders did not occur with great frequency, they happened on enough occasions to make rhetoric concerning the contented slave a known fallacy among Virginians. In one particular case, "the public sensibility [was] so much excited, and the public curiosity so much awakened" when a case involving Andrew, Lucinda, and Caroline was tried in the Bath County courthouse. On August 22, 1838, locals awaited details of the fate of the three enslaved persons who stood accused of murdering Margaret and Mary Mayse, the daughters of George and Sarah Mayse. Most of the evidence came from Caroline, Lucinda's fourteen-year-old daughter. According to Caroline, on August 10, 1838, Lucinda and Andrew disclosed details of an appealing blackberry patch to pick from. Areas from which to pick berries, herbs, and various plants offered a burst of sweetness to the bland meals and rations many enslaved people were offered by slaveholders. As chapter 2 showed, foraging also provided much-needed roots and plants for remedies. In this instance, Caroline likely seemed interested in the possibility of picking sweet berries for their delicious taste. Time spent foraging, walking, and chatting with her mother, Lucinda, and Andrew provided a break from the backbreaking toil of farming, cooking, and housekeeping. But in this instance, Lucinda and Andrew did not plan an excursion for themselves alone, and Caroline became embroiled in a scheme of her mother's design.[40]

Lucinda instructed Caroline that after meeting Mary and Margaret at school to walk them back, she was to bring them to a large gate located near the Mayse homestead. When Caroline arrived, Andrew stood leaning against the gate, and Lucinda appeared next to him. Caroline inquired about the blackberry patch, but, rather than reply, Andrew seized Mary, and Lucinda grabbed her by the head and pulled it back as Andrew cut her throat with a shoe knife. Margaret immediately took off, but before she could gain any distance Andrew caught her, and Lucinda held her down as he cut her throat. Andrew and Lucinda jumped the fence, but Caroline headed to the house, and on her way there she noticed that Andrew briskly walked toward the well, where he attempted to wash off the blood on his shirt, hands, and arms. As Caroline picked up speed, she abruptly felt compelled to stop, as she considered the deadly outcomes that awaited her. She explained "her fears of being murdered herself, from disclosing the event to her mistress immediately upon getting to the house." She also disclosed that her mother "told her she would be hung if she told any thing about it."[41]

Lucinda walked "leisurely" to the house, and when she saw Sarah Mayse, she inquired into the whereabouts of the girls. The light of day began to dim, and evening approached as Mayse became increasingly concerned. She initiated a search for the girls, to which Lucinda suggested that they might have drowned in crossing the run. Mayse thought this impossible given the depth of the water and her strict instructions to the girls to avoid it. Caroline told the search party that the girls might be near the blackberry patch, and when they arrived at the gate, she pointed to their bodies. The search party immediately returned to Mayse to explain that they found the girls dead. She stood "inexpressibly shocked, and incapable of moving from the spot where she stood." She stoically instructed Lucinda to retrieve the bodies of her daughters, and Lucinda proceeded in the direction of the gate and returned without the girls to notify Mayse that she saw a large man standing by the bodies with a club in his hand and "a great dog sitting near." Local men went in search of the man but found no one. Neighbors brought the bodies to the house, and witnesses saw "Mrs. Mayse almost frantic with grief," "shrieking and screaming like one beside herself," and "Lucinda looking intently upon her and smiling with apparent satisfaction."[42]

The three enslaved defendants arrived at the Bath County courthouse eleven days later to learn of their fate. The magistrates and counsel attempted to extract both evidence and motives associated with the case, as the public outcry against the deaths of two white children demanded an explanation. Lucinda and Andrew wore clothing that showed signs of blood, but Lucinda explained that the blood resulted from having a tooth pulled. Another enslaved woman who was deposed stated that she witnessed the tooth extraction but did not see any blood from the cavity. Witnesses also noticed blood on Andrew's shirt, to which he explained that infected flea bites and a cut on his finger created the specks of blood on his shirt. The court did not find these accounts of the bloodstains on their garments compelling. It proceeded to examine possible motives. Sarah Mayse explained that George Mayse attempted to whip Lucinda a few days prior to the murder, but she escaped. She later recalled hearing that "Lucinda declared that neither her master nor any other man should ever whip her—if they did, there would be murder committed, for she had as soon die one death as another." George Mayse testified that he attempted to prevent Lucinda from "beating one of her children in the most cruel manner." Both testify to the violent dynamics that shaped life in bondage. The historian Jeff Forret aptly notes that "the very same owners who viewed whipping as a necessary form of correction for their bondpeople constructed an alternate narrative to explain the violence that took place on the plantation, one that recast paternalistic whites as the guardians and protectors of their enslaved people from the dangers posed by other slaves."[43] Lucinda faced the looming threats of her own beating as she allegedly inflicted her own forms of corporal punishment on her children. She demanded their loyalty and their obedience and refuted any attempts at inference. We see this with Caroline, who provides the most substantial testimony that the court admits as compelling evidence of Lucinda's culpability.

Why would Caroline testify against her mother? In some cases, enslaved people, young and old, might be coerced into confessions and testimonies implicating another enslaved person. But in this instance, Caroline explains the life-and-death circumstances in which she found herself. Her mother warned her that death awaited her if she told Sarah Mayse details of Mary's and Margaret's murders. Caroline waited to see how this incident played out, and when the search party solicited her help, she led them to the bodies, but she did not yet disclose details about her mother's involvement. If George Mayse is to be believed, Lucinda vigorously disciplined her children, which might clarify Caroline's involvement and subsequent hesitation. Caroline seemed conflicted between allegiance to her mother and her own convictions about her disapproval of Lucinda's and Andrew's actions. Caroline labored for the Mayses, and Sarah Mayse assigned to her the task of caring for the girls in particular. She even attempted to shield the younger girl from the sight of her sister's death, a testament to her own ethos about what adults exposed children to, even as she herself, a child, witnessed a murder in which she did not want to play a part. Details about her shielding the child made locals believe that she "turned the child's head away, knowing that she was so much attached to her sister that she would cry out if she saw them do any harm to her." According to local opinion, "This single act shewed conclusively that she knew the purpose for which the children were decoyed to the scene of murder." But seen from her view, a child's view, Caroline's instincts led her to shield the child even as Andrew pried the girl away from her. She guided the search party to the bodies after her mother led them in the opposite direction, to the creek. Caroline saw the world violently unraveling around her, to which she responded with as much cooperation as she could muster.[44]

The conflicts that shaped the power dynamics on the Mayse homestead formed the basis of public understandings of the motivations behind the murder. According to George Mayse, Lucinda became "exceedingly insolent," and he threatened to whip her. But Lucinda's youngest child, an infant, became ill and died soon after. How did Lucinda's baby die? And in what state did Lucinda find herself while caring for an infant and performing the endless labor that slavery demanded? Mayse seemed to acknowledge the exceptional circumstances of Lucinda's anger and delayed the punishment. But his sympathy reached certain limits, since news of the death of her infant did not prevent him from buying a fresh cowhide, which he deliberately displayed for all to see what awaited Lucinda and anyone else who crossed him. Grievances against George and Sarah Mayse did not end with Lucinda. Andrew also made threats. On numerous occasions he expressed his desire to be sold to another owner and his general discontent with life at the Mayses' homestead. In the past, Andrew escaped from George Mayse and avoided him in hopes of evading a whipping. According to Sarah Mayse, Andrew declared that "he would do something to make his master sell him, for he would not live with him." The court called four enslaved men as witnesses to confirm Andrew's alibi, which put him in the fields at the time of the incident. But the court found inconsistencies in each of their testimonies, and Sarah Mayse explained that Andrew stood at the well during the time the witnesses claimed that he labored in the fields. The court sentenced Andrew and Lucinda to death, and Caroline received an acquittal that involved George Mayse paying a bond of $2,000 to ensure her good behavior, which ultimately led to her sale and transportation. The court paid Mayse $1,200 from the public treasury for the value of Andrew and Lucinda.[45]

Public news accounts featured opinions and insights imbued with interpretations about the criminality of the defendants and the function of clemency as a form of justice.[46] One reporter underscored the incident as a symptom of George Mayse's mismanagement of the enslaved people under his charge. "It appears from all accounts, that the family had been very indulgent towards the slaves—that the want of authority operated upon such too malignant and reckless spirits, so as to produce the perpetration of two of the most emboldened and atrocious murders which the present day has produced," the *Richmond Enquirer* reported.[47] The nature of the murder and the manner in which the defendants seemed to target the children triggered the moral sensibilities of the public. The reporter lamented, "It thrills the blood of every humane person, to see two such tender and helpless innocents fall victims to the demon-like passions of two such fiends." According to reports in the news, Lucinda and Andrew became notorious for performing a heinous act against humanity and represented the grave lessons of the unchecked will and power of enslaved people. The two defendants remained at fault, but as the editorial makes clear, Mayse failed to exercise proper authority over them. To onlookers, Mayse led a household characterized by disorder. The social contract forged between slaveholding and nonslaveholding locals emphasized the tolerance of the institution in exchange for the assurance of peace and order. Proper discipline ensured that the enslaved posed minimal threat to the locale. Mayse attempted to intimidate Lucinda and Andrew with threats of violence, but the consequences no longer seemed as menacing as before. Witnesses recalled earlier that Lucinda stated that should her master or any other man ever whip her, "there would be murder committed, for she had as soon die one death as another." The exigencies of slavery weighed on Lucinda and Andrew in ways that informed their decision to initiate an explosive blow to the Mayse family with the full knowledge of what it meant for them. To them, death did not matter anymore.[48]

Governors considered the possibility of reprieve or clemency involving the capital crimes of enslaved people, and, in this case, Caroline appeared as a likely candidate, but the fate of her mother and Andrew seemed fixed. One editorial informed readers of the news that the case went to the governor's office, which, according to the writer, was "a wise and humane provision of our criminal law." This statement reflected the general sentiment of lawmakers and Virginians who understood the demand for ensuring the economic viability of slavery and the corresponding aim of discouraging slave resistance. He further explained the logic of this provision, stating, "The slaves, not having the benefit of a trial by jury, nor before the Magistrates of the County Courts, whose sentence for good or for ill, is conclusive, it was thought proper and humane to transmit the Record of the trial to the Executive of the Commonwealth—who might, if they saw fit, interpose their province of mercy to reprieve, to pardon, or to commute the sentence of death into transportation (as is frequently the case)."[49] Southerners viewed the very existence of clemency, an avenue of appeal for the enslaved people accused of capital crimes, as a measure of benevolence. The "proper and humane" technologies of the law made the outcome of acquittal not freedom but sale and transportation in order to provide assurance of good behavior and the general peace of the commonwealth. Even in the rare instances of acquittals, the best outcome for an enslaved person led to a return to slavery. This meant that to ensure the peace of the commonwealth, officials and slave owners sold enslaved people convicted of capital crimes. But the editorial writer shared doubts, stating, "In the present instance, the record is so dark and bloody, that no attempt has been made to soften the sentence—and there is no prospect of the Executive interfering to change the decision of the Court." The court arranged for Caroline to be sold, but Andrew and Lucinda died on the gallows, just as they predicted.[50] The murders that enslaved people stood accused of drew the broader attention of Virginians across county lines as a reminder of the constant potential for violent resistance and to reassure citizens of the legal protections and the justice available to slaveholders and other white victims of these crimes.

While legal conditions of reprieve remained a possibility, in many cases the court ordered the execution of enslaved women for murder convictions. During the summer of 1857, Catherine, a young enslaved woman likely hired out to Salena J. Hall by her owner, Maria Thomson, died at the gallows after the court found her guilty for Hall's murder. The sheriff, M. J. Gooch, confirmed to the clerk, "I have executed the within sentence by causing the within named negro girl Catherine to be hung by the neck on the public gallows on the 21st day of August 1857 til she be dead."[51] The court valued Catherine at $800. In Lynchburg, Peggy appeared before the court for attempted murder. According to records, Peggy somehow came into possession of a spade that she used to wound Lydia Pritchard, the wife of John L. Pritchard, allegedly inflicting cuts that caused "great bodily injury." The court determined Peggy's value at $400 and sold her.[52] During the summer of 1840, Betsey appeared before the Fauquier County court of oyer and terminer for the murder of John Somerfield Wilson, the infant son of Joseph C. Wilson. While the court found her guilty, it also unanimously recommended Betsey for transportation instead of the death sentence. The counsel assigned to her case verified that she died by execution. Typically, the records include a note from the sheriff who performed the act, but in this instance the counsel explained that, while he did not see Betsey hung on the gallows, he witnessed her being "carried out for that purpose and the crowd that followed her" and he verified her death. The gallows became a site of spectacle, drawing groups of people with sizes depending on the locale in which the hanging occurred and the public magnitude of the case. This case drew a crowd of locals who witnessed Betsey's death, a scene that presumed her guilt.[53]

Violent conflicts often erupted on news of the transfer of enslaved property through an inheritance, a transaction that shifted the lives and relationships that enslaved women worked tirelessly to preserve. In the spring of 1853, Margaret Buckner, an enslaved woman bestowed on Reuben Gaines by his parents, partnered with Jim Phillips, who is listed as a free Black man, in a plan to murder Gaines. The court records explain how Buckner and her daughter, Betty, became the property inherited by Gaines and that any money from the sale of Buckner and Betty, and their increase, be split among his sons when they reached the age of twenty-one. The transfer of property and the resolving of estates meant that women like Buckner, along with "her increase," moved from one person in the Gaines family to the next. The reality of Reuben Gaines's inheritance or perhaps even the dynamics of the Gaines homestead triggered Buckner, and the court determined her guilt and sentenced her to death for murder in the first degree. According to news reports of the executions of Buckner and Phillips, "a smile was on their countenance from the jail to the gallows."[54] Onlookers observed that "they expressed a willingness to die, and met their fate with a hope of happiness in the world to come." The gallows, a public space that could draw a crowd consisting of hundreds of locals, became the site from which Virginians scrutinized the bodies, faces, and emotional state of convicted enslaved people. Before they took their final breath, onlookers searched for any final sentiments that might tell them more about the people forcibly fastened to the gallows. But the inner lives of enslaved people, as well as free Black people, remained outside the purview of newspaper reporters, crowds, and even court records. Only Buckner and Phillips understood the full extent of their motivations and the reasons behind their actions. The intimate worlds of households that employed enslaved people and the financial transactions that forcibly moved them from one place to the next prompted a number of responses.

Laboring in Southern homes might mean that enslaved women and girls attended to the care of white families in swaths of time that demanded their ongoing attention. Such demands particularly in the context of care work afforded limited, if any, time for oneself. In Powhatan County, Jane, described as a "negro girl slave," attended to the care of a certain Mrs. Beasley, the woman who hired her. Beasley struggled with a long-term illness, which also involved her confinement to bed. Jane likely served as a nurse, tending to Beasley's health and responding to her requests. The care of a woman stationed in her bed might also require that Jane bathe and clothe her, administer her medicine, and change out her chamber pot. At some point, Jane reached a breaking point. By breaking point, I mean to underscore the possible presence of some exceptional moment, perhaps one that accumulated over years of turmoil, or even the everyday demands that extracted from the bodies of enslaved girls. If Jane never reached this sort of watershed moment, she certainly registered her own decision to end whatever endless cycle of labor and attention Beasley extracted from her. According to records, Jane confessed to suffocating Beasley as she lay in bed. One news report explained that "in a shocking manner," she attacked Beasley, who "choked to death, without having the power to help herself."[55] The sheriff executed Jane the following month. Her age is not recorded in these records, and we can only surmise that she faced her fate at a relatively young age compared to the enslaved women who stood trial for murder. Gustavus Depp, the man who claimed ownership of Jane, received $520 from the state treasury.

Enslaved women expressed a number of grievances that resulted in their deaths and the deaths of others tied to their everyday lives in bondage. In one case, Molly labored on the homestead belonging to Charles B. Champion. Champion hired an overseer, John R. Magee, who not only supervised the labor of the enslaved but also issued food rations on a daily basis. On one occasion, Molly accused Magee of withholding rations and demanded that he provide more food. She hurled her complaints about inadequate food, to which Magee hit her for calling him a liar. Disputes about the size of rations were common throughout the South, as many slaveholders instructed over-seers to limit provisions to bare necessities. Slaveholders wedded to ideals of paternalism might appear more generous by providing better-quality rations and clothing. Some enslaved people maintained certain expectations about what they were entitled to, and, here, Molly was no exception. She informed Magee that "no white man should whip her" and that "she meant to have a meal out of the house or lose the last drop of her blood." Magee explained that he typically issued more food than Champion allotted and never pos-sessed reason to whip Molly. Something shifted for her that day, however, that does not appear in the record. A scuffle ensued, and Molly followed up on her promise and stabbed Magee. The court found her guilty of assault with intent to kill, then ordered her execution, and Molly died on the gallows in September 1852.[56]

Virginians read about murder cases in the news, and when they learned of an enslaved woman making an attempt on the life of a white person, they ex-pressed their horror, but not their surprise. On the morning of July 19, 1852, the residents on the far end of Seventh Street in Richmond grappled with a terrifying scene at the Winston residence. According to the news, "Mr. and Mrs. Winston were found lying on their bed with several gashes and deep brain cuts upon their heads, evidently made with a sharp, heavy instrument." The couple's nine-month-old daughter was found in a cradle, "dying from se-vere contusions on the side of the head."[57] Jane Williams, an enslaved female described as "a yellow woman of ordinary size, apparently 35 or 40 years of age, hair nearly straight, and with features indicative of great firmness," testi-fied that when she entered the room and picked up the baby, she noticed that she felt limp. After placing the baby back into the crib, she noticed the bloody stains on the bed and notified another enslaved woman that she found every-one in the house dead.[58]

After news spread of the ghastly scene at the Winston homestead, doctors arrived and confirmed the death of the mistress and the critical condition of her husband and child. In addition to deep cuts near the eyes and the nose, the doctors noted that "four or five other wounds extend[ed] to the frontal bone, fracturing the skull." The coroner found a large hatchet stained with blood in the kitchen and a set of clothes also stained in blood in Williams's bed-room. The testimony of enslaved and free witnesses included information that conflicted with Williams's testimony. For instance, Williams stated that she went to the market to get beef to cut up for a soup. But her husband and other enslaved people in the neighborhood recalled that they ate cabbage and bacon with apple dumplings and that they did not notice any beef in their possession. Williams claimed that she cut the beef with the hatchet, which covered it in blood, but another enslaved woman testified that Williams cooked in the kitchen and did not prepare beef that day. When the police asked Williams to take them to the spot where she cut the meat, "there were no spots, marks or indentations there."[59]

Throughout the course of the trial, Williams continued to deny any involvement and even tried to accuse another enslaved woman, Anna, despite testimony that confirmed her own contempt for the family. Other witnesses recalled that Anna courted men outside of the household and that her reputation appeared increasingly "base." Williams told the jury that one evening Anna attempted to talk to a man through her window since she did not receive permission to leave. According to Williams, "if it happened so again," the man Anna courted planned to "knock Winston in the head some of these times."[60] According to one witness, however, "There always seemed to be some difficulty between Mrs. Winston and Jane, and her husband. Jane has said she did not like Mr. and Mrs. W."[61] Both Jane and John Williams, her husband, vocally expressed their disdain for the Winstons.

The court turned its attention to John Williams, now a suspect and alleged accomplice in the homicide. One witness claimed that Williams confided in him and told him that "three or four weeks before the murder took place, his wife Jane told him she intended to kill Mr. and Mrs. Winston, but that he did not believe it any more than that he could fly to the sky."[62] In fact, enslaved women's violent crimes did not occur frequently, but when they did, some struggled to come to terms with the ways these acts disrupted their ideas about gender. According to this witness, John Williams "said he did not think any woman would attempt such a thing, although they might be disposed to talk of it." John Wortham occasionally hired out Williams from Joseph Winston and testified that Williams explained that "hardships were imposed on him by his master." According to Wortham, Williams disclosed that "he meant to put a stop to it and would stop it." Indeed, Wortham personally received threats from Williams and recalled an incident when he threatened Wortham with a hammer.[63] Wortham explained that Williams gave him trouble and that he "was afraid of him all the time he was at the factory." Locals believed that, while Jane Williams was the culprit, John Williams served as an accessory and accomplice for her actions. One news report declared, "It should not be forgotten that Jane Williams, the most execrable wretch of whom we have ever read or heard, was a communicant, and so was John."[64] The reporter went further, stating, "These devils incarnate considered it perfectly consistent with the creed to murder the innocent infant in its cradle— the sleeping and unsuspecting parents in their beds!"

A few days following the cross-examination of the enslaved members of the Winston household, Jane Williams confessed to the pastor of the local Black church in Richmond that she committed the murder on her own. According to her confession, she woke up early in the morning as her husband slept, and she took his hatchet and proceeded to the Winstons' bedroom. She attacked Joseph Winston first, after which "he scarcely struggled," then "commenced cutting into the head of Mrs. Winston."[65] She recalled that Virginia Winston's "struggles were so great" that she "inflicted stronger and more frequent blows upon her head than she did upon Mr. W's in order to silence her quickly." Once Virginia Winston appeared unconscious, Williams killed the infant and washed the hatchet. She claimed that the devil "had such possession of her that morning, that she believed she could have went further than she did, if necessary." On August 9, 1852, "in a clear and composed tone of voice," Williams pleaded guilty for the murder of Virginia Winston and professed sole responsibility for the violent attacks on the Winstons.[66] Before she approached the gallows, she was asked once again whether anyone aided her in the crime, and she "denied positively that any person aided her in committing the murder."[67]

On September 10, 1852, a crowd of reportedly 6,000 onlookers, "of all sexes, colors, and ages," formed around the gallows, so infamously creating a sensation near the hustings court. White Southerners expressed their vitriol and launched a series of tirades against Jane and John Williams. One report referred to her as "one of the vilest wretches that ever disgraced humanity." She served as a mere confirmation of the perceived depravity of Black women, but Black Virginians responded differently. As Jane Williams's body hung on the gallows, one observer noted, "She has gone home," while another determined, "She is in glory." The reporter identified spiritual declarations and expressions of a heavenly afterlife after having suffered on earth and endured a life of bondage. These adages gave hope in moments of despair and death even as they sparked outrage among others. The reporter stated, "Innumerable expressions of that kind were heard on the ground, and have since been repeated all over this city!" The court spent an extensive period of time investigating who Jane and John Williams were, but the responses of Black observers also beg the question of who Virginia and Joseph Winston were. Another Black observer stated, "Her seat is far higher in Heaven than that of Mrs. Winston."[68]

Locals who knew Jane Williams described her as a mulatto woman with one eye. The story of her eye remains absent, but injuries from the violent realities of slavery were common and led to manifestations of bitter resentment toward those who benefited from the system of bondage that circumscribed her life.[69] Furthermore, one enslaved woman testified, "Jane was mad at one time because master Joe threatened to sell her without her child." Why would Joseph Winston threaten to sell her without her child? While selling families apart occurred regularly in the interstate slave trade, the threat signaled a power move on Winston's part. Additionally, the witness stated, "I suspect Jane because she always had such bitter feelings towards Mrs. W. and her child. I heard that she was suspected of poisoning the other child of Mr. W's that died."[70] Virginia Winston specifically assigned Williams the responsibility of caring for her children, which likely happened at the expense of caring for her own daughter. Indeed, during the week leading into the incident, Williams's husband expressed frustration with her because she chose to sleep in the same room as her daughter rather than in her marriage bed. He found this disagreeable, but she remained at her daughter's bedside. The courts deposed Anna, also enslaved in the Winston home. The Friday before the incident, Anna attempted an escape from the Winston household. While it became clear that Joseph Winston forbade her from meeting with her paramour, the reasons for her detainment point to her recent flight. At least three enslaved people owned by the Winstons demonstrated various degrees of recalcitrance. Additional information about conditions within the Winston household remain largely absent except that white residents argued that enslaved people owned by the Winstons were some of the most privileged in Richmond. Jane Williams, however, stated that she "had been ill-treated by Mr. and Mrs. Winston, and had been brooding over her bloody revenge for some time." In the social economy of the enslaved, the Winstons violated values and expectations determined by those held in bondage which provided just cause to shirk their authority. The law, however, did not recognize, and in fact criminalized, actions that served as a violent rejection of obedience to the authority of slaveholders.[71]

John Williams also expressed resentment toward the Winstons, but did his frustrations actually inspire him to kill them? The following month after Jane Williams's execution, her husband was found guilty of murder despite the fact that she confessed to committing the act alone. The cross-examinations focused on John Williams's reputation for being defiant and difficult to work with. Overseers and other white locals who hired him or directly interacted with him took note of instances when he openly challenged them over labor disputes and working conditions. Locals, however, undoubtedly sought retribution for the murder that cracked open a renewed sense of vulnerability reminiscent of the Southampton Rebellion, which occurred two decades prior to the incident (see chapter 5).[72] One resident of Richmond lamented, "What guarantee then shall we have, that we will not lie down on our beds at night, as did they, and sleep in unconscious security, all dreamless of danger, and yet the morning sun arise on our bloody and maligned corpses?"[73] Still, some white Virginians doubted that the court based Williams's sentence on sufficient evidence. One report observed that some locals "ha[d] been led to doubt whether the evidence was of sufficient strength to justify conviction."[74] The narrative that prevailed, however, focused on the brutal violence of the incident. At the funeral, the presiding minister, the Reverend T. V. Moore, declared, "Never, perhaps, since this city had an existence, did such a thrill of horror vibrate through its population."[75] He lamented the death of Virginia Winston, who he described as "one of the gentlest and loveliest of her sex, one whose heart never throbbed but with love, and whose tongue never spake but with kindness." The minister offered a gendered juxtaposition between virtuous white Southern womanhood and deviant Black women. In another sermon, not far from where the Winstons' funeral services were held, the Reverend Robert Ryland, pastor of the local African church, urged Black residents of the city to be "obedient and submissive." A slave owner himself, he reminded them, "God has given this country to the white people. They are the law-makers," and went further to state, "[They are] the superiors."[76] He made clear that rather than defending white Virginians, he pleaded with them for the "especial benefit" of Black residents. Invoking the biblical maxim "Vengeance is mine!," he instructed his audience to let God have the final word in the spirit of divine retribution.[77] Both ministers actually underscored the stakes for white Southerners.

While acts of murder committed by enslaved women were not typical, the case raised alarming concerns for white residents of Richmond. The reactions from both the Black and white residents of the city also reveal how violent resistance undermined the relatively cooperative interracial relationship that became a common feature of Virginia society.[78] Historians might look to the story of Jane Williams to understand that enslaved women's violent resistance did not have to occur in overwhelming numbers to disrupt life in Southern towns. One writer aptly captured the magnitude of Williams's actions when he stated, "Never, in the whole history of the city of Richmond, has an occurrence taken place within its borders, so shocking as the inhuman massacre of the Winston family."[79] The case made a lasting impression on the residents of Richmond, but it also created symbolic value for the court.

The local justices understood the kind of visibility that the case gained, and this became evident with the thousands that thronged the gallows for Jane Williams's execution. One person declared, "It is to be regarded as at once [a] matter for thankfulness to the Almighty, who restrains the hearts of men." The Rev. T. V. Moore understood that, for an enslaved woman to be accused of murdering the family that owned her, Williams triggered the greatest fears and vulnerabilities of white Southerners. Moreover, he added, "[The handling of the case was] a most signal tribute to the orderly and law abiding temper of our citizens; and the forbearing wisdom of the friends of the murdered family, that the evident perpetrators of this crime were not hurried to some swift and lawless punishment by which the majesty of law would have been dishonored, and the dignity of justice degraded."[80] The minister understood, as did most Southerners, that an act of violent resistance, such as the one for which Williams died, could possibly lead to violent execution at the hands of mobs comprising outraged locals or those related to the slaveholding family. According to the minister, the citizens and the court upheld "the dignity of justice" and affirmed the sanctity of Southern law and its practitioners. Slavery itself did not appear on trial, but the integrity of the prosecution of the case and the legal processes that protected white Southerners from Black retribution gave the trial its meaning for the broader public. The actions of one enslaved woman confirmed Richmond's worst fears. The criminal legal proceedings for enslaved people convicted of capital offenses allowed for enslaved, free, and expert witnesses, which reinforced ideas about the "orderly" design and "majesty" of slave law and Southern justice.[81] A murder case in Prince William County unfolded with the same level of publicity but ignited a very different debate about the sexual exploitation of enslaved women and the reputations of white men.

In the winter of 1850, an enslaved woman named Agnes sparked rumor and debate as she appeared on trial for the murder of the slaveholder Gerard Mason. Several different news accounts emerged, with mixed ideas about how Mason's death occurred. The *Baltimore Sun* reported that, one evening, Mason stumbled into his home "under the influence of liquor" and that "he became offended with something the woman had done" and threatened to kill her with his ax.[82] The article stated that Agnes, "wresting the axe from him, struck the blow that killed him." This account of what happened seemed to suggest that Agnes acted out of self-defense rather than premeditation. Mason appeared as a master whose drinking led to his demise at the hands of the enslaved woman. Another interpretation read by locals, an article published by the *Alexandria Gazette*, told a more decisive story. One witness to the trial offered that "beyond a rational doubt, that Mr. Mason was killed in his bed, most probably whilst asleep, by blows inflicted with an axe by the accused."[83] In this account, the reporter circumvented the prospect of her acting in self-defense and instead presented a case that portrayed her actions as a calculated effort to murder Mason. The degree of premeditation determined her sentence, but the reputation of Mason also shaped the possibility for the recommendation of leniency.

Mason came from a family line of prominent Virginians.[84] Conflict was not uncommon within Virginian families and institutions that boasted long and wealthy lineages.[85] In 1829, Mason received an appointment as a trustee of the town of Occoquan in Prince William County to oversee the economic development of Mill Street.[86] His grandfather, George Mason, slaveholder and delegate to the U.S. Constitutional Convention of 1787, notably stated at that convention: "Every master is born a petty tyrant."[87] Not far from George Mason's Gunston Hall, Gerard Mason's plantation faced opposite the village of Colchester, along the Occoquan River, in Woodbridge. The sprawling property spanned 500 acres and included a primary residence, a barn and stable, slave quarters, and a large limekiln. Later advertised as a particularly "valuable" farm, the productive plantation did not appear without conflict.[88]

Mason placed advertisements in local newspapers for runaway slaves as early as 1822. Runaway advertisements reveal general details about enslaved people's appearances and reputations, but also the disagreements and struggles that unfolded in slaveholding households.[89] While it was not uncommon for enslaved men and women to run away, those enslaved on Mason's plantation seemed particularly determined to escape. On October 15, 1822, a man named Bill, around twenty or twenty-five years of age, left the plantation wearing "country cloth much worn."[90] The description revealed that Bill's hand could not open because of a severe burning he suffered as a child. During the summer of 1823, another man, Will, described as forty or forty-five years of age with two missing front teeth, ran away from Mason's plantation.[91] Bill did not successfully escape the first time, but he reappeared in a second runaway advertisement during the winter of 1840, this time as a forty-year-old man, bearing the same burn on one of his hands.[92] His being poorly clothed and showing visible signs of physical injury reveal some indication of what life might have been like on Mason's plantation. The fact that Bill risked his life repeatedly to escape Mason's grip provides a glimpse into his tendencies as one of the "petty tyrants" that his grandfather warned against at the Constitutional Convention. On Gerard Mason's plantation, Agnes, like other enslaved people on the property, experienced the hardships and the volatility that came with lifelong bondage on his estate.

News sources that originated outside of Prince William County largely read the implications and motives of Agnes's actions as inherently criminal or as a form of "malice," which described first-degree murder charges. For instance, the cross-examinations included the standard language that Agnes "willfully, deliberately, maliciously and with malice aforethought, killed and murdered her master Gerard Mason, by striking him repeated blows on the head with an axe."[93] The justices of the peace for Prince William County decided on the death penalty and offered "under thorough conviction" that "she committed the murder willful and premeditated, whilst he was in bed, and the strong presumption asleep."[94] Over seventy citizens of Prince William County signed petitions that argued that "the extreme penalty of the law should not be inflicted upon the negro woman, Agnes, under sentence of death." Instead, they regarded pardon and sale to another plantation as a more appropriate sentence.[95] It was not uncommon for locals to weigh in on cases ranging from minor disputes to those widely publicized involving slave resistance.[96] Local citizens again introduced an alternative set of guiding mores to contextualize the case and Agnes's circumstances more specifically.

Following the trial proceedings, witnesses believed Agnes to be five weeks pregnant and "visibly swollen."[97] The court postponed the scheduled execution in anticipation of the further development of her pregnancy.[98] The execution of a pregnant woman raised important moral questions about hanging an enslaved woman with her unborn child, but, most likely, the hesitation pointed to economic reasons for assessing the total value accrued as a result of the loss of two lives. In Virginia, reproductive considerations may or may not forestall the execution of a pregnant woman, but, in this case, the possibility convinced justices to postpone execution. G. W. Clifford, the jailer of Prince William County, wrote a letter stating, [Agnes "was] very much swollen all the winter and spring, and Dr. Thornton (who examined her) says it is very natural that she should have come to the conclusion that she was pregnant, indeed it was the opinion of all who saw her at that time, but now the swelling has left her, it is evident she is not in that situation."[99] Agnes could very well have been pregnant, particularly given the noticeable weight gain observed by witnesses, but after waiting a few months to see if she advanced in pregnancy, the court concluded the absence of any visible signs of a child and proceeded with the execution. Pregnancy was particularly difficult to detect and sustain through the arduous labor demands required of enslaved women.[100] Hard physical labor and emotional and mental duress could stave off a woman's menses or trigger miscarriage.[101] Many accounts in the transcripts suggest that she lied about her pregnancy, but those who confirmed her visibly swollen belly might also support circumspection of involuntary or voluntary abortion. The debate concerning whether or not Agnes carried a child underscored the manner in which courts accounted for the gendered and economic dimensions that came with the reproductive condition of enslaved women defendants. Contestations about Agnes's body not only circulated in letters debating her pregnancy but also appeared in deliberations about what precisely led to the conflict between Agnes and Mason.[102]

Publications that reported the details of the death of Mason left out critical components of Agnes's cross-examinations, underscoring the gendered assumptions about Black women's criminality and culpability in the antebellum South. Several witness accounts, however, explained that "the deceased wanted to handle her and she would not submit to it."[103] Testimony placed the spotlight on Mason's behavior and reputation in ways that contextualized the sexual terror that galvanized enslaved women's murders of white Southerners. In response, Mason grabbed for his gun and threatened to kill her, and she in turn reached for the gun and put it away. Mason demanded that Agnes get the ax and start a fire, and Agnes reportedly claimed that the ax appeared too dull for use and showed it to him. A fight ensued, and Agnes struck him with the ax, and he ended up unconscious on his bed. Another account offered that, after the gun incident, Mason sent Agnes to cut wood and then told her she took too long. In response, Agnes informed him that she could not sharpen the ax herself in order to chop the wood. The cross-examiner stated, "He wanted to turn up her clothes and take privilege with her, she told him she was too old for that now," and he grabbed the ax and threatened to kill her.[104] She snatched the ax and struck him with it, and he fell on the bed dead. The legal argument against Agnes focused on efforts to prove that she killed Mason under premeditated circumstances, and news reporters framed her disclosure of Mason's sexual violence as evidence of the premeditated nature of the act rather than believing Agnes defended her life.[105] County locals, however, understood the power dynamics on Mason's homestead firsthand and proposed a revision to the sentence.[106]

The petition of local county citizens deepens our understanding of Mason's death in *Commonwealth v. Agnes*. Petitioners contributed layers of complexity to debates about the sentencing of those charged with crimes, often having no direct relationship to the person they defended, as was the case with those who defended Agnes. Two signatories of the petition submitted by the citizens of Prince William County included Henry Duvall and Hugh

Hammill.[107] Although news reporters and justices obfuscated Agnes's testimony, the petition reveals the insights of those with closer proximity to what life looked like on Mason's plantation.[108] Four years earlier, in *Commonwealth v. Gerard Mason*, Duvall offered testimony in a trial that brought Mason before the court on murder charges.[109] This case involved the murder of an enslaved woman named Katy.

Witnesses testified that Mason notoriously demonstrated a penchant for sadistic violence against enslaved women. William Johnson, a witness in the case, testified that he watched Mason knock two Black children out of the way as he stormed "apparently in a violent rage" into Katy's living quarters.[110] Johnson stated that Mason went into the cabin, "where he made a great noise as if thumping or knocking people about." Returning at about eleven o'clock to unload wood, Johnson "saw Negro Katy lying in the yard at the quarters, she seemed to be in great pain as if from a beating—just breathing, just talking, not able to turn about."[111] James Foster, who claimed to be ignorant of any recent incidents, recalled that in the fall of the year before, he "saw Gerard Mason stomp Katy in his yard at his dwelling."[112] Within two months of the court proceedings, William Bates saw that "Katy was unable to walk about and ha[d] continued so ever since," and he stated further that he saw her "crawling about her cabin and when crawling would sometimes fall some."[113] The violence Mason committed against Katy's already disabled body did not stop. Henry Duvall testified to what he saw when he went to Mason to sell wood: "[Mason] beat Katy with a large stick at the home, drove her back to the field, pursued and beat her a second time—knocked her down and left her lying on the ground."[114] Every person who witnessed this violence recalled the manner in which Katy always remained lying on the ground. The imagery of Katy is a snapshot of how Mason expressed power through sadistic violence. Duvall added that, just days after, he saw Katy "get another beating from Mason in which he seemed to strike with anything he could get hold of."[115] As they conducted daily business transactions with Mason, witnesses viewed firsthand the terror he inflicted on Katy. On October 23, 1845, Mason killed Katy and buried her on his property.

The court initiated an inquest of Katy's buried body six days later to uncover the details of her death. The examination by the coroner and the observations of the jury indicated that Mason, "being moved and seduced by the instigation of the devil, a short time before the death of his negro woman slave Katy, with force and arms at a cabin, in and upon the aforesaid slave voluntarily made an assault."[116] They stated further that Mason "then and there with some instrument violently struck and cut and gave the said slave" several "severe wounds." These wounds, located on the "back and lower part of the head" with "one and half inches cutting into and taking off a part of the skull," fatally wounded her already battered body. Mason spent a brief period of time in jail for the duration of the trial, but justices exonerated him.[117]

Locals who testified against Mason in the case involving Katy reappeared to submit a petition in favor of Agnes's deportation instead of execution. The signers of the petition, through their daily interactions with Mason, learned firsthand the incredible degree of violence he inflicted on enslaved women he legally owned. Men like Mason were supposed to embody the virtues of Southern white male honor and paternalism, but life within the plantation household also served as the site of merciless violence.[118] Southern honor did not preclude the murder of enslaved people, but the excessive and recurring violence on display on Mason's plantation offended local sensibilities. Historians show that Southern honor, and the character and reputation of men like Mason, required affirmation from the public.[119] Thus, the petition did not protest slavery, but comprised a collection of grievances that spoke to Mason's offensive behavior and violation of social codes of conduct. Even as locals expressed their dissent, Mason's deadly transgressions receded as Agnes emerged from the trial a murderer. These popular discourses about enslaved women's criminality, despite overwhelming evidence of sexual and other forms of physical violence, gained critical attention beyond Virginia.[120]

Antebellum law did not recognize any acts of attempted or actual rape of an enslaved woman committed by a white person.[121] Testimonies from witnesses included in both the *Commonwealth v. Gerard Mason* and *Commonwealth v. Agnes* cases indicate that Mason tormented enslaved women through physical and sexual violence. Similarly, in *State of Missouri v. Celia, a Slave*, the courts tried Celia for the murder of Robert Newsom, a slaveholder who raped her from the moment of her purchase at fourteen years of age.[122] After bearing two of Newsom's children, Celia became pregnant with a third while maintaining a relationship with an enslaved man named George. Newsom continued to violate her, until one evening Celia struck him in the head and killed him. Missouri law regarded as a crime actions that involved men who took "any woman unlawfully against her will and by force, menace, or duress, compel[led] her to be defiled."[123] The defense counsel applied this statute to his argument; however, judge William Hall refused to recognize any claims to self-defense or even the idea that the law recognized Celia as a "woman." On October 10, 1855, Celia received a death sentence. Saidiya Hartman theorizes that, without enslaved women's ability to offer consent or testimony, the courts applied gendered ideas about the women's sexual depravity to support the absence of their voices from the evidentiary record. Therefore, the courts rendered the notion of enslaved women's sexual consent and the virtue of their testimony wholly impossible. These silences reinforced the presumption of both culpability and acquiescence on the part of Black women.[124] Hartman argues further that "Newsom's constant violations were eclipsed by the criminal agency of Celia."[125] In one account of Agnes's testimony, Mason attempted to "turn up her clothes and take privilege," but she told him "she was too old for that now." Her statements reveal that Mason repeatedly and lawfully raped her as a young girl and into her years as a young woman.[126] Similarly, the inquest of Katy's body and accompanying witness accounts indicate that she, too, suffered through physical and sexual violence at the hands of Mason. The proceedings that determined the sentences of enslaved women who defended themselves against sexual violence show that too often verdicts that accentuated the criminality of enslaved women worked in tandem to expunge white culpability.

Crime and fatal punishment, for enslaved women, involved execution practices woven into the jurisprudence of the legal system as well as violent "discipline" *ex juris* of the courts within the private and legally protected spaces of white households. Agnes reacted to Mason's threats to kill her by hitting his head with the ax, while Katy could barely physically defend herself as a result of the destruction he inflicted on her body.[127] Agnes received the death penalty at the public gallows, and Mason executed Katy's death sentence at his home. The legal proceedings unsurprisingly demonstrate that the racial and gendered violence experienced by these women did not play a role in the jurisprudence exercised by the justices involved. The petitions of locals at various points during the trials momentarily disrupted the conversation in their efforts to intervene in the future of these women. Ultimately, the legal value of whiteness outweighed the scales of human justice. The resistance and deaths of enslaved women, however, invoke meanings of tragedy and retribution in ways that underscore alternative epistemologies of justice. This view of justice also provides an important perspective for how we understand the possibilities of leniency in the Old Dominion.[128]

The trials of enslaved women accused of murder not only show how ideas about race, gender, age, and sex influenced their prospects for leniency, but they also reveal stories that shape how we understand a place like Virginia. Throughout Agnes's trial, officials detained her in the Brentsville Jail, located in the seat of Prince William County, Virginia, in a centrally situated compound that included the county courthouse and a church. Visibly and centrally located, courthouses in Virginia provided the stage from which slaveholders sold enslaved people and statutes, including those pertaining to slaves, were read aloud. The courthouse accommodated the space in which justices deliberated over the futures of enslaved women, men, and children. Today, the jail has undergone extensive renovation to reflect the structure as it appeared when Agnes was on trial. Characteristic of local jails in nineteenth-century Virginia, the jail stands two stories high, with a hallway leading to a staircase beyond the front entrance.[129] The jail keeper typically lived at the jail, on the first floor, just off to the left side of the entrance upon walking in. White persons convicted of crimes occupied one of two designated cells on the first floor, to the right upon entry. Enslaved and free Black persons held in the jail occupied cells located on the second floor. For the duration of Agnes's trial, and during her final days alive, the jailer confined her to the rear cell to the left on the second floor. In that room, Agnes possibly looked out of a cross-barred window that offered a direct view of the gallows on which she eventually died. The strategic placement of Black and white persons detained in the jail gave Black defendants greater physical proximity to the gallows—a striking metaphor for Black people's disproportionate vulnerability to execution. To understand Agnes's experience in the jail is impossible. We can only discern the conditions and presume that following the violent terrorism she experienced on Mason's plantation, the room functioned as yet another vestibule of bondage and that she traveled through private and public spaces threaded together by violence against women like her.

Today, the public visits the space and consumes the details of Agnes's violent end, just as the nineteenth-century community of citizens did. Her experience is exhumed while visitors vacillate between the spectacle of the trial and execution of an enslaved woman and the grim realities of violence and slavery. Visiting the jail with Agnes at the forefront shifts the consumption of the space from a family-friendly excursion of exploring nineteenth-century architecture and daily life to an encounter with a woman who lived in a society with a violent past. To listen to Agnes's story is to confront a complicated history of Virginia, a commonwealth with coveted and protected historical narratives of looming figures such as Mason's grandfather and contemporaries who deliberated over justice and Southern law. Placing slavery at the center of public memory and history transforms the way people experience historic courthouses, churches, and plantations to show that the beautified landscapes and intricate designs of the historic mansions were cultivated and built at a shattering expense.[130]

We learn from these cases that the administration of both punishment and pardon in Southern courts upheld slave law and preserved the racial and gendered hierarchies that made slavery possible.[131] For white Southerners, moral understandings of evenhandedness did not pose a conflict with the institution of slavery. Whether enslaved women's testimony featured prominently in debates or not, they articulated a counternarrative of justice through their experiences and their actions. Moreover, most verdicts ended with the acquittal of the white party involved and the perpetuation of bondage even when the courts heard testimony verifying that white Southerners subjected enslaved women to particularly harsh or cruel abuse.[132] In cases that prosecuted an enslaved woman for the death of a white man or woman, most courts assumed, through gendered ideas about Black women's proclivity toward violence and moral depravity, the provocation and fault of the enslaved woman.

The interconnectedness of gender, slavery and Southern law appears in considerations of leniency in each of these cases as Southern courts and locals considered a range of factors including gender, race, age, sexual violence, community mores, and perceptions of slaveholders. Katy received no justice, Mason evaded culpability, but Agnes was charged with killing Mason "with malice aforethought," as courts typically framed such crimes, and received the death penalty despite the fact that white witnesses testified against Mason. The term *malice* distinguished a murder from manslaughter or murder in the second degree.[133] Measured violence could be tolerated locally, but in instances where slaveholders failed to adhere to a paternalist ethos of moderation, locals decidedly weighed in to temper the discourse to reflect a morally critical community. These debates unfolded with very little consideration for the interests of the enslaved. The court decisively convicted Nelly and her older children for the murder of Green, and yet the pardon of the twins Ellen and Elias represented a calculated decision "all sufficient for public justice and example"—a nod toward Southern paternalism. Jane Williams, however, confessed to the murder of Virginia Winston and her child and the attempted murder of Joseph Winston. Something compelled her to end their lives, but the record offers limited detail about life on their homestead. In Virginia, the law offered continued bondage as the best possible alternative. Murder cases, deemed the most egregious of crimes, reveal the gendered contours of leniency in cases involving enslaved women. As the experiences of these women show, gendered considerations of acquittal and pardon proved to be a complementary gesture that white Southerners used to support a broader defense for the "moral good" and "necessity" of slavery in the antebellum South.

CHAPTER FOUR

Infanticide

A negro woman belonging to Mr. James Thornton, of Rappahannock County, was committed to jail on Monday last charged with drowning her child. She confesses the crime, but says she intended to drown herself also, and jumped in the river with the child in her arms, but floated to the bank.

—*Alexandria Gazette*, August 7, 1858

In 1823, *Elements of Medical Jurisprudence* by Theodoric Romeyn Beck became the first substantial study of forensic medicine to be published in the United States. Notice of the publication appeared in the *Phenix Gazette* and the *Richmond Enquirer*, informing Virginians of this latest treatise on medical jurisprudence. Beck's brother, John Brodhead Beck, contributed a seminal essay on infanticide to the book. The brothers were from Schenectady, New York, and trained as medical physicians at Columbia College of Physicians and Surgeons. By the late 1820s, John Beck gained a reputation as an authority on forensic approaches to infanticide, miscarriage, and infant physiology. *Elements of Medical Jurisprudence* became a guide for medical examiners and coroners investigating cases of infanticide in the United States. Southern newspapers included announcements of this publication and details about its contents for the broader public to consider.[1] Medical experts today typically view the processes for discovering the details of pregnancy and death in the nineteenth century rudimentary, but the emergence of medical jurisprudence coincided with the establishment of the formal legal profession. Uncertainties about death and crime demanded answers of a medical discipline with a limited understanding of reproductive medicine. The historian Deirdre Cooper Owens explains the significance of this dynamic relationship between medicine and the law in her research, stating, "As both the legal and the medical systems worked out the processes of how Black women were to be defined and treated by doctors, jurists, slave owners, and southern society, individual American doctors were adding their perspectives to the discussion, medical case by medical case."[2] These examinations were cursory at best but initiated an invasive method for giving an account of the medical dimensions of a case and, therefore, the bodies of enslaved women and infants. Indeed, the haphazard and violent nature of such exams and medical knowledge itself placed enslaved women in a precarious position of legal defense. As scholars have shown, the advancements of medicine can be attributed to the exploitative uses of bodies of enslaved and free Black people for further study and examination.[3] The relationship between medical knowledge and jurisprudence, however, did not emerge without precedent.

Lawmaking entities employed the application of medical knowledge for the purposes of the administration of justice, a process that dates back to antiquity, beginning with the Code of Hammurabi in 1755–1750 B.C., which established laws that addressed incidents of medical malpractice and diseases that slaves might contract that, in turn, had an impact on labor agreements. In ancient Egypt, studies of poisons were commissioned, and in Rome, laws were instituted that required the removal of fetuses from women who died during pregnancy.[4] Over time, societies in northern Africa, the Middle East, and, later, Europe established processes that required medical knowledge for clarity in legal matters. Even though these inquiries date back to ancient times, the knowledge of medical examiners remained incomplete and limited at best late into the nineteenth century. Yet the role of medical examiners factored in cases in increasingly more significant ways as jurists determined critical information that involved the bodies of the enslaved. The medical procedures appear infrequently, if at all, in the legal record, but the academic manuals created by nineteenth-century medical experts became a blueprint for Southern doctors who served as expert witnesses in the courts that prosecuted the alleged crimes of the enslaved. Cases involving infanticide raised a number of questions about what the bodies of the enslaved might tell the court about the cause of death and the parties responsible for any deaths. In this chapter, enslaved women stand accused of killing their children.[5] Not only did they undergo great scrutiny in the cross-examinations and the trial proceedings, but their bodies, and the bodies of the fetuses, were thoroughly examined and at various points dissected to arrive at a conclusion about the cause of death.

Central to these examinations were procedures outlined in medical examination texts that instructed the expert witnesses on how to rule out different causes and conditions in which the child might be discovered. These procedures were put in place to establish culpability and the degree of legal charges against the defendant. Felonies, in such cases, were distinguished by murder in the first degree, with evidence of malice and intent, and murder in the second degree, an offense in which premeditation remained absent. But in order to uncover these details, enslaved women and their infants underwent intimate and intrusive procedures, even if the examiner viewed the process as a formal medical procedure or a scientific method used to determine a cause. According to the historian Marie Jenkins Schwartz, enslaved women understood the intrusive role of slaveholders and physicians, and "out of concern that they might be subjected to painful and dangerous procedures, abortions, or degrading treatment, some slaves hid miscarriages, pregnancies, even the onset of labor from owners, despite life-threatening complications."[6] The lack of accuracy, knowledge, and proven methods for medical treatment and diagnoses in America, and the violent outcomes of examinations and experiments, is perhaps the most disturbing aspect of this burgeoning approach to legal medicine. In Europe, legal medicine might be viewed as "always academically turbulent and against the intellectual current of the times."[7] European universities viewed legal medicine as a controversial and less established discipline since so much of the legal traditions was steeped in superstitious and supernatural conclusions tied to religious beliefs.[8] The American South was no exception to this trend. Indeed, even in the early modern Atlantic, Europeans, Indigenous peoples, and Africans created epistemologies of phenomenological and unexplainable illnesses and therapeutics, which African-descended people harnessed in ways that confounded European approaches to early medicine. In the context of Black Caribbean healers, the historian Pablo Gómez offers that "just as there were outstanding historical actors associated with the European epistemological revolutions about the natural world in the seventeenth century (be they surgeons, natural philosophers, natural historians, or physicians), there were also exceptional black Caribbean creators of the New World's wondrous realities."[9] Centuries of therapeutic and medicinal experiments and approaches preceded the establishment of the formal medical institutions that peppered the commonwealth and shaped the laws that directly affected enslaved women's reproductive lives.

The reproductive and sexual lives of enslaved women became commodified through the 1662 law that made slavery inheritable through "the condition of the mother." The law allowed for the sexual exploitation of women and girls, posing a contradiction between consent and culpability. During the colonial era, white women who arrived in Virginia as indentured servants most certainly experienced sexual exploitation from men who employed their labor for a specified term. The colonial statutes stipulated that women servants who appeared pregnant by the "master" faced two additional years of labor after their original term ended.[10] This punishment did not account for the culpability of the "master" or the power dynamics of indentured servitude that shaped a woman's access to consent. In the case of interracial sex involving white women and Black men, fines were doubled and owed to the church. The church was authorized to sell the white women involved to another parish as indentured servants and the children of interracial unions were sold to church wardens to serve a term of labor until they turned thirty years of age. Intermarriage between white women and Black men led to banishment "from th[e] dominion forever."[11] In the seventeenth century, white men, however, only faced repercussions for legitimizing a relationship with a Black woman through marriage. White women could end up in prison for six months without bail for marrying a Black man.[12] In these instances, the women appeared in the courts as recipients of the consequences of any sexual encounters they experienced, and Black men could easily face charges of rape. The courts condemned women for the pregnancies, even as the laws invalidated consent. Furthermore, colonial law created a framework of Black men's sexuality that bore consequences many centuries after the statutes became law.

These statutes governing the sexual interactions among Virginia's inhabitants served the purposes not of legal protection but of social engineering on the basis of race and sex. The sexuality of Black men became a source of criminalization outside the context of slaveholders harnessing the sexuality of enslaved men and women to reap the financial advantages that came with inheritable bondage. Black men were to be kept from white women, and white men wielded violent power reinforced by the law. For instance, a 1705 statute allowed for slaveholders to be absolved of any murder charges in the instance of killing an enslaved person for discipline; a 1769 provision of the law banned dismemberment, as it ran "contrary to the principles of humanity."[13] The law allowed for enslavers to "accidentally" kill an enslaved person, but the dismemberment statute spoke to the sensibilities of the polity.[14] Black male castration became the only exception to this rule, and the sentiment around interracial sex reached particular limits in the case of Black men and white women, while making space for certain tolerated allowances in the instances of white men and Black women.[15] The collection of laws governing the lives of enslaved people and white servants shaped the sexual dynamics among the various classes of people who populated Virginia. This meant that white men wielded unchecked sexual power over enslaved, free Black, and white women in ways that temper any conceptualization of consent. How does sexual consent configure in a society where the legal apparatus governing it allows for unbridled access to the bodies of women? For enslaved women, their sexual encounters took place within this legal context, but these women also found ways to navigate their sexuality and reproductive lives on their terms. In cases of abortion and infanticide, legal and medical experts struggled to understand how enslaved women shaped the outcomes of these dynamics.

By the nineteenth century, the legal and medical professions appeared more formalized in the United States, offering more opportunities for jurists to draw on the medical expertise of new doctors. American medical examiners like Theodoric Romeyn Beck traveled to Europe to receive formal education in legal medicine at pioneering institutions such as the University of Edinburgh, since many of the younger colleges in the United States could not accommodate the curriculum needed to study the more specialized field of legal medicine. In Virginia, medical examiners appeared in Richmond, Staunton, and Alexandria, many having been trained at institutions in the state. As early as the 1820s, the University of Virginia Medical School hosted a series of lectures on medical jurisprudence that were available for students to attend.[16] In 1827, students such as William H. Meriwether of Albemarle, William Michie of Hanover, and Robert Taylor of Norfolk distinguished themselves with high marks in the field of medical jurisprudence.[17] Staunton Law School offered lectures in medical jurisprudence taught by A. Waddle, "a gentleman of eminence in his profession, whose instructive and entertaining lectures were received with entire approbation."[18] Universities in Virginia offered instruction in medical jurisprudence at both medical and law schools, showing the interdisciplinary study and application of this knowledge. Medical jurisprudence shaped not only legal outcomes in cases involving infanticide but also transactional disputes and insurance claims involved in purchasing enslaved people.[19] Training in legal medicine and local medical associations provided the foundations from which examiners established the basis of cause of death and ultimately justice. Physicians recorded their medical investigations of the bodies of enslaved patients in medical journals that appeared in the nineteenth century. Unlike scholarly publications today, these journals did not involve formal processes of peer review.[20] The journals also show ways that medical professionals tested new therapies on the bodies of enslaved women to advance medical approaches for the health and well-being of white women.[21] Theories and ideas about culpability, criminality, and the body, too, were tested out on the bodies of the enslaved.

Manuals for procedures associated with medical jurisprudence established definitions of key terms and guidelines for examination. Beck defined *infanticide* as "the criminal destruction of the fetus in utero, or of the newborn child."[22] First, the examiners confirmed the existence of recent pregnancy through an "anatomical inspection of the uterus and its appendages."[23]

If a pregnancy did not exist, Beck stated that the uterus likely measured at three inches, but in the instance of pregnancy the uterus might measure up to ten inches and or evidence of the placenta and vascular fallopian tubes appears present.[24] Scrutiny of the uterus in instances of death meant that enslaved women's bodies were dissected and examined with very little regard for the value of the women's bodies to kin who sought to mourn the loss of the women and children and perhaps provide a meaningful homegoing and burial. Furthermore, if examined alive, enslaved women experienced invasive and lengthy procedures that involved the constant prodding of the most intimate parts of their bodies at the hands of a typically male stranger entrusted with providing medical facts and details to determine their culpability. During the nineteenth century, an obsession with empiricism and advancing research in reproductive medicine led many physicians to take advantage of opportunities to examine complicated pregnancy cases among enslaved women. In their efforts to scrutinize the developments of gestation, they often triggered abortion through their instruments and the physical intrusion of the women's uteruses. Since the court did not permit enslaved women to testify against white men, one historian notes that "the attitude among elite men that only they could accurately judge one another helped ensure that any blame for miscarriage remained with the expectant mother or her female attendant."[25] When slaveholders or the courts called on medical examiners for expert testimony, consent from enslaved women mattered very little, as the case tried the enslaved woman for a criminal offense.

To determine a case of miscarriage or abortion, examiners searched for evidence of the "use and application of various criminal agents," which might include objects inserted to puncture or terminate the pregnancy or traces of herbal agents used to initiate abortion.[26] Plants such as *Juniperus sabina* and *Mentha pulegium* led to cases of miscarriage or abortion, while *Polygala senega* aided in the restoration of the menstrual cycle. Enslaved women from the colonial era drew on African practices of contraception, and that knowledge likely passed down to younger women. The historian Barbara Bush explains that "apart from wide birth spacing through long lactation, ritual abstinence, abortion, and other elaborate forms of contraception are more widespread in traditional African societies than is generally recognized."[27] Research from historian Liese Perrin reveals that enslaved women used the cotton plant as a contraceptive to prevent any unwanted pregnancies.[28] Some pregnancies might be terminated from the consumption of *Actaea racemosa*, or what locals referred to as squawroot, a plant named as a result of Native American discovery and knowledge of its medicinal properties.[29] Beck's manual offered a blueprint for medical examinations, a road map to narrowing down the cause of an infant's death, but the information also reveals the botanical knowledge of women and how they might make use of herbal medicines in lieu of consultation with a medical practitioner. This knowledge developed from Indigenous and African epistemologies of plant properties that they experimented with well before the publication of Beck's manual. Not mentioned in the manual is the use of cotton root both to trigger the menses for women who desired children and to initiate abortion for those who did not.[30] Collective knowledge of remedies and plants shaped the use of these methods and substances among locals of all races and ethnicities. Indeed, many white women utilized these methods to "avoid the disgrace which would attach to them from having a living child" with someone they did not marry or for married women hoping to avoid a life-threatening pregnancy.[31] Enslaved women, too, carefully guarded their inner lives and developed reputations that locals expressly defended.[32] In the case of enslaved women, their reproductive lives might be shaped by the sexual violence that slave law permitted and the subsequent commodification of these pregnancies.[33] In other instances, motivations might be determined by personal decisions to shield future children from the prospect of bondage. White women, particularly in instances where the mother's marital status remained in question, also confronted accusations of infanticide and faced specified terms in jail or prolonged periods of indenture.[34] The calculations of miscarriage, abortion, and infanticide that enslaved women contemplated bear minimal resemblance to the gendered configurations white women were subjected to; however, the reproductive realities of enslaved women must be understood in the contexts of chattel slavery and the limited room for refusal available to enslaved women.[35] Some slaveholders expressed confusion in instances where enslaved women dealt with infertility, but as the historian Deborah Gray White explains, these matters remained protected secrets among enslaved women.[36] If the examiner ruled out the presence of any damage created by an object or a poisonous substance, the fetus or infant underwent even greater scrutiny as the next step for ruling out the cause of death.

Once medical experts established evidence of pregnancy, they pursued two specific lines of inquiry: "Has the foetus in utero been actually destroyed? Has this been brought about by criminal means, or by accidental and natural causes?"[37] These two questions proved difficult to accurately determine in many cases. Some women experienced complications related to retention of the placenta, ectopic pregnancies, the breech of the baby, premature labor, and uterine rigidity.[38] Reproductive medicine remained underdeveloped, as obstetrics and gynecology, as a discipline, did not appear until after the Civil War. Women, drawing on years of experience with assisting in the delivery of babies, even as they were excluded from formal medical education and the authority that came with it, addressed issues associated with pregnancy, miscarriage, and abortion.[39] Planters called on enslaved women who served as midwives, a testament to the ways that slaveholders depended on them given that many of these women practitioners boasted an impressive record for successful deliveries.[40] After birthing a child, many unexplained factors might be at work in the sudden death of an infant, which could be tied to suffocation, fever, and what today is known as sudden infant death syndrome, or SIDS.[41] Moreover, Black women drew on their own experiences, knowledge, and spirituality to provide obstetrical care or initiate abortions. The maintenance, complications, delivery, and destruction of pregnancies reveal the ways that enslaved women also applied their own therapeutic and medicinal epistemologies to the developments of the reproductive aspects of their bodies. Nevertheless, when an enslaved woman stood accused of infanticide, both her body and the body of the fetus were thoroughly examined to determine her culpability, but many of the reasons for the loss of a child remained unanswered in an underdeveloped medical profession. English common law recognized the life of a fetus after the period in which the woman begins to feel movement around week sixteen, making a vague distinction between the "animate" and "inanimate" fetus.[42] These considerations very seldom took into account the labor conditions enslaved women endured during pregnancy. Backbreaking labor, the hazardous conditions of extreme heat, the untenable pace of work, malnutrition, and brutal punishment presented possible explanations for the death of a child in utero. Local witnesses might attest to the work conditions, but they hardly viewed such work arrangements as unusual or even sufficient evidence to absolve enslaved women of accusations of infanticide. Sudden deaths of infants occurred at higher rates among free Black and enslaved people in Virginia, although many white Virginians were less likely to report incidents of sudden death. Births, deaths, and marriages did not appear systematically recorded in the commonwealth until 1853.[43]

In 1815, the court of oyer and terminer in Powhatan County convened to try the case of Jenny, an enslaved woman accused of drowning her three children, Anderson, Julius, and Violett. According to witnesses, she committed the act in a nearby creek while pregnant with another child. Stumbling on the scene of Jenny and her floating children in the creek, an enslaved woman alerted Peter Stratton, her enslaver, to news of Jenny's three drowned children and just barely made it in time to prevent Jenny from similarly ending her own life. The court postponed her execution based on the knowledge of her pregnancy. As it waited, locals petitioned for her reprieve, as they read her actions as an indicator of both desperation and possible insanity. The court considered her particularly valuable, not only for her ability to bear children but also "in consequence of her having been an excellent weaver."[44] Jenny made clear that she did not want to bear more children—did she consent to the ones she had prior to this pregnancy? Her voice does not appear within the record beyond the steps she took to end her children's life and her own. She received a commuted sentence, relegating her to more of what she tried to end. The auditor signed off on her sale and transportation, which required more weaving, more sexual labor, more children, and endless bondage.[45]

In Brooke County, the court heard a case involving Letty, an enslaved woman accused of murdering her newborn girl within hours of giving birth. Witnesses testified that after she gave birth, she crushed the girl's skull, swaddled her, and then left her in the woods. Letty explained, "If the child had been one of her own colour, she would not have done as she did."[46] Letty's testimony is both an admission of what she stood accused of and a refusal of any burden of guilt. Over the years, Letty developed an understanding of the sexually predatory practices of slaveholders and local white men. Did she hope to end what she believed to be an untenable life for her daughter? Moreover, her decision speaks to her own experience of violation and violence as she offers a clear explication of her rejection of those "not of her own colour." The sexual encounter and subsequent pregnancy became realities that she protested. She pleaded not guilty, because in her social economy the circumstances in which she came to have the child, and that the child would be subjected to, were wrong. The court found her guilty of the offense and sentenced her to death. Fifteen locals, however, submitted a petition to support a commutation of her sentence. Perhaps many of them understood that her experience with sexual violence informed her decision to end the child's life? They explained that a "free white man" fathered the child and "may have moved her to the commission of the crime." The community knew details that Letty perhaps felt too afraid to disclose for fear of repercussions. And yet they, too, wanted to be rid of the stain that came with the turmoil that slavery created. The local peace and the peace of the commonwealth remained at odds with lifeless bodies that turned up in the woods and the women who disclosed harrowing details of their lives in bondage. The court sold Letty for $300 and arranged for her transportation out of Virginia. She did not die on the gallows, and we do not know of her desired outcome, but her destination to another slaveholding locale would not erase the memory of what she endured and what she felt compelled to do.

In November 1819, Lucy, an enslaved woman who legally belonged to Thomas Batton, stood before the court of oyer and terminer in Lewis County for charges of infanticide.[47] The courts permitted enslaved defendants to testify with the intention to issue a confession. When asked why the court should not pronounce a murder judgment against her for infanticide, she coolly replied that "she has or knows nothing." Lucy pleaded not guilty, but the question of her plea might be viewed as a gesture rather than a reality of justice in the court proceedings, which gave enslaved defendants a brief moment to confess, but not to testify. Even if enslaved defendants issued a confession, legal counsels served as intermediaries to convey the admission. Lucy understood that the courts did not serve as a space in which her voice held the kind of weight that effectively countered the accusations against her. "She has or knows nothing" underscored this understanding and might be read as her own form of refusal, the dismissal of any need to offer explanation to a court populated by men who supported slavery, even as a nuisance, and yet refused to resolve the tensions between the institution and the state's aspirations for justice. The court sentenced Lucy to death and placed her value at $500. Regarding Lucy's case, the news reported, "A mother murdering the offspring of her womb, almost as soon as it saw the light of day; oh, inhuman! Oh, monstrous!"[48] Lucy appeared in the news as a murderous mother, and the article went further, stating, "Servants take warning by the fate of Lucy. Know that vice will be punished, justice will overtake you either in this world or the world to come."[49] Lucy became viewed as "monstrous" and "inhuman" even as the monstrosity of bondage dimmed behind the narrow dimensions of justice. Vice, or wickedness, as the term connoted in the early nineteenth century, did not account for the dilemma in which enslaved women found themselves when pregnant. The decision to bring children into a world in which the ones closest to them provided love coincided with deliberations of what it meant to rear children under the oppression of slavery. These circumscribed considerations of bearing children, and parenting, unfolded in the context of slavery where the slaveholder wielded power and ownership over their lives and futures. Even as avenues for reconciling the conflicted feelings that came with pregnancy remained limited, enslaved women used what power they possessed over their bodies.

The news emphasized a burden of responsibility placed on Lucy and her actions. Everyone, however, did not share the view of Lucy as "inhuman" or "monstrous." On receipt of a petition of locals from Lewis County, the governor commuted her sentence to sale and transportation. As evident in cases discussed in previous chapters, locals weighed in on cases that stirred the attention of the public. Sensational accounts were tempered by local encounters with women like Lucy, in ways that make clemency a possibility even for a crime deemed as heinous as infanticide. To complicate matters, Lucy's case reportedly contained enough evidence for conviction. One account offers that "she delivered herself of the child in the woods and then abandoned it to its fate—some marks of violence were discovered by the inquest—the child was a mulatto."[50] Southern society used the term *mulatto* for both official and pejorative purposes. The term described people viewed as mixed race, as an outcome of the fairly common occurrence of interracial sex. If the account of what happened in the woods holds true, the last remark might have played into the motivations of the petitioners. White Virginians certainly did not shy away from interracial sex, but, for some, an overt or distasteful disregard for the sensibilities of locals might lead Southerners to petition for a commuted sentence. Rape and interracial sexual relationships became a largely accepted practice in the South. But local reputations and sensibilities added layers of complexity to cases such as Lucy's. Reputations mattered for the white men involved, but also for the enslaved women. The news developed a portrait of a "murderous mother," but locals weighed in to support the commutation of her sentence, perhaps because they felt compelled by a context of her life that remained absent in the trial record. To leave the child in the woods signals her own moment of refusal. Perhaps the action translates into a refusal to become a mother or a response to the white man who fathered the child? These silences and declarations that "she has and knows nothing" can be treated as a dead end or the possibility of a different account of what happened. Batton, her owner, received the full amount of her projected value; petitioners were pleased to see the governor grant clemency; and Lucy was prepared in chains for the long trek to the Deep South.

In 1819, the Buckingham County court examined Polly, a young girl on trial for "having murdered her own infant child." "Her own infant child" is a curious turn of phrase that appeared in court dockets after the first decade of the nineteenth century. The phrase bespeaks the irony of a girl like Polly making a decision over "her own infant child" even as the person who legally owned Polly, William Toney, also claimed ownership of the child she bore. The contradictions give pause and gesture toward the inconsistencies that the court grafted into the language of the record almost as if to impose a set of moralizing norms that emphasized the unsettling charge against her rather than the fact that she owned neither herself nor the child in the eyes of the law. In other ways, the phrase acknowledges the powerful bonds between mother and child that existed among many enslaved women and the children they reared, loved, and cared for during the tumultuous and arduous years of lifelong bondage. Slaveholders exploited the loving bonds among kin even as the enslaved observed meanings they developed regarding their heartfelt affections independent of the law. Whether Polly shared this attachment to the child she birthed seems uncertain, particularly in light of the details of the case. The court found that the evidence supported the charge against her and found her guilty of ending the life of the child. The court, however, recommended an executive pardon on "account of her youth, and former good character."[51] The courts took age under consideration in deliberations over clemency. One such case that the court tried the same year that Polly appeared in court involved Mary, an enslaved girl accused of arson. The court decided that the evidence did not support any malicious motive, and it recommended reprieve based on "consideration of her youth."[52] Enslaved girls became entangled in the criminal court proceedings as a result of the demands placed on their labor. In the case of Polly, such labor went beyond the tasks of household work, farming, sewing, and cooking, to less visible sexual and reproductive work that made girlhood a porous boundary for the enslaved. This young girl, of an age that remains a mystery in the court record, might have found the very fact of pregnancy so foreign and terrifying that the child never became "her own" because she, too, found herself still in the throes of childhood slavery. Given that she was known as a young girl of "good character" and all of the complexity that phrase provokes, one must ask: Who tried to push her into the exigencies of adulthood? The legal calculus of reprieve withholds such details even as they remain critical to the possibility of clemency.

Infanticide undermined Southern arguments that promoted slavery as a positive good and depicted enslaved people as happy and contented. In this context, enslaved women's decisions exposed the contradictions and inconsistencies of Southern paternalism, and often petitions for clemency marked one of many ways Virginians attempted to reconcile these tensions. Despite the fact that locals viewed the act as a profound measure of desperation, infanticide did not always inspire leniency. During the summer of 1826, Milly was accused of murdering her child, and based on "examination of her person and character" the court sentenced her to death.[53] The courts considered multiple factors in decisions to commute sentences, including public perceptions of an enslaved woman's personality and reputation. A number of locals in the county likely met her during visits to the homestead owned by Gabriel

Hanky, the estate on which she lived. If Hanky did business with locals, or maintained regular correspondence with neighbors, it is possible that in visits to his residence, they encountered Milly working or perhaps serving them. Alternatively, Hanky might have had limited interactions with neighbors, and, as a result, locals possessed very little knowledge about Milly and based their opinions on hearsay. In the absence of any possible petitioners to testify to her character, the court could base its assessment of her personality on the allegations alone. But the court also "examined" her "person and character," which reveals that court officials engaged in their own line of questioning. Without details of these exchanges, perhaps her responses did not align with the behavioral attributes demanded of the enslaved. Just as her "person and character" shaped broader perceptions of her, how might the enslaved view this case? Did she express values and judgments that reveal her rejection of the customs of slavery? Did she use her voice or remain reservedly silent in defiance? There were no locals compelled to submit a petition for clemency, and the court proceeded with a death sentence. Milly attempted suicide, and the governor commuted her sentence to sale and transportation, for which Hanky received $400 in compensation.

The year after Milly's trial, Martha of Prince Edward County faced the possibility of the gallows for the death of her son.[54] James Dearman, the son of the man listed as Martha's enslaver, had taken notice of her pregnancy. He made an unusual proposition. He requested that he keep Martha at his home until the birth of the child. His father agreed, and "the prisoner actually slept in the chamber of the witness and the door was locked."[55] He questioned her about the details of her pregnancy, to which she replied that "time would show." One day, an enslaved person entered the bedchambers Martha remained confined to, in order to prepare a fire to warm the room. Martha left the room and walked about 100 yards from the house, where she gave birth in a garden. She returned to the house, and Dearman interrogated her, to which she replied that she did not have any child. He "threatened to correct her if she did not produce it," he testified. Dearman discovered the child bleeding from the eyes, mouth, and nose. The child lived for a brief time that day, but by two o'clock in the afternoon breath had left his body.[56] Although the court found Martha guilty, the presiding justices recommended her for executive clemency. The presence of locals willing to testify to Martha's character and her counsel's compelling case on her behalf convinced the court to recommend a commuted sentence before the governor even read the details of the case. Such cases reveal the complexity of local relationships between enslaved people and white Virginians and the weight that local testimony held in such matters. Infanticide was often an indictment on locales that presumed the presence of contented slaves and the paternalist slaveholders who adhered to the Southern ethics of honor. News spread of these cases and caused some to quietly call into question the abilities of planters to maintain order and authority and the conditions that might inspire a mother to take the life of her child. As scholars have shown, collective agreement regarding what justice required in order to maintain the peace often overruled what others might perceive as a predictable outcome.[57]

Commutation functioned as a legal technology that upheld the business of slavery and the ideology of paternalism. In 1833, Governor John Floyd approved the commutation of the death sentence that Ally, an enslaved woman, faced after being accused of "murdering her own children." She spent several days in jail that spring, awaiting the details of her fate as the court and the governor deliberated the outcome of the case. A few months later, the governor recommended sale and transportation.[58] Kesiah, an enslaved woman, appeared on trial at the Henrico County courthouse in 1834. According to Henry L. Carter, her enslaver, Kesiah "murdered her own female infant child" on the night of April 13, 1834. The court found her guilty and sentenced her to death on June 6, 1834. Kesiah waited in jail, until she learned that the governor granted her a "reprieve" from the death sentence, as she was "not more than seventeen years old," and the constable prepared her for sale and transportation instead. The court issued Carter $440 in compensation.[59] Similar to the cases discussed in previous chapters, the legal considerations were financial ones as well. Additionally, these cases and the role of clemency responded to growing criticisms of slavery in the South.

The antebellum decades of slavery in Virginia, as in much of the South, drew criticism from abolitionists, who increasingly mounted attacks on the institution by assisting fugitives, launching campaigns to boycott goods produced in the South, and establishing national organizations and political parties to undermine slavery.[60] During the antebellum decades, infanticide became a well-known phenomenon as news spread nationally of Margaret Garner's desperate attempt to flee U.S. marshals who threatened to return her and her children back to slavery. Stories like hers appeared in Harriet Beecher Stowe's *Uncle Tom's Cabin*, stirring the sympathies of Northerners and the ire of slaveholders. Stowe wrote her novel prior to the incident, however, revealing the fact that abolitionist circles became increasingly aware of infanticide and the sexual exploitation of enslaved women.[61] Garner's case presented complex legal questions as she committed infanticide in Ohio, just across the Kentucky border.

In the frigid winter of 1856, Margaret and Robert Garner plotted an escape from Kentucky with plans to take their children in tow. Some enslaved parents decided on a series of escapes that involved perhaps a parent leaving another parent and children behind in order to gain a head start on free soil and reduce the risks of traveling while being hunted down. Children might not be able to travel the same distances as the adults charged with their care. Margaret and Robert Garner made their way across the frozen Ohio River and found refuge at the home of Elijah Kite, her cousin. Not even twenty-four hours passed before U.S. marshals along with slaveholder Archibald K. Gaines surrounded the family, forcing them into siege warfare. Robert Garner quickly grabbed the gun he carried and fired at the group in an effort to defend his family. Margaret Garner gathered her children and retreated to a room nearby, where she reportedly declared, "Before my children shall be taken back to Kentucky, I will kill every one of them." According to records, she killed her two-year-old daughter, Mary, and injured the remaining children to prevent their return to slavery. The case posed questions about whether Garner should be tried for murder in Ohio or Kentucky. If tried in Ohio, she faced charges of murder and remained subject to the criminal law of Ohio on the assumption of her freedom. Locals, however, assumed that the governor, antislavery politician Salmon P. Chase, planned to grant her clemency if the court found her guilty. By the 1850s, however, Gaines possessed federal rights under the Fugitive Slave Law, and he intended to use them toward his economic advantage. If tried in the state of Kentucky, the place from which she fled, Garner might be executed or sold further south. The jurists in Ohio needed to determine whether Garner's case should be treated as an issue of crime or property.[62]

Three of Garner's children were believed to be fathered by Gaines, the man who legally owned her and her children. Nineteenth-century accounts described Garner as a "mulatto, showing from one-fourth to one-third white blood." Virginians described persons who had "one-fourth part or more of negro blood" as "mulatto."[63] The common occurrence of children born to parents who were white and Black or biracial meant that Americans continued to do the work of making distinctions of race. These distinctions configured neatly in the creation of slave law and medical study in the South to support the purported veracity of race and gender categories. Descriptions also figured prominently in newspaper accounts of Garner's appearance: "Her eyebrows are delicate lines finely arched, and her eyes though not remarkably large are bright and intelligent. The African appears in the lower part of her face—in the broad nose and thick lips. Her ear is small, her wrist and hand large, and she wears a plain gold or brass ring on the little finger of the left hand. She is twenty-two or three years of age."[64] Her eyes, portrayed as "bright and intelligent," most certainly speak to the qualities of a person who makes strategic decisions for herself. The "plain gold or brass ring" is a symbol of her commitment to her chosen partner, Robert Garner, with whom she made vows and also dreamed up a different future for their family. Gaines constantly disrupted this bond she shared with Robert, inciting fear and force in any given moment he sought to satisfy his lust for her. The antislavery activist and Oberlin graduate Lucy Stone appeared in court to offer testimony of her interview with Margaret Garner. The Fugitive Slave Law did not allow Garner to testify in her defense or against her owner. According to the historian Steven Weisenburger, however, the court allowed her to testify in separate proceedings.[65] Serving as an intermediary, Stone provided context that reveals the gendered and sexual experiences that informed Garner's decision. Stone stated, "The faded faces of the negro children tell too plainly to what degradation female slaves must submit. Rather than give her little daughter to that life, she killed it. If in her deep maternal love she felt the impulse to send her child back to God, to save it from coming woe, who shall say she had no right to do so?"[66] By disclosing details of her experiences with sexual violence, Garner and Stone offered an alternative understanding of that which might be interpreted as wrongdoing. Newspapers described Gaines as "an agreeable and intelligent gentleman," but her testimony offers another glimpse into his character.[67] Beyond the legal opinions of the jurists, this disclosure offered an indictment of slavery and the sexual exploitation that the law allowed for. Furthermore, the epistemologies of enslaved women's experiences with abuse struck a nerve at the heart of national politics, typically characterized by a general tolerance and acceptance of slavery. The case gained widespread attention and triggered responses from proslavery, moderate, and antislavery voices throughout the nation. For white Americans, infanticide became an uncomfortable reality associated with the cruelty of slavery. Enslaved women, however, knew all too well the realities of rape and reproductive exploitation that featured prominently in slavery. The understandings that Garner and countless enslaved women developed concerning the gendered realities of bondage emerged in the national spotlight during the antebellum era, thus fueling the arsenal of abolitionist allies in the fight to dismantle slavery in the Union.

Before the court decided the case, it returned Garner and her family to Gaines, who absconded with her in an attempt to sell her in Louisiana. Abolitionists remarked, "This is done not only in defiance of justice and humanity, but also over the prostrate sovereignty of the State."[68] The case, and Garner's actions more specifically, offered an indictment on the law and administration of justice. Many Ohioans responded not only in alignment with abolitionist sentiment but also with criticism of the encroaching influence of Southern slave law. Regarding the innovation of slave law in the Garner case, the scholar Christina Sharpe notes, "Its atmospheric density increased; slavery undeniably became the total environment."[69] Virginia newspapers never mentioned Garner's name, but simply referred to the incident as the "Cincinnati slave case," with writers emphasizing the legal property rights of Gaines.[70] Infanticide stood at the center of the debate about the constitutional application of the Fugitive Slave Law. The only legal options to consider focused not on the impact of slavery on cases of infanticide but on whether Garner should be legally treated as a fugitive chattel or a criminal. Even as the parties involved weighed the possible legal approaches to the case, what the case unsurprisingly reveals is the absence of the possibilities of justice that enslaved women might envision in these instances. While this might seem obvious to students of nineteenth-century American history, we have been less attendant to how enslaved women created their own avenues of recourse, even as its effects proved profoundly disorienting and devastating.

Garner remained enslaved and Gaines forced her on a vessel headed south, a decision that the state of Virginia viewed as reprieve or clemency. But she knew better. The steamboat *Henry Lewis* carried the Garners south, but an *accident* jolted overboard Garner and her infant girl, Priscilla, or Cilla as her family affectionately called her. Cilla did not survive the collision, and scholars debate the extent to which her death might be read as an accident, since Garner expressed a reserved satisfaction with the fact that slavery no longer threatened the child's future.[71] After working in bondage in New Orleans and later in Tennessee, Garner died of typhoid fever in 1858. Her story still resonates in the most powerful critiques of slavery. The history of enslaved women in Virginia shows that acts of infanticide occurred well before and after Garner decided the fate of her children. In an act of both power and devastation, enslaved women sent ruptures of warfare that they waged on the sexual and reproductive claims on their bodies. Less noticeable in national headlines, but ever present and notable at the state and county level, were more cases of infanticide involving enslaved women in Virginia.

In 1850, Caroline started showing the first signs of pregnancy, and we can only imagine the thoughts that ran through her mind or the thoughts of countless enslaved women who navigated a range of emotions at the thought of delivering a child into the world of slavery that Virginia wrought. On

Friday, March 28, 1851, Caroline delivered a baby girl. We do not know the circumstances of her pregnancy or to whom to attribute the paternity of the child. Whether she decided in the moment of birth, nine months prior, or in the season of life where she understood the powerful devastation that comes with the sexual exploitation of an enslaved girl, at some point Caroline decided that this infant she held in her arms would not live to see the scenes that Virginia slavery and its masters subjected her to. That evening, she suffocated the child and, according to testimony, "then and there expose[d] the said female child to the night air," and the next morning the newborn was discovered "frozen and chilled."[72]

Those charged with examination of the case did not hesitate to employ the moral judgments that come with cases involving infanticide. The court recorded that "suffocating and cold the said female child died" and that Caroline "in manner and form aforesaid so willfully, feloniously and did kill and murder against the peace and dignity of the commonwealth of Virginia." The language of the courts assigned meanings of malice to Caroline's actions. The very "peace and dignity" of the commonwealth were disrupted, according to the record, but the death of Caroline's child leaves an enslaved woman living in the torment of a condition that she rejected on the child's behalf. Her refusal to bear the burdens of protection, care, and love under a system of tyranny, violence, and exploitation reveals a world much less defined by peace and dignity. Her actions were enough to offend the sensibilities of magistrates posturing toward justice, but slavery itself, and what it meant for enslaved women's bodies and progeny, somehow worked in harmony with the everyday demands of the commodification of their sexuality and reproductive capacities. Justice and its meanings underscore the contradictions and competing demands of the concept. Infanticide, an act of refusal and a profound use of power, reveals the gendered contours of enslaved women's resistance and exposes the moral entanglements of justice when competing articulations of its meaning rose to the fore.[73]

Caroline and enslaved women and girls in Virginia similarly accused of infanticide at some point in their lives decided that motherhood, and the life that awaited these children, proved too much to bear. These women and girls were the exception rather the rule, as many enslaved women forged family ties and reared children and younger kin according to the values of their respective communities. These kinship ties were not without conflict and tension; however, these ties were instrumental in the survival of generations of people of African descent.[74] Women were vital to these networks, forging bonds of intimacy and rituals of self-regard in the face of chattel slavery.

Infanticide tapped into the deep wells of trauma, a reminder that the life of the child was precarious well before a parent or guardian contemplated the child's death. On the basis of court documents, most incidents occurred immediately following the birth. Some enslaved women sought herbalists and nurses among the enslaved community to terminate pregnancies. Existing reproductive politics focused on acts of abortion among white women, but instances of abortion were discussed less in the context of capital crime even as it was relatively common. Just as enslaved women acted on their own ideas of justice, death also held different meanings. Caroline gave birth to a female infant, and her decision to end her life was likely shaped by the knowledge of all that it meant to be an enslaved girl in antebellum Virginia.

In the summer months of 1852, the Albemarle County court tried a case involving Fannie, who had recently given birth to a baby girl. A local doctor performed an invasive examination to confirm Fannie's recent pregnancy. Fannie denied the allegations at first, stating that the child was "born dead, and that she had thrown it to the hogs and had seen them eat it." The court reported that it discovered the baby "concealed in [a] bed" and that the infant's name "was unknown." According to the court, Fannie gave birth to a healthy baby around July, and "being moved and seduced by the instigation of the Devil," Fannie choked the baby until she could no longer breathe. The court found Fannie guilty of murder in the second degree and sentenced her to sale and transportation at the value of $650. If the court determined that Fannie committed the act "being moved and seduced by the instigation of the Devil," or with malicious intent, then why did it accuse her of murder in the second degree? She stood firm on her innocence; as her owner explained, "The prisoner is a woman of great pride, and thinks a great deal of her virtue." Fannie boasted a reputation well before the incident, a testament to the ways that she sought desperately to maintain aspects of her person on her terms even if her entire story could not be explained. The county courts applied these concepts in ways that show the broader inconsistencies of cases involving clemency and execution. Locals furnished details that shaped the dimensions of the case and the corresponding evidence, but these aspects did not always appear clearly articulated in the record. Jurists often recommended commutation for circumstances they deemed highly unusual, such as inconsistencies between the actions of enslaved persons and their reputation for cooperative behavior.[75]

The demands of impeccable character and deference from enslaved women and girls functioned as the imbalanced expectations used to groom them into trustworthy servants and laborers in the plantation households and urban homes of Virginia's cities. Judith Fore of Chesterfield County hired out Lucy Randolph, a young, enslaved girl, to John L. Weymouth. In 1852, Lucy discovered she was pregnant. For reasons that she kept to herself, she attempted to conceal her pregnancy, and the night she went into labor, she reportedly ingested "a great deal of camphor and laudanum."[76] Weymouth testified that Lucy appeared visibly disoriented and he believed her to be "out of her right mind."[77] Weymouth requested a doctor, who said Lucy initially denied she had delivered a baby at all, but, soon after his line of questioning, she confessed. Weymouth discovered the child covered in straw and an apron in a hogshead next door. Two enslaved women, Ann Willis and Peggy, were deposed and verified that they heard a child crying, and when they went out to the yard, they saw Lucy carrying something wrapped in her apron. It is likely that Ann assisted with Lucy's delivery or attempted to, as she confirmed that Lucy was ill after having taken "considerable medicine." According to reports, Lucy was "not quite 15 years of age" and "had always been a most excellent servant."[78] We know little of the circumstances of her pregnancy, only that she was young and that she desired to "hide her shame."[79] The source of that "shame" is unclear, but given the unchecked opportunities to violate enslaved girls, one does not need to reach far to understand the different circumstances that might have led to her pregnancy. According to reports, Lucy labored under arduous "mental and physical" turmoil during her delivery. This "excitement" was "produced by the stimulants she had taken, and the pains of nature, and the desire to hide her shame."[80] The court called in witnesses who volunteered their perspective on the matter. According to some locals, "they ha[d] never known a better character" than Lucy's.[81] While the court landed at a unanimous opinion that Lucy killed the child, it also submitted a recommendation to the governor for a commuted sentence of sale and transportation.

Right at the eve of Lucy's scheduled execution, Governor Joseph Johnson commuted her sentence, gaining the approval of the public regarding the matter. One news report offered, "We were much gratified at learning this decision of the governor, and we believe that such is the feeling of the community generally." To account for the "peculiar" circumstances of the case, observers emphasized knowledge of "her previous good character and extreme youth."[82] The general understanding of her "extreme youth" and her reputation for excellent character might offer a window into her world and her thinking behind the child's death. On the basis of her sense of "shame," it was clear she did not desire to mother a child, and public opinion concluded that her pregnancy appeared inconsistent with her character. Having established a notably agreeable and admirable reputation, it is quite possible that Lucy also carried herself with a sense of respectability. She worked in Richmond, a city where she might have encountered free Black Virginians who owned property, attended churches, and established their own community relief societies. Free Black women, many of whom worked as domestics and others as seamstresses, washerwomen, and nurses, established themselves in the city, and perhaps Lucy attempted to attend church services or interact with other enslaved women and girl hires in the city with aspirations to earn wages for themselves and to live in a place of their own in Richmond or even Alexandria or Washington, D.C.[83] Lucy made an impression on everyone she met, which tells us she carefully navigated the demands of deference imposed by slavery, the burdens of impeccable character that nineteenth-century Americans measured to judge one's reputation, and perhaps had some dreams for herself of freedom and a life on her own terms. This all came to a screeching halt, and the world she worked hard to navigate so that she might avoid "trouble" came crashing down.

Something went awry for Lucy before 1852, when the labor pains contorted her womb, and she consumed the stimulants offered to her. Lucy had a reputation for doing things in ways that met everyone's approval. Perhaps she bore the "shame" for which she was granted no choice in the matter. Enslaved girls, from "extreme youth" to adulthood, were vulnerable to sexual violence, as age did not present an adequate barrier against the appetites of predatory Southerners. Jeff Forret, in his treatment of infanticide, reminds us, "That it was often masters, overseers, and other white men who made enslaved women prematurely knowledgeable of sexual matters made no difference; the irony garnered the polite silence of the southern white masses."[84] White men in Virginia were not accused of rape in cases involving enslaved women and girls, making the legal culpability the purview and responsibility of the enslaved woman or girl accused of infanticide. The legal culture, while permitting the commutation of the death penalty, and petitions from locals, protected the property and sexual interests of slaveholders and white men who raped enslaved women and girls. Just as enslaved girls began to understand the social customs that kept them from punishment, they, too, learned the realities of evading predators and their own vulnerability to rape without legal recourse. The sexual lives of enslaved girls often appeared in the press, in courts, and in medical publications, making their experiences public in ways that white women of means were often shielded from.

Julia, another enslaved girl in her teens, appeared in the medical publication the *Stethoscope: A Monthly Journal of Medicine and the Collateral Sciences*, in a case study of abortion. The *Daily Dispatch* of Richmond explained that "the Stethoscope faithfully maintain[ed] its reputation," to attest to the scholarly authority of the publication.[85] The journal article introduced Julia as "a negro girl—17 years of age" and in "good health" and of "good constitution."[86] The doctor explained that, at five months pregnant, "sudden fright, over exertion and exposure" triggered her abortion. The case also included details of Julia surviving a house fire. "Sudden fright, over exertion and exposure" were possible reactions to the fire, pregnancy complications, and also slavery itself. The journal article casually mentions these factors in ways that reinforce terror and backbreaking labor as accepted and normalized features of the lives of the enslaved. The doctor stated further that while "she suffered from pain and some fever afterwards," "the symptoms were not so violent as to require much attention."[87] Regarding a white woman dealing with a similar uterine condition, the doctor explained, "As her long continued debility and suffering had made even life undesirable without relief, she readily consented to a thorough examination."[88] White women possessed access to consent in their interactions with medical professionals, but enslaved girls were treated as specimens, with consent often authorized by slaveholders and with very little attention to their need for relief from pain.[89] Even as the doctor attempted to prescribe remedies to heal their condition, he did so in order to achieve very specific ends based on the racial and legal status of each woman or girl under consideration. The doctor focused on Julia's improvement "so as to attend to her duties," but emphasized the degree to which the white woman could access a desirable life.[90] Slaveholders employed local doctors for both medical and economic reasons tied to the expectation that enslaved women and girls resumed their work after receiving treatment.

Following the miscarriage, Julia struggled to pull herself up and walk and continued to experience excessive hemorrhaging, typically a life-threatening postpartum condition. Along with the hemorrhaging that occurred monthly and lasted for one to two weeks, she experienced debilitating pain in the back and left ovarian region of the uterus. The doctor conducted a series of painful and invasive examinations to understand her condition. He explained that the vagina "was sensitive" and the cervix "enlarged" and "very painful to the touch when pressed upwards." The doctor conducted these examinations several times over a span of four years.[91] He discovered a rounded tumor in the uterine walls, also "painful to the touch," which he attributed to subacute inflammation. He treated her with cold water injections, a detergent vaginal wash, and creosote. Historically, medical professionals used creosote with the idea that it might serve as an antiseptic, astringent, anesthetic, expectorant, and laxative. It might also be used to burn dead tissue, and the doctor may have applied it to the tumor. One could find creosote for sale in Virginia newspaper advertisements placed by druggists.[92] But the plant-based carbonaceous substance contains extremely toxic properties that doctors today view as a carcinogenic that produces radiation.[93] Creosote is now used to create a tar that preserves wood and coal. Julia experienced bouts of recovery, which the doctor noted as occurring in instances when she neglected the remedies he prescribed. On the basis of his assessment, she applied the prescribed remedies only in moments when she appeared in grave condition. He concluded, "I have no doubt she might have been perfectly cured long since, if the proper course of treatment had been fully and perseveringly carried out and continued until she was secured against a return of the disease." But a "perfect restoration" of the uterus seemed impossible, since the condition itself remained simply and vaguely designated as "uterine disease." Her discomfort seemed to persist because of an unclear diagnosis and the ineffectiveness of the remedies the doctor prescribed. These violent experiments and inquiries performed on the bodies of enslaved women and girls supported the development of legal medicine and medical expertise called on in the courts.

Many known and unknown reasons accounted for infanticide among enslaved women and girls. White women also appeared before the court for charges of infanticide, but not to the extent that enslaved women were convicted for the crime. For some women, the idea of bringing a child into the world of slavery proved too much to bear. The social proscriptions against unwed mothers led white and Black women to commit acts of infanticide or orphan their children. For enslaved girls like Lucy, it is plausible that she simply did not want to become a mother. To bear children only to have them subjected to the same brutal experience of the mother posed a dilemma that white Virginians deemed a fact of Southern life. Furthermore, to parent a child with the understanding that a slaveholder could harm, sell, maim, or even kill without recourse made the prospects of building a family a precarious endeavor. Still, countless women and men built kinship ties, community, and a sense of collective identity and support that lasted through the generations. In many, but not all, instances, enslaved women and girls convicted of infanticide were the survivors of rape. The unwanted advances and predatory harassment they were subjected to reveal a life of everyday precarity and shattering violence. As jurists and witnesses deliberated the most "appropriate" sentence, years of unchecked violence and "punishment" often went unaccounted for as the burden of guilt fell on the shoulders of enslaved women and girls. At times, the petitions were a collective acknowledgment that perhaps an owner or overseer was known to be particularly cruel toward enslaved people. While the conditions these women and girls confronted appealed to the sensibilities of locals, such sentiment did not go so far as to transform the laws pertaining to the rape of enslaved women and girls or the possibilities of their testimonies against white Virginians. In Lucy's case, locals were relieved that the governor commuted the sentence "to one more mild, just and appropriate."[94] Sale and transportation were the rewards of good character. But for enslaved women, the judicial process could be silencing as well as traumatic. The legal structure of Virginia made impossible the kinds of recourse defined by enslaved women and approaches to justice that allowed for them to protect their person, remain close to kin, or bear children on their terms or even for the possibility of freedom. Enslaved women were afforded little to no opportunity to offer testimony, and much of what we know about infanticide is written in records penned by Virginia officials.

More women and girls witnessed the death of their offspring, whether through complications or deliberate initiation of abortion or infanticide. On August 8, 1852, Benjamin Richardson realized that the sewage from his water closet was backed up, so he hired Augustus Arsell to examine the pipes. Working through the waste that clogged the passageway, he noticed an unusual odor and removed the gooseneck of the pipe. He took the pipe outdoors to snake it, when he pushed against a small mass and the head of an infant came out. Lucy, described as a "mulatto slave girl," stood nearby as Arsell worked through the pipes, and as soon as he turned to speak with Richardson about the matter, Lucy "seized the head and made off with it out of the gate."[95] Arsell caught up to her and demanded that she return the infant, and she refused and declared her plans to "bury it." Afterward, Arsell witnessed her wrap the head and take it into her room. For Lucy, this was a matter deeply personal to her, one that Richardson and Arsell could not possibly understand. Richardson confronted her with demands to know where she placed the baby's head, but Lucy informed him that she "buried it."

Lucy's story began to shift and contradict her previous explanation after an official investigation was launched. The sheriff of Amelia County arrived and questioned Lucy about the baby, and Lucy "positively denied having seen or heard anything of the child's head." The sheriff performed a search and found the baby's head "wrapped up in one of Lucy's skirts." He immediately arrested her and brought her to jail to await trial. Richardson remained unsure whether the enslaved young woman he hired delivered the infant, but she appeared to be pregnant for several months. A doctor examined Lucy and determined that "there were strong and almost undoubted symptoms of her recent confinement."[96] Lucy underwent an invasive examination that involved measuring her uterus to determine whether a pregnancy and possible delivery occurred. In addition to the medical examination, the coroner questioned Lucy, and she responded by stating that she recently miscarried that year and that a doctor H. Cabell attended to her. According to the coroner's account, "she denied to him knowing anything about the remains found" and that prior to the discovery "she was delivered of the child in the privy of Mr. R's house, on Wednesday last; that the child was dead when born and passed down the pipe entire."[97] She stated further that, although she experienced pain, she "repressed all noise." Another doctor examined the child's head and determined "it to have been that of a new born full-timed infant." Lucy delivered at full term, unlike her previous pregnancy, in which she miscarried. According to Lucy, the child did not appear alive, but the doctor noted that "the head looked as if it had been severed from the body and not fallen from it by reason of decay."[98] Enslaved women employed remedies to abort unwanted pregnancies, and some lost children because they experienced complications that made a successful delivery untenable. This pregnancy marked one of two known incidents in which her pregnancies ended in the death of the fetus, but the medical examinations did not offer explanations concerning whether she experienced any condition that triggered complications. George W. Randolph served as legal counsel, but he offered very little argument to compel the court to commute the sentence. Indeed, the press stated, "The case was one of the most horrible infanticides that we have ever had to record."[99] To the reporter's astonishment, Lucy "exhibited no sort of feeling for the deed which was said to have been committed by her, which she at first stoutly denied." Lucy's inner feelings about the matter never emerged in court, whether by her own volition or based on the procedures permitted by the court. This form of dissemblance to shield her thoughts and deny any culpability reveals a deeply personal commitment to wrestle with the decision on her own terms. She found the wherewithal to hide the infant's head in the gooseneck of a pipe, and she carefully wrapped the head and placed it among her skirts. She knew the spirit of the baby was long gone, but the physical head of the child was hers to hide and hers to bury. She "buried it." And all that factored into her decision to remove the child far from the surface of life on the Richardson homestead, too, was buried. The profound silencing of her voice and experiences means that we cannot comprehend the trepidation that led her to commit the act in the manner in which she did.

Factors involving insufficient evidence to measure intent, and the sexual exploitation of enslaved women's bodies, shaped understandings of motives. This was evident in a case that emerged in Powhatan County, where Opha Jane, an enslaved woman, stood trial for the death of her child. The court found her guilty of infanticide. Although Opha Jane faced the sentence of death, Governor Henry A. Wise determined that the evidence remained uncertain. He commuted her sentence to sale and transportation after careful scrutiny of the details of her case.[100] That same year, the governor commuted another death sentence in a case involving Suckey. The county court of Culpeper tried Suckey for infanticide, on finding her infant with a "string of linsey cloth" that she "wrapped twice tightly around the neck and tied fast." Because of Suckey's "previous good character," the court recommended clemency, and officials arranged for her sale and transportation. In Suckey's case, the physician administered a hydrostatic test to determine the cause of the infant's death. This procedure involved removing the lungs of the baby and placing them in water to examine the buoyancy of the organs. Floating lungs served as an indicator of air and, thus, infanticide.[101]

In 1857, one woman in Richmond attempted to end the life of her child when she "threw it over a high fence."[102] Another enslaved person discovered the child, and the infant made a remarkable recovery. Throwing the child over the fence appeared to be a very public act. In many cases involving infanticide, women discreetly hid children following their death. Perhaps the woman, Margaret, hoped that someone might discover the child and care for it or that she might even abscond with plans to carry the child off the property. But in many of these instances, women also responded to the weight of bearing children in a system that might force their separation and that normalized the harm and exploitation of these children. Days before the court announced the verdict, locals thought they discovered that the infant was white. They soon identified Margaret as "a mulatto woman," rather than a white woman as originally stated by the coroner.[103] Margaret appeared on trial in Abingdon, Virginia, for infanticide, and her sentence to sale brought her owner, Joseph M. Crocket, the handsome sum of $1,050. The price enumerated for her sale and transportation, and the details about her fair skin, likely meant that slave traders prepared her for the lucrative markets that sexually trafficked enslaved women. The sexual commodification of enslaved women such as Margaret often meant that women found it undesirable to produce children who might meet a similar fate.[104]

In 1858, young men of Rappahannock County discovered an enslaved woman wandering in distress in the woods. For five or six days, she wandered through the woods in despair, primarily living off of whortleberries. The young men discovered Ellen, an enslaved woman owned by James Thornton, in a state of anguish. She confessed that she drowned her child and explained that she also attempted to drown herself by jumping in the river. "Thinking her clothes the cause of her not sinking, she undressed and made a second attempt, when she again floated to the bank," the news reported.[105] The conditions of life for herself and her child weighed heavily on her as she contemplated an end to whatever she found unbearable about the prospects for her future and the life that awaited her and her child. The court sentenced Ellen to transportation, and the auditor signed off on the journey ahead, which involved more of the same unless she discovered a way to survive the devastation that brought her to the banks of the river.[106]

The gestational period of pregnancy gave ample time to consider the possible outcomes of bearing children, as enslaved women and girls studied their growing and changing bodies. In the summer of 1860, Emily, an enslaved woman hired out to Henry N. Bowers in Richmond, proceeded with her usual duties with the hopes that Bowers might avoid noticing the transformation of her body. She spent the spring visibly pregnant, but something seemed off according to Bowers. He testified that, in searching through his basement, he "made discoveries that induced him to believe his servant woman had given birth to a child." Perhaps he saw traces of blood and fluids on the floor or soiled rags, typically left over after a delivery. Emily denied that she gave birth, but Bowers sent her to her room to prevent her from taking any further steps to evade investigation. As Bowers continued to search for answers, Emily managed to escape, but she did not make it far before bounty hunters tracked her down and committed her to a private jail. These private jails, like the ones discussed in previous chapters, functioned not only as sites of slave sales, auctioning, and temporary confinement but also as brutal sites of discipline and terror. The local slave jails were lucrative for the premium placed on the distasteful work of torture and punishment. Not long after Emily's stint in the jail, she "confessed" that immediately after she gave birth to the child, "she threw it into the sink in the yard."[107] Did her time in jail involve measures to extract a confession? Emily explained that she arranged for a Black man to carry the child away for her. Officials never discovered the child and made efforts to hunt down the accomplice who carried the child away. Did Emily attempt to kill the child? Without the body of the infant, these charges were difficult to prove. One particular detail that slaveholders remained undoubtedly aware of pointed to the fact that Emily also confessed that the child remained alive when the accomplice carried it away. Do Emily's

the west side of Shockoe Creek.   It occupied a portion of the ground now covered by the establishment of Chamblin, Delaney & Scott.   A narrow
lane known as Wall Street, properly Fifteenth
Street, led to it.   This establishment, which has
been often spoken of as the "old slave pen," con-
sisted of four buildings, which were of brick.   One

LUMPKIN'S JAIL.

was used by the proprietor as his residence and his
office.   Another was used as a boarding-house for
the accommodation of those who came to sell their
slaves or to buy.   A third served as a bar-room and
a kitchen.   The "old jail" stood in a field a few
rods from the other buildings.   It was forty-one feet
long and two stories in height, with a piazza to both
stories on the north side of the building.   Here

"Lumpkin's Jail." Carter Lumpkin used this structure to confine enslaved people for sale
and to torture enslaved people sent there for discipline. The jail was leased to the seminary
that became Virginia Union University. Charles Henry Corey (1834–1899), *A History of the
Richmond Theological Seminary, with Reminiscences of Thirty Years' Work among the Colored
People of the South* (LC2852.R4 T3 1895), Special Collections, University of Virginia,
Charlottesville.

actions conclusively point to attempted infanticide, or might other possibilities be at work? Might the act point to her planned effort to arrange and ensure the freedom of the child? We might never know Emily's motivations, but relevant to the story is that her decision implied a rejection of slavery as part of the future of her child. Whether the act represented an attempt at death or freedom, the infant became inaccessible to her owner and any local officials employed to resolve such matters. This interposition of her will, like that of the women and girls who preceded her, struck a powerful chord.

Infanticide cases proved difficult for jurists and locals to substantiate in the face of limited evidence and medical expertise. The courts went to lengths to determine the culpability of enslaved women in ways that appeared invasive, coercive, and inconclusive. As medical examiners blundered through damaging procedures on the bodies of enslaved women and their children, the women, too, discovered ways to wield and claim their bodies as their own. Moving beyond criminality and culpability, the actions of these women force us to question the parameters of justice more broadly and the systemic apparatus that makes death, continued bondage, or sale outside of Virginia the best possible outcome. What is clemency in instances where enslaved women decide that death is better than a life in the slave South? Infanticide revealed the gendered contours of antebellum law that offered limited recourse in instances where slaveholders wielded violent power over the bodies of enslaved women. The law, by design, offered no protection for instances in which enslaved women were subject to rape or forced reproduction. In Virginia, these cases were tried in such a way to make space for the claims and rights of slaveholders.

Infanticide cases also shed light on the legal complexities involved in trying such cases. These women, tried for murder and treated as inhuman, reveal the contradictory nature of slave law and the fact that these women were anything but inhuman. They harnessed the limited power they had even if the avenues toward refusal led to both a literal and metaphorical dead end. What was the law to an enslaved mother? What did justice look like for women deemed by the law as unrapable? Justice reached its limits as long as the property interests in enslaved women, their reproductive labor, their profit-focused disposability, and their sexual exploitation remained encoded in American law. These women shed light on the institution of slavery in ways that inspired the radicalism of abolitionist politics in the antebellum era.

The actions of these women sparked a national outcry against the Fugitive Slave Law, but also the sexual and reproductive violence that shaped their experiences. Prominent cases such as the Margaret Garner trial and the lesser-known cases of the women in Virginia featured in this chapter reveal that enslaved women across the nation and within the oldest slaveholding state in the Union understood their own capacity for refusal, even as it came at a tremendous personal cost. Their experiences underscored alternative understandings of wrongdoing in a way that bears on the reputations of slaveholders and the integrity of slave law. But many white locals upheld the sanctity of the rule of law, while also challenging the use of the death penalty through petitioning. The weight of local sentiment and opinion underscores the ways that the law and administration of justice required the support of those who constituted the citizenry, as historians have shown. The cases called into question and disputed the honor of men deemed respectable and representative of Southern paternalism. Paternalism allowed for the kind of reprieve exclusively defined by slaveholders. This fact made freedom and justice that accounted for white culpability an impossibility. As abolitionists got wind of notable cases involving infanticide and the sexualized experiences of enslaved women, the shift from local intervention to the mobilization of national intervention threatened the political foundations of the commonwealth and Southern slaveholding states throughout the Union. The assault on slavery, however, did not originate from abolitionists alone. The actions of enslaved women sent rumblings that signaled that the foundation of slave society faced an enemy within.

CHAPTER FIVE

Insurgency

At a court of Oyer and Terminer for the County of New Kent held at the Court House on Friday the 10th day of September 1830 for the trial of Peggy, Patrick, Franky and Caroline slaves belonging to the estate of John Francis dec'd of this county charged with murder and arson.

—Auditor of Public Accounts

August in Virginia left a sweltering haze over its victims as the heat and humidity reached peak levels at the close of summer in 1830. Peggy, an enslaved woman in New Kent County, found herself battling the heat while laboring for John Francis. Something about this year, this month, felt different. Francis made a habit of terrorizing Peggy, and by the end of the summer his violence proved particularly acute. Over the years, however, she retained the wisdom of her mother, a woman forced to bear children with Francis, their enslaver, who warned her of his plans for Peggy. Could she anticipate the events that followed? This story is not a new one, as we have seen in the previous chapters.

Here, I return to murder to show that the insurgent behavior of enslaved women and their comrades preceded the end of chattel slavery. These stories remind us that by the end of the Civil War, enslaved people set in motion a series of rejoinders reminiscent of the battles they fought in the decades leading up to the conflict. Historian Vincent Brown argues that the slave trade catalyzed ongoing diasporic warfare, and although his work attends to the eighteenth century, the same might hold true in the antebellum South. Brown asserts, "This was not war in the conventional sense, however, involving disciplined armies directed by the rulers of states. Rather, it was the simmering violence inherent in mastery, by its nature a forceful assault, and the slaves' countervailing resentment of slaveholders' 'fraud, rapine, and cruelty.'"[1] Stephanie M. H. Camp reminds us in *Closer to Freedom* that enslaved women engaged in everyday acts of resistance that preceded wartime actions waged against their former owners, and in Virginia this fact holds true.[2] Thavolia Glymph offers that "slave resistance—the burning of planter homes, murders, conspiracies, and flight—confirmed how much enslaved people knew and understood about the conflict and put their experience as 'knowledge brokers' to new use."[3] Manifestations of enslaved women's acts of insurgency revealed their antislavery and liberation politics. The Civil War allowed for them to act on stores of knowledge, memory, and strategies of resistance passed down and developed over time and geography. These tactics were not novel; indeed, they appeared repeatedly throughout previous chapters in history and in the decades leading up to the war. The story of Peggy and the enslaved women, men, and children who follow reveals the ways that they became the knowledge brokers whom Glymph speaks of, through murder, conspiracies, arson, and flight.

John Francis taunted Peggy, his daughter, with numerous threats of assaulting her. In one incident, he vowed to have two enslaved men, Jesse and Patrick, hold her down as he acted out his sexual desires, despite her clear rejection of him. Testimony later revealed that he regularly kept Peggy chained to a block and locked up in a house on the property. In another instance, Francis chained her to a block and hurled violent threats and promises to sell her further south, which he, like countless others taking revenge on enslaved women and girls, believed would subject her to the same fate he prepared for her on his estate. Perhaps he hoped that she would acquiesce with the prospect of remaining near the people and place she knew well. But what comfort might she find in either place in the face of sexual terror? Peggy's half sister would later testify, "I know the deceased wanted to cohabit with Peggy to which she objected and that was the cause of the difference between them. I know the deceased threatened Peggy to beat her almost to death and to send her off if she did not yield to his wishes." Peggy decided on a different fate.[4]

On the evening of August 22, 1830, Peggy enlisted the help of Patrick, Franky, and Caroline to murder Francis and set his home ablaze. Who were Patrick, Franky, and Caroline in Peggy's life? Witnesses explained that Patrick suffered from a mental disability and could hardly be seen as a culpable participant in the incident. People on the plantation, however, knew Patrick from his strength, a physical advantage that Francis called on when Peggy refused his advances. Franky and Caroline joined in the effort, but on what basis? Perhaps they were motivated by their kinship with Peggy, or they possessed their own set of grievances that motivated their actions. Collective and sporadic action might be the result of numerous injuries incurred by the enslaved along with mutual ties that pull others toward a particular conflict. In this instance, they all seemed to be in agreement that something must be done.

Peggy and Patrick approached the entrance to the Francis home with a sharpened ax and wooden stick. According to Patrick, Peggy held the ax.

Witnesses heard knocking, thumping, and wailing within the house. Those were the sounds of Peggy and Patrick beating Francis to his death, and upon the final blows to his body, witnesses heard him cry out, "O lord have mercy!," until he fell silent. Peggy, Patrick, and Caroline left his body and proceeded to gather bales of hay, which they used to stuff large quilts. The three of them approached the house with the stuffed quilts, tossed them inside, and lit them on fire. The flames quickly engulfed the house, where Francis's body lay limp against a wall. When a neighbor noticed the glow coming from the house, he rushed over and took in the sight of the ravenous fire. The house collapsed, and a charred body appeared at the corner of what remained of the dwelling.[5]

Not long after the defendants arrived in court on September 10, 1830, locals began to assemble a petition. After hearing the testimony of witnesses, the court dismissed charges against Caroline, but the court found Peggy, Patrick, and Franky guilty. Perhaps the affair came as no surprise since the sexual appetite Francis possessed appeared as general knowledge, even as it offended local sensibilities. One white witness testified that "it was currently reported in the neighborhood that the deceased was the father of Peggy and that he wished to have illicit intercourse with her." Several witnesses confirmed that they knew Francis to be Peggy's father. This history of his violent exploitation of enslaved women and incestuous behavior became an unsettling fact for the residents of New Kent. One hundred residents of New Kent signed a petition to request executive clemency for the enslaved people involved in the incident. The petition included the following statement: "There are circumstances attending the case of the poor ignorant slaves although not sufficient to justify the act for which they are condemned yet in the opinion of the undersigners should mitigate the punishment." In the petition, the signers expressed knowledge of circumstances that did not appear "sufficient to justify the act," yet the punishment of sale had "the same effect on Society, as the punishment by death."[6]

The petitioners revealed an important aspect of the legal history of clemency in cases involving enslaved women—that the sale of criminalized enslaved people possessed the "same effect on Society, as the punishment by death." In Virginia, the circulation of money, bodies, deeds, and receipts for the value of enslaved people remained a constant feature of sentencing outcomes. These practices shaped the meanings of justice for those removed from slavery's chains, but for the enslaved, the possibilities for justice demanded new interpretations and methodologies for meting out these claims. Peggy, her mother, and perhaps a number of women suffered on the Francis homestead under laws that permitted his violent use of power. Locals used petitions to express their disapproval of such behavior, and yet they knew of his antics and like most Southerners displayed their silent tolerance and indifference prior to the incident. What changed? As many locals watched the Francis home go up in flames, Peggy's actions sent a ripple through New Kent that brought his behavior to the surface. Francis and his reputation threatened the integrity of the overall reputation of the local community. Through the petition, locals sent a signal to Richmond that Francis did not represent the values of county residents. A judge, the sheriff, and constables all signed the petition in favor of a commuted sentence. But as they remind us, the sentence was less about favorable circumstances for the enslaved, since commutation produced the "same effect," and more about a consensus that made Francis an outsider. The governor approved commuted sentences for Peggy, Patrick, and Franky. Peggy explained her decision, declaring that "she had as well die with the ague as the fever." Virginia's brand of justice did not protect her from Francis, and she resolved to do whatever remained in her power to end the torment. Peggy's fight might be understood as a matter of insurgency or a posture of revolt, even in the absence of an immediately transformative revolution of society.[7] Patrick, Franky, and Caroline collectively joined the effort, even as they understood the grave consequences that awaited them. They were compelled by values and ideas that transcended the legal and social logic of the slave South. And they were not alone.

On September 19, 1831, Lucy, an enslaved woman who labored for John T. Barrow in Southampton County, appeared before the court on charges of conspiring to rebel. But Barrow did not live to bear witness in the trial. He died at the hands of Black men who marched from home to home ending the lives of as many white men, women, and children as they could find. In the summer of 1831, locals targeted Nat Turner, a Black preacher from Southampton County who they presumed to be the leader of a collective effort to kill white Virginians. Turner, born enslaved and taught to read and write, became proficient in religious teachings and used this knowledge to make the theological case for freedom. Turner believed himself to be chosen for the task of ushering the enslaved of Southampton County out of bondage.[8] He acted on the epistemologies of enslaved Virginians developed generations before the summer of 1831. Still, Turner enlisted the participation of over seventy-five enslaved residents of the county, which led to the deaths of fifty-five white locals.[9] College of William and Mary professor and a defender of slavery Thomas Roderick Dew reported that "in the county of Southampton in Virginia, a few slaves, led on by Nat Turner, rose in the night, and murdered in the most inhuman and shocking manner, between sixty and seventy of the unsuspecting whites of that county."[10] The story of the Southampton Rebellion, often referred to as Nat Turner's rebellion, emphasized the preacher and his male comrades as the primary agents in their collective resistance. In *Surviving Southampton*, the historian Vanessa M. Holden allows us to see the role of women in creating strategies of resistance and survival that shaped the world that Turner inhabited. Because of the work of historians who examine Black women's history, we can begin to imagine the possibility of enslaved women's work of insurgency and disentangle the gendered exclusion of enslaved women from the histories of collective resistance in the South. An assessment of court records and secondary accounts reveals that the Southampton Rebellion appeared to be less the work of one man and more a reflection of the collective resistance and kinship that shaped the dynamics among enslaved and free Black Virginians. From this framework, we can place Lucy and other enslaved women in acts of rebellion leading up to the American Civil War.[11]

That summer of 1831, when enslaved men approached the Barrows' house, John T. Barrow confronted them, while Mary Barrow, his wife, attempted to escape through the rear of their home. According to one account, Mary Barrow picked up speed, only to be abruptly stopped by Lucy, the enslaved woman who worked countless hours serving the Barrow household.[12] Barrow's testimony revealed that Lucy allegedly grabbed her arm in an effort to stop her. Barrow managed to disentangle herself from Lucy's grasp and fled to the swamp. Lucy declared her innocence, but faced the death sentence, as the court read her actions as complicit with the rebellion. "We succeeded in taking 12 men and one woman prisoners, who it appeared had taken an active part in the massacre of the inhabitants of this county," the news reported.[13] Perhaps Lucy feared that Mary Barrow might be safer under her care, or it might be possible that Lucy acted in alignment with the collective effort to end the lives of those who wielded unchecked power over her life. These lines of resistance were not always as clear as murder, but the insurgent actions of enslaved women took on various forms. Charlotte and Ester offer another case in point, as they toiled in the household of Nathaniel and Lavinia Francis while the rebellion unfolded.[14]

The Francises were expecting a child, which meant that an extensive list of preparations fell on the enslaved women to address. These women would include Charlotte and Ester. The rebels approached the Francis property and killed an overseer and two white boys. They could not find the Francises, so they proceeded to the next house with the intention to return. Once Lavinia Francis appeared in the kitchen, Charlotte reportedly grabbed a knife and wielded toward her to finish what Turner's band started, only to have it intercepted by Ester. Francis then escaped to the woods. According to author William Sidney Drewry, Nathaniel Francis spared Ester any punishment and even expressed gratitude for her "loyalty," but Charlotte met her death after he tied her to a tree and shot her multiple times.[15] This account of Charlotte's death lacks any documentation, but this book has shown that slaveholders exercised their own forms of discipline at their own discretion in Virginia. Nathaniel Francis determined Charlotte's and Ester's futures, but the court formally ordered Lucy's execution.[16]

The memory of the incident sent shock waves into Virginia and sparked national debate about the future of slavery. White Southerners remembered the rebellion as an important justification for preserving the hierarchies of slavery and protecting the rights to property they felt entitled to.[17] Enslaved women and their progeny remembered it very differently. Virginia legislators, particularly those less invested in slaveholding, seized the moment to consider the plausibility of abolition as either a gradual measure or one that involved colonization, or both. Led by Thomas Jefferson Randolph, the grandson of the venerated founder, the movement to seriously consider the possibilities of gradual emancipation revealed the intrastate fissures between the western portion of the commonwealth and the eastern planter aristocracy. Randolph proposed an amended version of a motion presented by William Osborne Goode of Mecklenburg, who opposed any serious organization of the legislature to address the possibility of manumission. In an effort to push the matter, Randolph proposed the following: "That the children of all female slaves who may be born in this state on or after the fourth day of July, 1840, shall become the property of the commonwealth, the males at the age of twenty-one years, and females at the age of eighteen, if detained by their owners within the limits of Virginia, until they shall respectively arrive at the ages aforesaid; to be hired out until the net sum arising therefrom shall be sufficient to defray the expense of their removal beyond the limits of the United States."[18] This gradualist proposal brought the legislature back to where it all began—the reproductive lives of enslaved women. To undo the work of slavery, whether immediately or gradually, lawmakers needed to address the source of the legal inheritability of slavery as Virginia law assigned it in 1662. The gendered age distinction here allowed for slaveholders to benefit longer from the labor of men than of women, but slightly influenced the likelihood of a growing enslaved population. This approach might allow for Virginia to benefit from the labor of enslaved women and men, while also managing the costs of emancipation and possibly colonization by manumitting women some years earlier. Dew, however, viewed these considerations as improprietous, arguing that "any scheme of abolition proposed so soon after the Southampton tragedy, would necessarily appear to be the result of that most inhuman massacre."[19] The *Southern Planter* reported Randolph's remarks in the debate and dismissed them as "ludicrous."[20] "Who could have anticipated, that the bloody horrors of the Southampton massacre, instead of suggesting plans for stricter discipline, would give birth to schemes of emancipation?" declared Benjamin Watkins Leigh, a member of the state legislature.[21] Slaveholding Virginians went to work to protect slavery in the state.

Virginians, particularly political thinkers of the state, set out to make the case for more harsh laws that restricted access to literacy and literature, gatherings of groups of enslaved and free Black people, and movement between the counties. Strategic and collective insurgency among the enslaved, as opposed to acts of hysteria and fanaticism featured in the press and public memory of the rebellion, triggered an important debate about the plausibility of gradual emancipation. Randolph and supporters of gradual emancipation made compelling arguments for the overall financial and physical security that the measure might bring. Defenders of slavery, however, namely Virginians who came from regions of the state that relied on the institution, shifted the discussion sharply in the direction of the economic and political calamity such a measure might cause. Dew, in his *Review of the Debates*, captured this division within Virginia, stating, "The people of the west, in which there are comparatively few slaves, in which there never can be any great increase of that kind of property, because their agriculture does not require it"—that opposing faction regards slavery as "a 'nuisance' to them."[22] Dew argued that slavery became a burden imposed on the colonies by the British Crown and that "Divine Authority" and philosophers of the classical tradition all affirmed the practice of slavery. In other words, Virginians bore limited, if any, moral responsibility for the institution. He wrote, "Aristotle, and the great men of antiquity, believed slavery necessary to keep alive the spirit of freedom."[23] Dew crafted an argument that moved away from slavery conceived as a "nuisance"; rather, it was the product of enslaved people's good fortune. The historian Alfred L. Brophy observes that "Dew's essay harnessed fear of change, indeed the impracticality of change, along with a narrative of the benefits of slavery for the slave owners, non-slave-owners, and the slaves, too."[24] As opposed to the death of enslaved people, the habit and customs of Western laws of war pertaining to captives meant that Virginians and countless Southerners in the region generously introduced the enslaved to productive labor.[25]

Many Southerners emphasized ideas about the benevolence of the institution within the context of staving off potential deaths warranted by the threat of warfare. The myth of benevolence gets reinforced with Dew's argument where he insists that the enslaved find themselves in "infinitely better condition than that of savage independence" and that slavery "gives rise to greater production" and "increases the provisions in nature's great storehouse," where the enslaved are "better fed and better provided."[26] But the result of reaping the bounty of "nature's great storehouse" relied on the labor of the enslaved and the premise that the fruits of their labor served the purposes of enriching the economic lives of slaveholders. Dew couched productive labor exclusively within terms that supported the economic prospects and social mobility and security of white Southerners. This becomes clear when Dew explains that the impact of the gradual emancipation proposition would lead to catastrophe for Virginia, stating, "It is gravely recommended to the state of Virginia to give us a species of property which constitutes nearly one-third of the wealth of the whole state, and almost one-half of that of Lower Virginia, and with the remaining two-thirds to encounter additional enormous expense of transportation and colonization on the coast of Africa."[27] In addition to an economic argument, Dew proposes an oft-cited treatise on the moral fitness of people of African descent. "The slave is not only economically, but morally unfit for freedom," he asserts.[28] He explains that "idleness and consequent of want, are of themselves sufficient to generate a catalogue of vices of the most mischievous and destructive character."[29] These claims about the moral depravity of Black people certainly do not originate from Dew's essay, but his remarks signal the culmination and evolution of racial discourse that reaches back as far as Jefferson's *Notes on the State of Virginia*. Even as Jefferson presented his theories of race in the infamous publication, Randolph's support for gradual emancipation builds on his grandfather's own ideas about the political liability and encumbrance of slavery. Jefferson might have sided more with his grandson, but his racial views corresponded with Dew's. Dew, however, deployed these racialized ideas to different ends, namely, the defense of slavery as an institution that the enslaved and enslavers benefited from. Dew made a remarkable statement concerning Black people's fitness for freedom, a racist claim that historians built on in the early publications of slavery historiography.[30] He concluded, "The blacks have now all the habits and feelings of slaves, the whites have those of masters; the prejudices are formed, and mere legislation cannot remove them."[31] Thus, gradual emancipation did not become the engine for slavery's demise in Virginia. The enslaved continued with their everyday acts of insurgency.

With the possibility of gradual emancipation stifled by a reinvigorated argument for the suitability of Black people for slavery, the 1850s and undoubtedly the first half of the subsequent decade ushered the commonwealth into an unprecedented era of insurgency. Virginia became an important site of a broader political crisis among Americans who organized against the expansion of slavery, those who worked for the immediate abolishment of lifelong bondage, and people in favor of maintaining and even expanding the institution. The Southampton Rebellion sparked an important debate from those who supported gradual emancipation, while Southern intellectuals and politicians launched a new theory about the benefits of slavery for the enslaved and the greater good of American society, but even radical abolitionists made their way to the commonwealth.

In 1858, John Brown along with thirty-four Black men began to conceptualize an overthrow of slavery that brought the abolition war to one of the South's most esteemed states. The elaborate plan involved the conceptualization of a constitution for a republic of free Black people, along with strategic efforts to court potential financial support from Gerrit Smith, Thomas Wentworth Higginson, Theodore Parker, Samuel Gridley Howe, George L. Stearns, and Franklin B. Sanborn—all men of means and champions of abolition, referred to as the Secret Six.[32] With their support, Brown rented land in Harper's Ferry, Virginia, with plans to seize the armory and arm the enslaved in an invasion. But enslaved people did not join in the large numbers that he anticipated. As he seized the armory that October, he and his small band of soldiers managed to take some hostages, including a descendant of George Washington. The next day, militiamen from Virginia and Maryland converged and exchanged fire with Brown and his men. With the assistance of the marines, the fighting ended, with many wounded and sixteen people dead, including two of Brown's sons. Three of the Secret Six, Stearns, Howe, and Sanborn, fled to Canada, and Brown along with six of his comrades, two of whom were Black, received the death penalty. Brown's raid became a manifestation of white Virginians' worst fears.

The reverberations of insurgency most certainly caught the attention of enslaved women. While these women were not typically the ones tapped to serve as soldiers in these matters, the Southampton Rebellion and historians such as Holden remind us that enslaved women were active participants in the culture of insurrection. Moreover, enslaved women developed a keen ability to read the landscape, its volatility, and then decide to what degree they might lend support to such efforts. In this case, the record does not confirm any direct involvement of enslaved women in Brown's raid. Perhaps the women in the area held suspicions of a white man they knew nothing about except for his intentions to start a war in Harper's Ferry. Enslaved women understood the dynamics of the community, the white residents and their capacity to retaliate, and made their own assessments about the degree of risk they were willing to take in such an enterprise. This is not to suggest, however, that enslaved women withheld their support because they favored bondage or even their owners. These matters underscored the autonomy of their politics and the precarity of their lives and most treasured bonds, lives that they fought to protect. The raid, however, reminded Virginians that the threat of abolition appeared not in rhetoric alone, but right on Virginia soil.

Governor Henry A. Wise delivered a message that reminded Virginians and the federal government that every state remained entitled to protection from "invasion" and "domestic violence." He made clear that "here, there was no 'insurrection'; no ease of force from within" and that "invasion was threatened from without, by citizens of one State against another State."[33] Wise expressed frustration that President James Buchanan did not offer more substantive support and speak out against the Northern states that Virginians believed to be responsible for the raid on Harper's Ferry. "I did not call on the President to protect Virginia, and would not do so. I apprised him of apprehensions 'in order that he might take steps to preserve peace between the States.'"[34] The president interpreted matters differently, pointing out that Brown and his supporters did not come from foreign nations or Indian country and thus did not fall within the category of invaders, but were mere fanatics. Wise vocally disagreed, and relations between the executive office and Virginia began to sour. The presidential election only made matters worse. Divisions emerged more vehemently in the years following Brown's raid, because slaveholding states feared that the election of a Republican meant the destruction of slavery's future. In the 1860 election, Republican candidate Abraham Lincoln made clear his intentions to prevent the further expansion of slavery beyond where it already existed, but leaders in the South remained unconvinced that he did not intend to target slavery where it continued to be practiced.[35]

Irreparable political divisions brought the South to warfare, and Virginia became part of a different kind of insurgency, one that protected the rights of the commonwealth and the institution of slavery. As in previous conflicts where the U.S. military fought on North American soil, enslaved people took advantage of the conditions of war to reach lines of refuge and opportunity. The war, however, created the kinds of conditions that slaveholders always threatened and feared. Threats of secession became reality once Southern states faced the challenge of establishing a new government, and the fear of warfare between seceded states and the Union, slaveholders, and the enslaved became an increasingly conceivable danger to the stability of this new government. Stealth attempts to remind slaveholders of their own vulnerability had an impact on the health, happiness, and property that shaped the power dynamics of slaveholders and slave societies. With a few exceptions, most historical accounts of the wartime experiences of the enslaved emphasize the accounts of men arriving to Union lines to avail themselves to the military in hopes of freedom and wages in exchange.[36] But what exists in the record reveals the many ways enslaved women, too, leveraged the conditions of war to abandon farms, burn houses, take food, and begin life anew.

By the end of the war, residents of Richmond braced themselves for an imminent march led by General William Tecumseh Sherman and Union troops making their way to the capital of the Confederacy. "The enemy, it is reported, are burning all the good houses along the route of their march," warned the *Richmond Whig*.[37] Confederate Virginians were losing their grip on what remained of the Old South. With the South embroiled in chaos, Southern jurisprudence and sentencing practices became increasingly subject to the exigencies of war and martial law passed by the Union government just across Virginia's northeastern border. Political leaders within the Union passed a series of wartime measures under martial law that allowed for the layered disintegration of slave law in the Confederate states. Enslaved people abandoned slaveholding households with the hope of making their way to Union lines and securing their freedom.[38] But as this book has shown, before all the notable transformations of the American Civil War unfolded, enslaved women waged war on the households in which they were held in bondage prior to Southern secession. Throughout the decade leading up to the war, ruptures of violence, flight, and flames spread within and beyond Virginia households as political tensions mounted and the foundations of paternalism began to crumble. Political turmoil triggered a sense of insecurity, and enslaved women could sense the shift in tone among white Virginians in the 1850s. Insurgency swelled at the most opportune moments.

During the 1850s, more Americans celebrated the Christmas holiday, and while many New Englanders found such celebrations frivolous, Virginians and Southerners alike used the occasion to display gestures of grandeur and gentility, but also paternalism. With these gestures some enslaved people received a day or two off, perhaps a piece of clothing, or a jug of liquor and prized foodstuffs such as meat. This was an occasion in which slaveholders performed the role of patriarch and benefactor and enslaved people relished much-needed time for rest, leisure, and pleasure. Enslaved women might plait their hair and make a new apron or dress, and others nearby might prepare special meals, songs, and dances that brought a number of people from various households and plantations to their quarters.[39] Enslaved women prepared delicious meals with rare ingredients foraged and saved throughout the year, while some kinfolk might prepare small homemade gifts for children. But for some enslaved women, the holiday presented a strategic opening for escape, burning, stealing, and violence.

With the attention briefly suspended away from labor, jubilant celebrations and the ceremonies of paternalism converged with plots of refusal. As this became a rare respite from the backbreaking work demanded of enslaved women, slaveholders remained on their guard. In an article titled "Advice to Slaveholders," one writer warned, "At no season of the year are negroes more liable to contract vicious habits and to impair their usefulness as during the Christmas holydays."[40] Unlike at any other moment, especially with the combustible political climate of the 1850s, the laws governing slavery in Virginia proved even more pertinent to slaveholders. The political assault on slavery from nonslaveholding partisans pooled with the on-the-ground realities of everyday resistance meant that slaveholding Virginians looked to the law to protect their property interest in slavery and their political power in the South.[41] "The stringent and wise laws of this State, if properly enforced, afford ample protection to the slaveholder," the article's author offered.[42] These laws criminalized enslaved and free people for unlawful assembly, violating curfews, engaging in disorderly behavior, and the like. He warned, "The laxity and criminal disregard of those laws renders our Christmas holidays the time for the most dangerous orgies with the slave population of Virginia."[43] But the general concern surfaced not from moralizing about the leisure pursuits of enslaved Virginians, but from the possibilities of collective fellowship and the potential for rebellion. Indeed, with regard to assemblages of celebratory gatherings among the enslaved, he opined, "Robbery, arson and bloodshed are not unfrequently the results of these gatherings." Fellowship and merriment inspired suspicion, and demanding work and a stringent law provided the only contexts in which slaveholders might momentarily rest at ease. "We trust that for the next few weeks the magistracy of Virginia will assume the responsibility of enforcing with great rigor the laws," he concluded. A time for levity was also a signal to be on one's guard. They were on the lookout for missing slaves, goods, and fire.

Arson caused a considerable amount of damage, not only to the structures set ablaze but also to the property and equipment within those structures. Although enslaved people appeared before the court for charges of arson, often some cases were attributed to accidents associated with the everyday tasks that came with dangerous work. Barns, in particular, caught fire often. In one instance, Jenny, an enslaved woman who worked on the estate of Colonel Robert Pickett, appeared before the court in Henrico County for setting fire to "one of her master's barns, containing a quantity of farming machinery."[44] After the court examined witnesses, it concluded that "the evidence proved conclusively that the fire was caused by accident, and not design, as at first supposed." Nineteenth-century barns and structures created in addition to the primary residence were often built with wooden frames and shingles. They were typically kept dry for the storage of wheat, corn, and livestock, and it would not take much for one to catch fire. As is the case with Jenny, incidents involving the burning of buildings remained a mystery in the absence of compelling evidence that provided answers about who the culprit might be. Acts of arson could set slaveholders back by significant sums, whether by design or accident. Once they incurred the losses brought on by fire, they hardly held any motivation to risk the loss of valuable slave labor that might disrupt homestead operations in the event of sale or execution. Slaveholders faced the loss of or damage to the structures, and the materials housed within them, but also the temporary loss of labor as enslaved women and girls stood trial to face the accusations against them. Many of them were held in the custody of the court or sheriff in preparation for legal proceedings.

Described as a "young girl," Adaline was found guilty by the court of burning the dwelling of Richard Stonnell. Sarah Cockrell actually legally owned Adaline, but she likely hired her out to Stonnell. Perhaps taking her younger age into account, the court did not issue a capital sentence that led to Adaline's sale or execution.[45] The court ordered fifteen lashes on her bare back. In this sense, leniency might be inferred as a generous measure that took into consideration her age, but from the perspective of a young girl, baring her back to be publicly whipped came with a healthy dose of pain and trauma. The typical number of lashes ordered for adults was thirty, but Adaline received half that number. The logic of slave law meant that courts viewed this calculation as an evenhanded and measured execution of the law and punishment. As the whip repeatedly tore into her flesh, it is less likely that she experienced the beating as an expression of evenhandedness. A young girl learning her way around the duties of a home that belonged to a stranger might be cause for a series of accidents or mishaps; however, the courts made these incidents matters of criminality.

Helena Robinson hired out an enslaved woman, Frances, to a local man, who accused Frances of setting his house on fire in Richmond.[46] The house was located on the south side of Cary Street, between Twelfth and Thirteenth Streets, and the man argued that at the time the house appeared smoking and in flames, Frances was the only person with access to the garret in which the flames originated.[47] According to Frances, she took a candle up to the garret to look for pigeons. The man who hired her purported that her motive was driven by dissatisfaction "with her home, because she had no place to entertain company," an interesting claim and potential motive given that Frances worked as an enslaved woman.[48] Perhaps as a hire, she believed that she was entitled to private living quarters that made space for socializing during moments when her services were not required. Kinship became a vital source of survival and belonging, and for Frances, life in the state capital provided many opportunities to cross paths with enslaved and free Black Virginians. While Frances acknowledged being in the garret at the time, she explained that when she lit the candle, it must have caught on something that made the flame spread. The court found Frances not guilty and discharged her, but after the damages he incurred, the man who hired her likely sent her back to Robinson. Whether or not Frances intentionally set the attic ablaze out of discontent, she made him aware of her criticisms of the space. As an enslaved hire, Frances expressed her own preferences for how she desired to inhabit and use the space she called "home." *Home*, as a space, became a tenuous concept subject to conflict and competing interests between the enslaved and enslavers, but *home* might also be the liminal space through which the enslaved forged meaningful ties and bonds of trust. Enslaved women faced degrees of vulnerability and uncertainty within the hire system in Virginia, and the extent to which this form of labor allowed them some flexibility can be understood from the ways they advocated for themselves and a proprietor's willingness to concede to these requests. Someone who leases an enslaved woman might find incentive to comply in hopes of cooperation and good quality work output and to reduce the likelihood of permanent or temporary escape. As this book has shown, however, the law gave slaveholders authority over living and laboring conditions, as well as discipline and punishment. In this instance, Frances did not belong to the man who leased her, and therefore his authority was circumscribed to a degree by the fact that he might be responsible for the recovery of any damages associated with her ability or inability to continue to labor and generate revenue for the owner.

In 1849, Fanny, an enslaved woman legally owned by John W. Morris, worked in the home of Emanuel Seaman in Richmond and stood accused of arson.[49] Evidence seemed to support her guilt and the court arrived at the decision that Fanny be executed for the offense. The court scheduled Fanny's execution for the following month, when her death would be on display for countless city dwellers in the state capital. These public displays of gallows punishment not only conveyed the imperatives of promulgating the rule of law but also sent warning signals to those enslaved women hired out in the city and contemplating resistance. But Fanny remained in jail for the next several months and beyond the scheduled date of her execution when she received a commuted sentence. Valued at $500, Fanny was prepared for sale and transportation by the jailer. The court, however, left clear instructions that she be sold "with knowledge of the circumstances of her guilt." Enslaved people sold under the knowledge of their resistance might be subjected to particularly brutal treatment between the time of their transportation and sale and the first months of laboring at another plantation. Even as the courts engaged in legally designated acts of mercy, the violent dimensions of slavery persisted in the various legal outcomes of capital cases. Knowledge of these circumstances led planters to initiate a process of "breaking" to ensure that enslaved women like Fanny understood that defiance would not be tolerated. But as the historian Walter Johnson makes clear, breaking "represented a fantasy of mastery."[50] Southerners accepted "breaking" as a necessity to uphold the paternalist authority wielded by slave owners. A clear delineation of Fanny's guilt in the court record signals to slave traders and future owners that extra measures to suppress the possibility of her refusals were warranted. In most cases, the shift in sentencing did not include a postscript for communicating to buyers the nature of the offense, but it was not difficult for them to find out the reasons for the sale.

Not all cases of arson identified a motive on the part of enslaved women. In the summer of 1857, Lucy, an enslaved woman accused of arson, appeared before the court for setting fire to a home belonging to Daniel Hagerty, a man whom she worked for as a hire. Hagerty left Lucy in charge of the house while he and his wife called on a neighbor. According to him, "When he left his room, his coat was lying upon the bed, but when he returned on hearing the alarm bell, the coat had been placed upon a chair, and the bed was enveloped in a sheet of flames."[51] Perhaps, Lucy attempted to use the coat to put out the flames. There was no sense that Lucy held any specific grievances against Hagerty, although slavery appeared to be reason enough if this were to be read as an act of resistance. Candles catching fire, however, were common occurrences in nineteenth-century homes, and the coat that might point to Lucy's effort to put the fire out could also absolve her of the offense. With Hagerty and his wife gone, their absence could be the right moment to set the house on fire or simply a coincidence and consequence of Lucy being forced to labor and oversee the home while they visited their friends. Working as an enslaved hire proved hazardous for the ways it made enslaved women not only vulnerable to abuse but also prone to accusation for the everyday accidents associated with nineteenth-century domestic labor.

Property owners might view instances of arson as accidents and subsequently might appeal for a commuted sentence on the basis of a woman's character and reputation. In one instance, Nancy, an enslaved woman in Franklin County, received a sentence of death for burning the barn house belonging to William Brooks, presumably a man who leased her.[52] Nancy pleaded not guilty, and numerous witnesses attested to her character and innocence. The justices found the appeal to her reputation a compelling reason to unanimously recommend her to clemency, and the governor commuted her sentence to sale and transportation. A commuted sentence still ensured the recovery of damages from the proceeds of sale and transportation, leaving her owner at an inconvenience, but with the financial resources necessary to replace Nancy. If Nancy's intentions were harmless and absolved her of execution, the best possible outcome for her resulted in continued enslavement within or beyond Virginia. Even as locals attested to her character, reprieve only existed in the form of fueling the slave economy and its interstate trade. The limited scope and logic of justice framed the decisions of jurists who found compelling reasons to be convinced of the innocence of enslaved women and yet perpetuated their punishment. The law supported a state of recurring discipline to ensure the compliance of the enslaved and thus the peace of the commonwealth.

Trials involving enslaved women accused of capital crimes yoke together the ideological commitments of the courts, local slaveholders, and the domestic slave trade. Cases involving arson raised questions about the value that enslaved women could be sold for in the domestic slave market. On the frigid night of January 6, 1851, Mary Raines woke up startled as smoke rose and flames rapidly collected throughout her home. The sheriff of Sussex County arrived at the scene of the blaze and arrested Lucy Barker, an enslaved woman who labored at Raines's home. Officials interrogated Barker hoping for a confession; however, with "nothing being offered or alleged in arrest or delay of judgment," the court sentenced her to death.[53] The court delayed proceedings for two months, which, from the perspective of officials, gave Barker ample time to confess. Three of the justices determined that Barker should be sold at $400, while the remaining two justices believed her worth to be $375. Justices at times disagreed on the value of an enslaved person sentenced to sale and transportation. The problem of marketing an enslaved person charged with a crime posed an issue that emerged in clemency cases. The right price might be a compelling reason to purchase an enslaved person with a record of resistance. Ultimately, the court decided to place her value at $390, having reached somewhat of a compromise. These considerations illuminate the entanglements of Virginia's courts, legislature, slaveholders, and the domestic slave trade.

The valuation determined by the court stipulated not only the amount that Barker was sold for but also the figure for which Mary Raines, and in this case her son, William Raines, would be compensated. The amount they decided on had an impact on the legislature's coffers that compensated slaveholders in the event of execution or sale in capital cases.[54] When justices agreed on the "legal value" of enslaved women and girls who were convicted, they codified meanings associated with their refusal. Justices reduced their legal value on the basis of their reputation for resistance, for fear that word might spread of the enslaved person's infractions and buyers would be unwilling to pay the going rate. Moreover, these convictions determined how they might be treated in the slave market. As scholars have shown, countless enslaved people with reputations for resistance were sent to markets in the Caribbean, Latin America, and Louisiana and Mississippi and fell into the hands of slaveholders with overseers skilled at "breaking" enslaved people with criminalized pasts. Assumptions about who these women and girls were, and fears about what they were capable of, shaped their experiences as they were sold, transported, and acclimatized to their final destination. Many were subjected to harsh discipline and sexual violence to stave off the possibilities of defiance. This, then, offers a window into how we might understand commuted sentencing and the considerations of paternalism.[55]

In the fall of 1857, one woman faced charges for burning the barn of John Booton, the slaveholder who owned her. The record shows that she confessed to the act, but the court believed that the confession "had been extorted from her under circumstances which would not justify hanging or transportation."[56] As mentioned in previous chapters, some cases involved prompted confessions of the enslaved through violent and intimidating methods. The title of the article "Acquittal of a Prisoner" suggests the woman's innocence, and if deemed innocent by the court, why sell her further south? Acquittal, clemency, and innocence became synonymous with sale and transportation. Thus, the outcome did not favor the woman, but rather perpetuated her subjugation to the domestic slave trade. When jurists spoke of justice in the contexts of slave courts, outcomes tied to the domestic slave trade signaled the benevolence of the courts as opposed to the horrors of the slave trade. From the perspectives of enslaved women, we find that the possibilities of justice remained deferential to the interests of slaveholders.

After 1858, commutation from the death penalty shifted the sentence to sale and transportation or a life at the penitentiary laboring on the public works.[57] Virginia built one of the earliest and largest prisons in the South. In the winter months of 1859, Alberta, an enslaved woman, stood accused of "house burning" in Madison County.[58] Alberta pleaded not guilty, but the court unanimously agreed that she committed the crime. The court sentenced her to sale further south, but the governor revised her sentence to labor for life on the public works. In 1859, this form of sentencing appeared as a departure from the trends in the court records. Indeed, the value of enslaved people reached unprecedented levels, and the court determined that Alberta was worth $1,200. The Virginia legislature articulated a set of sentencing practices that anchored death as the worst possible form of punishment. In the minds of white Virginians, sale and transportation or a life sentence of laboring on the public works placed enslaved women and girls into more fortunate circumstances. This might hold true for some who were desperate to leave their current forced arrangements; however, the life that awaited them after trial did not translate into a desired end or any form of restitution. Indeed, many of the enslaved women and girls were transported for sale in Louisiana because locals believed that they acted under extraordinary circumstances. Extraordinary circumstances often point to possible confrontations with unreasonable or particularly violent demands. If innocence was a possibility, sale and transportation was the form of recourse used most consistently. Innocence, then, did not remove culpability, and enslaved women and girls were rarely, if ever, completely absolved of accusations of capital crime. To be granted clemency as an enslaved woman or girl meant persistent encounters with bondage. Depending on what they understood about life in prison or laboring on a Louisiana plantation, enslaved women and girls likely viewed "leniency" with varied perspectives. What form might leniency take in the middle of war? The question of leniency increasingly declined in significance with the pressing demand to mobilize a viable army for the Confederate States of America. Jurists often struggled to prove whether arson occurred by accident or whether enslaved women were motivated by their own wartime politics. Escape, however, became one particular act that left no question about the intentions of enslaved women and girls.

As tensions brewed and eventually led to gunfire and combat, enslaved women placed their bets on the possibility of freedom. They set more houses and barns on fire, stole food, and left plantations and households in search of refuge and kin. While remaining in Virginia, one woman stole pork valued at $500—"the property of the Confederate States."[59] Lucy, an enslaved woman who legally belonged to Robert Collins, stood accused of "receiving two hundred dollars in Confederate States notes, stolen from George W. Bagby."[60] For some, reaching Union lines could be nearly impossible or came with its own challenges, and refugee women who escaped Confederate territory did not do so simply because the Confiscation Act or the Emancipation Proclamation gave them indisputable authority to do so.[61] Instead, they charted hazardous terrain, evaded detection of Confederate troops, and fought nearby residents willing to expose them.[62] Wartime emancipation sparked a violent backlash across regional boundaries from those who maintained the view that African Americans burdened the nation and should by every means be returned to slavery or relegated to second-class citizenship. The Fugitive Slave Law was still in effect during the bulk of the war to maintain the loyalty of the Unionist border states. During the war and toward its end, Maryland remained a point of contention for refugee women and slaveholders, even after the state adopted a new constitution banning the practice of slavery. When Virginia seceded from the Union, however, the new emancipation measures made the viability of slavery incredibly perilous.[63]

Virginia newspapers reveal how slaveholders continued to act as though slavery remained firmly intact, and they had reason to believe this at the beginning of the war. They submitted their notices of runaways and advertisements of enslaved people for sale or available for hire, and local municipalities adhered to the prewar customs that governed slavery in the face of Unionist encroachments. In 1863, an advertisement offered "a girl for hire," between the age of twelve and fourteen, available for the balance of the year and only within Confederate territory.[64] In the midst of warfare, a girl as young as twelve might continue to experience the displacement of slave hiring within the commonwealth. The enduring operation of prewar financial transactions, which shifted the lives of enslaved girls, coupled with the exigencies of war meant that they were often forced to confront profound levels of uncertainty, especially as many of the girls were hired away from kin. Presumably, the owner of the girl believed his property rights to be protected under the laws of the new government. But enforcement proved difficult as the war made increasing demands on the men used to police the enslaved. Moreover, Union policies threatened the stability of slavery within the Confederacy as martial law made possible the legal emancipation of the enslaved who resided in the seceded territories. For Virginians, however, joining the Confederate States of America made the laws of the Union null and void. The enslaved women who escaped were not refugees but, in the eyes of the Confederate government, fugitives. As the historian Crystal Feimster reminds us, even escape to Union lines did not ensure an enslaved girl's safety, as she might also face vulnerability to physical and sexual violence.[65]

Enslaved women absconded from the plantations and households of slaveholders and Virginians who hired enslaved people under a contract that stipulated a specific term of service. Escape, then, did not simply occur in a linear fashion that led women from these homes directly to Union lines. Depending on their location, they might leave and head toward other parts of Virginia in order to connect with children, partners, and other kin. Others left within cities and towns such as Richmond, Norfolk, Alexandria, and Petersburg by folding their lives into the vibrant community of free and enslaved Virginians who lived separate from white families. Some women, however, did set their sights on searching for refuge within Union military encampments. Regardless of the destination, enslaved women leveraged the conditions of war that demanded the mobilization of white men who typically provided surveillance of the behavior, movement, and labor of the enslaved. As the Confederacy stood in need of filling the ranks of an unprecedented army, and the western half of the state remained loyal to the Union, the commonwealth changed indefinitely and thus redefined the political geography of insurgency for the enslaved. Virginia shifted from a haven of the Old South and a symbol of stability to a place of both mutability and vulnerability. Enslaved women, just as they did in the Revolutionary War and the War of 1812, knew that this was a moment in which they could set their claims to freedom in motion.

The escapes of enslaved women sent ruptures throughout the South as slaveholders struggled to maintain control of the enslaved population while trying to mobilize resources and military support for the Confederate cause. As Thavolia Glymph so aptly argues, the resistance and actions of enslaved women reflect their political commitments. Glymph states, "In refugee camps and on plantations, Black women sharpened the politics of freedom born in slavery."[66] The politics of enslaved women and girls manifested within the context of their disenfranchisement and the economic inhibitions that came with being Black, female, and enslaved in the American South. Nevertheless, they mobilized a politics that emphasized their entitlements to freedom and acted on their own articulations of justice premised by the idea that slavery, and all that they endured, was wrong. Enslaved women and girls also became political actors by virtue of the ways their actions had an impact on the war, exposed slaveholders, and shaped meanings of freedom and justice.

On the morning of Monday, May 6, 1861, Agnes, a sixteen-year-old girl, escaped from a man who hired her for the year. Agnes made this prodigious decision right at the beginning of the war, at a time of grave uncertainty concerning the possible outcomes of the conflict.[67] As the subscriber who advertised Agnes's escape warned, "The law will be enforced in such cases"; however, slaveholders knew that a groundswell of resistance became an unprecedented possibility given the geographic proximity of the theaters of war and enemy lines. Agnes, a young girl with a whole life ahead of her should the escape lead her out of the grips of slavery, sought freedom. She stepped out in search of a new way of life and acted on the idea that she should be free. But even as the runaway notice appears in a small box, lost amid advertisements for "SPRING AND SUMMER SUPPLY OF BOOKS AND STATIONERY" and the sale of "THREE YOUNG MARES," few might notice that Agnes legally belonged to none other than the revered general of the Confederate army, Robert E. Lee. As he corralled Southern soldiers in the eastern theater of the war, Agnes slipped away.

As Agnes's story reminds us, both slaveholders and renters of the enslaved lost returns on their economic investments in the labor of enslaved people when they fled during the war. Jennie escaped from a "Mrs. Hagan," who resided near Mayo Street in Richmond and hired her from her owner.[68] At forty years old, Jennie could sense that the war made the possibilities of life in Virginia different from anything she ever witnessed. Indeed, countless women like her never made it to Union lines but fled within cities nearby instead. Such a decision, made by a woman of her experience, might lead to more promising employment prospects. Even in the Confederacy, and in similar instances of escape prior to the war, enslaved women absconded within Southern cities and made attempts to hire themselves out. Union lines did not serve as the only destination for enslaved women who escaped. The possibility of blending within communities of free or hired Black residents who lived apart from slave owners allowed for opportunities to remain hidden in plain sight. Some believed they spotted Jennie at the Exchange Hotel located on the southwest corner of Franklin and Fourteenth Streets, where "she [was] no doubt hiring herself somewhere in the city."[69]

Histories of slave escapes often point to the lower numbers of enslaved women who fled compared to those of enslaved men and boys.[70] The archival record shows that this holds true during the war, since many men fled to serve in the Union military. In *The Women's Fight*, Glymph offers that "the number of black women and children fugitives grew with the mobilization of black men as soldiers and laborers in the Union army."[71] Similarly, enslaved women took flight with children in tow or in search of children who resided on separate but local plantations. Just as soon as Benjamin Rose purchased Lucinda, a "medium sized" woman of copper color, and her daughter, Clara, a girl with "white hair and blue eyes," they were both gone.[72] They were recently hired out to the overseer who supervised the estate belonging to the Bricker family of Culpeper County, just after they were purchased. Interestingly, the Brickers also hired Lucinda's husband, but he did not appear in the escape notice. This does not mean, however, that he did not escape or possess plans to. Just below the notice of Lucinda and Clara's escape is one for twenty-year-old Dick, who left a slaveholder donning a "blue Yankee uniform coat." The advertisement listed just before these alerted readers of the escape of a young man who was "no doubt making his way to the Federal lines." We also do not know if Lucinda and her husband decided to part ways, as many enslaved people did following the war.[73] Furthermore, it is unclear whether Lucinda's husband fathered Clara, since the advertisement described the girl as blond-haired and blue-eyed. The prospect of freedom meant that the enslaved acted on their desires to choose for themselves, regarding partners or other significant details pertaining to life after slavery. Similarly, Betty left Joseph Davis, the man who hired her from the slaveholder who owned her.[74] She left Davis's homestead and made her way to Cumberland County, where her children remained held in bondage. Tempy escaped from a property located near Oakwood Cemetery in Richmond.[75] Her owner suspected that she planned to head toward Goochland County to reunite with her husband. Enslaved women used the years of the war to plot their futures and made important decisions about where they planned to go and who to take with them.

Enslaved women in Virginia created their own rituals of freedom, including the adoption of preferred names and surnames, choices of dress and manners.[76] Winney Morton escaped on the morning of July 3, 1862, just before Independence Day and right on the heels of General Lee's successful defense against the invading Union Army of the Potomac in the Seven Days Battles.[77] The Army of Northern Virginia managed to stave off Union general George McClellan's campaign, but the war within the commonwealth waged on as women like Morton slipped from the watchful eye of slaveholders. Most runaway notices included the first name of an enslaved person, but in this case Winney Morton appears with a last name, likely a surname she insisted on being referred to by. In addition to wearing a "black silk handkerchief" and a hood bonnet, she appeared very "ladylike." Perhaps she planned to head in the direction of Manchester, where her sister resided, or meet up with her husband, who waited on a Captain Sales in the army. Mary Jane, described in a notice as "a small, delicate-featured woman, of a dark ginger-bread color," escaped from Joseph Jackson, the man who hired her in Richmond.[78] As I have shown in earlier scholarship, enslaved women engaged in their own processes of self-making even as slavery and racial inequality circumscribed the possibilities of these rituals.[79] Falling somewhere between the age of twenty and twenty-five years old, Mary Jane "call[ed] herself Mary Jane Jackson" and "generally dress[ed] in black." When nineteenth-century women in America wore black, the choice of color typically signaled a state of mourning; however, when we consider the epistemological creativity of enslaved women, we must ponder alternative meanings assigned to sartorial choices, names, decisions, and so forth. Even as the subscriber who placed a notice of Mary Jane Jackson's escape might express reluctance to take seriously her appointed dress and surname, he understood the necessity of acknowledging these choices in order to strengthen the chances of her retrieval.

Enslaved women looked to kin and community to assist with wartime escapes and provide much-needed support to evade slave traders commissioned to find them. In the spring of 1862, Daphney, a thirty-year-old woman purchased by Nathaniel Tyler of Richmond, escaped from his household.[80] He described her as "tall and black," with a "high forehead," and made a point to explain that he viewed her as "quite good looking." The explicit mention of this in the advertisement reveals the scope of surveillance slave catchers employed to prey on enslaved women on the run. The sexualized tenor of the advertisement did not appear uncommon or unsavory for a city known for funneling scores of attractive enslaved women into sexualized bondage. Perhaps this description might also offer a window into what she experienced with slavery in Richmond, but the advertisement and record do not go into such detail. Eighteen-year-old Cora fled from a slaveholder who described her appearance as "gingerbread color; full face; thick lips, having the appearance of being swollen; a remarkably nice figure."[81] These descriptions, while designed to increase the effectiveness of reconnaissance, drew attention to the bodies of enslaved women that projected sexualized desires and predatory innuendo as part of the surveillance apparatus of retrieving women runaways. These discrete yet public understandings of the forced intimacies that slaveholders demanded were both widely and tacitly accepted. If enslaved women were fortunate to maintain some proximity to kin, they might temporarily or permanently abscond. Tyler noted of Daphney, "She has a sister living on Franklin street, below Johnson's livery stable," revealing the ways that slaveholders took extra care to decipher important relations among the en-slaved. Tyler instructed those who discovered Daphney's whereabouts to se-cure her in the jail owned by the prominent slave trader Hector Davis. Davis welcomed handsome profits, which exceeded many of the returns from area crop yields. He did the dirty work of hunting and selling the enslaved, while slaveholders filled his coffers in return. He became so prosperous that he served as the president of Traders Bank, an institution that he helped charter. His ability to find an attractive runaway would not be difficult given his own affinity for Black women. He fathered a number of children with an enslaved woman, Ann Banks Davis, for whom he made arrangements to be sent to Philadelphia by the time of the notice of Daphney's escape. Davis died dur-ing the war not long after the advertisement appeared. His death, and the accumulating misfortune that slaveholders experienced as the war raged on, created critical opportunities for bondwomen.

Some women and girls escaped while fighting off diseases and physical ob-stacles to their plans to flee. Parthena escaped right at the beginning of the war, wearing a "dark brown and white calico dress," and was described as "me-dium size" and of a "ginger bread color."[82] The subscriber who placed the ad-vertisement also instructed those searching for her to look for a shortened forefinger on the right hand, a result of a painful infection of the finger known as whitlow, a type of herpes simplex virus. Slaveholders made note of par-ticular physical attributes that underscore the range of challenges enslaved women and girls learned to navigate in the absence of therapy, medical care, and resources. Nineteen-year-old Hannah did not let anything get in the way of her plans to escape from Dinwiddie County.[83] If freedom became a viable possibility, a young woman of her age had years to look forward to that did not involve her remaining in bondage. The subscriber explained that Hannah spoke with a stammer, particularly when excited, but this did not pose a bar-rier to her making her way to Union lines, as her owner suspected. Milly, at just fourteen years of age, appeared particularly determined to escape. She appeared in a notice as having "gingerbread color, full head of hair" and "not quite recovered from a severe spell of sickness."[84] Her case is remarkable not only for the relatively young age at which she fled, but also because she ran with an eight-pound ball fastened to the chains on her legs. The adver-tisement tells the reader more about the conditions of her bondage and the kinds of treatment she experienced than it reveals about her whereabouts.

The women fleeing bondage within and beyond Virginia sought freedom along pathways that allowed for them to live economically viable lives. Owners struggled to trace their steps, as they understood firsthand the intellectual capacities of these women and even attempted to downplay them. Martha, approximately forty-five years old, was described as "of gingerbread color, flat face," with "bad teeth, of ordinary size, and remarkably shrewd."[85] The subscriber remarks how her astute quality might position her to be rather cunning, but what we might also glean from this observation is how her ability to think strategically and intelligently works to mobilize her own efforts to realize freedom. These qualities that might threaten the ability of slave traders and bounty hunters to discern the whereabouts and maneuvers of the enslaved appear within the same newspaper. Just before the advertisement for Martha, one for Adeline alerts readers to her escape from a plantation in Chesterfield County. For the slaveholder, to understand Adeline is to take note of not only her "medium size" or "gingerbread color" but also her "genteel appearance."[86] Gentility, a term with origins in Virginia dating back to the eighteenth century, defined a class of people emerging in the colony as purveyors of taste and refinement. The enslaver's use of the term *genteel* to offer a portrait of Adeline suggests that self-making occurred well before emancipation, as she made particular choices about her disposition that led locals to understand her as someone known for cultivated deportment and sophistication. In Martha's case, the slaveholder suspected that she was "most likely in Richmond, passing herself off as a free negro washer and ironer."[87] Not only did he fear that he had lost her, but he knew she could pull it all off. Similarly, Nancy, a twenty-five-year-old woman, apparently "left home without cause," although bondage proved to be a sufficient cause and "home" was an unfitting term for what enslaved women experienced in Virginia households. This slaveholder suspected that Nancy, too, worked "about town in the capacity of a wash woman."[88] Sylvy, a twenty-year-old woman escaped within Richmond; her owner told those on the lookout to take note of her "pleasurable manners."[89] Emma, a "mulatto girl" about "5 feet 2 inches" in height with "tolerably straight hair," escaped from her owner, who attested that she "falsely pretend[ed] to be a free woman."[90] These qualities assisted the women in their efforts to secure employment, making freedom a more tenable possibility than if they did not demonstrate shrewd qualities.

Black women perceived by whites to be smart triggered much aggravation among slaveholders in search of their whereabouts. Harriet, known for her abilities to cook, escaped in Richmond, likely with the intentions of hiring herself as a *free* cook. She likely developed a reputation for doing things on her terms, especially given the rather vivid description of her in the runaway advertisement. The subscriber described Harriet as a "bright, thin-breasted, tall, sneaking mulatto."[91] Most threatening to those in search of her was that she knew how to read. Harriet's literacy put her in a position to forge necessary documents, make contracts with potential employers, and serve as an asset to members of her community. Adding to the frustration of the slaveholder, he noted, "[She] is a Methodist, sings very loud, and is disposed to argue." She wore a red bodice, black skirt, and a colored straw bonnet adorned with blue ribbons. Enslaved women possessed thoughts, desires, and methods for presenting themselves that confounded slaveholders. Donning a red bodice, Harriet might quickly revert from singing a spirited hymn to inflicting a listener with her sharp tongue. She might leave readers flummoxed. These were the qualities that enslaved women brought with them to their new lives, attributes that runaway advertisements warned readers of.

As the war progressed, enslaved women and girls in Virginia made plans to venture beyond the state, with some buying some time within the city until they could find their way to other places. Sarah left the man who owned her, "possibly making an effort to escape to the Yankees," or, as her runaway advertisement read, "It may be that she is lurking about the city to pass as free."[92] During the later years of the war, some women did not have a clear sense of where they might escape to, but the city and its changing population of soldiers, migrants, and refugees meant that Richmond allowed them connections with people who might share ideas and strategies for life beyond Virginia. For those on the lookout for Margaret, the subscriber instructed them to look for a twenty-two-year-old woman, "stout built, of ginger bread color." Margaret wore a green dress when she left the person who claimed ownership of her. The subscriber suspected that she "endeavor[ed] to make her way to North Carolina or Tennessee."[93] Women like Margaret might set their sights on places such as North Carolina or Tennessee, perhaps to follow the Union army or to find kin. Unlike in the antebellum era, enslaved women and girls who escaped during the war might target different destinations that did not always set them on the route toward Northern states.[94]

As it became increasingly clear that the Union made headway in the war, some women boldly escaped with and toward loved ones. Two women, Milly and Hannah, escaped from their owner along with one twelve-year-old boy and four girls at the ages of two, six, eight, and ten years old. With young children, the group might easily be detected, but the chaos of war and the spread of new information about the Confederate forces being pulled into more conflicts than they possessed the manpower to defend led many women with kin and children to take the next steps to seek new homes and lives. Kitty and Ben escaped together from the household their owner hired them

African American cabin. Edwin A. Forbes, *Spotsylvania Court House, Virginia*, 1864 (pencil), Library of Congress Prints and Photographs Division.

out to in Fluvanna County.[95] Similar in age, and owned by the same person, the pair likely headed to Goochland County, where Ben's mother lived.

Kinship and connections drove thousands of enslaved people to different parts of the South, where they searched for those from whom they were separated prior to the war.[96] Barbara left at the age of forty, with the intention to return to New Kent, where she came from before being forced under the custody of her enslaver.[97] Lucinda left the household of her owner in Henrico County, probably with plans to head to Mechanicsville in Hanover County, where her family raised her.[98] Jim and Ellen escaped together, likely headed toward Culpeper County, where they maintained relations. The owner caught wind of their intentions by a simple assessment of what they took with them. Jim, a young man about twenty-five years old, likely escaped before when he spent time in the army. The subscriber warned that Jim would "try to pass himself off as the servant of an officer." He carried with him "cavalry boots, a soldier's cap faced with red, a slouch hat, gray overcoat, jacket, a blue cloth

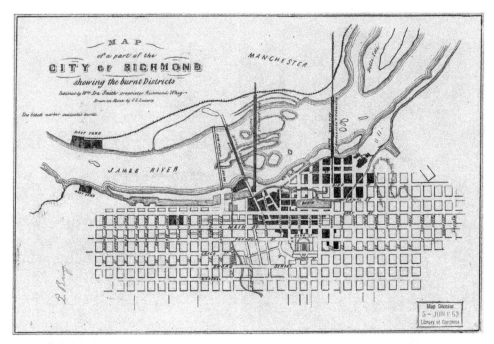

William Ira Smith, *Map of a Part of the City of Richmond Showing the Burnt Districts,* ca. 1865. Library of Congress Geography and Map Division.

military frock coat, blankets, etc."[99] Ellen did not leave empty-handed either. Described as rather "good looking," she intended to stay that way, taking with her a plaid dress, black calico, a hood, and blankets. Ellen, however, left her child at the homestead of her owner, which he hoped might "induce her to stop to see it."

In early September 1862, residents of Richmond came off the heels of victory in the Second Battle of Manassas, which led the Union army to retreat to Washington, D.C. A successful defense against John Pope's Army of Virginia led Confederate general Robert E. Lee to propose invasion of the North just before the November election. Lee desired to bring the war to an end, establish Confederate independence, and also shape the outcome of the Union election. But in a letter to Confederate president Jefferson Davis, Lee wrote from a posture that assumed the peace and stability of the Confederacy, as though Virginia existed solidly without the threat of internal vulnerability. In measures considered both significant and trivial, the thousands of enslaved people within the commonwealth did their part to shape the outcome of their own lives and thus the war itself. Just days before Lee penned his letter, a house on Richmond's Broad Street stood ablaze.

In the Confederate capital, Lavinia, an enslaved woman documented as the property of Martha Hill, stood trial for burning Hill's residence. Locals ran toward the large four-story brick dwelling to put out the flames that threatened to destroy not only any evidence of the structure but the neighboring edifices as well. As witnesses approached the house, they noticed four simultaneous fires dancing throughout the first and second floors. Hill was not present when the fire started, because she was promenading about the city visiting with acquaintances. With the house left in Lavinia's care, witnesses questioned where the keys to the house's doorways were to be found. Lavinia responded that the keys remained tucked away in her pocket, which meant that those attempting to extinguish the fire broke several doors just to get to the damaged areas. Lavinia remained in control, appearing and disappearing to observe the progress of the fire, while also withholding her assistance.[100]

Witnesses deposed testified that prior to the incident, and around the time of the death of Hill's husband, Alexander Hill, they noticed a "marked difference" in Lavinia's conduct. Not long before the fire, Lavinia attempted to escape from Martha Hill, a mistress who, after her husband died, now wielded unchecked authority over her. Lucy and William, two enslaved people who worked in the Hill household, notified a neighbor, who summoned firefighters. One door remained unlocked, but others required the keys from Lavinia. One witness testified that they could not find Lavinia when the firefighters arrived, but after they extinguished the basement flames, she noticed her standing among the crowd. Lavinia "had entire charge of the house, and the keys were in her pocket," Lucy testified. Mary Arnold, likely an acquaintance of Martha Hill, left trunks containing clothing, linens, and money at Hill's home. She informed the court that the fire damaged one of the trunks, but the remaining items were discovered in Lavinia's room and included a skirt and twenty-five dollars that belonged to Arnold. Hill, however, stated that she "always treated the prisoner kindly and had no cause to suspect that the prisoner would fire the house." Lavinia seemed clear in her resolve and did not confess to any wrongdoing.[101] Enslaved women in the capital felt the rumblings of war and leveraged these conditions to act in ways that appeared out of character to those who knew them years prior to the war.

Celia, an enslaved woman bound with her daughter to Charles Palmer of Richmond, became known for being "obedient and well behaved always." She gained a good reputation, which she cultivated for many years; however, by the time of the war, something had changed. One morning, when Sallie Law, the mistress of the household, left the house under Celia's charge, she could not anticipate what awaited her on her return. Palmer likely hired out Celia to Theodore Law and his wife, with assurances of Celia's good name. When the Laws returned home, they noticed the front door ajar, a door they distinctly remembered having locked. The Laws questioned Celia about the door, and she appeared "very much confused." Theodore Law headed toward the basement to ensure that there were no burglars lurking in hiding. As he inspected the premises, Law noticed smoke billowing through a bedroom door. Once he broke down the door, the house rapidly filled with smoke, but he could not help noticing that someone had pried open the bursar, or desk drawer, and set it on fire. As Hill, local police, and neighbors attempted to put out the fire, they set out to exit through the backdoor, but the door was locked. When they called for Celia, she again appeared "very much confused and brought the wrong key."[102]

Celia initially denied any knowledge of the fire and robbery. When the court deposed Sallie Law, she corroborated the account provided by her husband, but managed to include additional details about her interactions with Celia. As the flames roared throughout her home, Law entreated Celia to assist with the effort to put out the fire by bringing buckets of water to the second floor of the house. Celia again appeared quite confused and stated that she "did not know where the buckets were," leading Law to fetch them herself. Law testified that Celia "had been a very good servant" and she "had no cause to complain of her." Celia eventually confessed to the act, and the police searched for any missing property and discovered $3,820 hidden in Celia's stockings. In the chimney, the police discovered two missing watches along with jewelry. Tried, convicted, and found guilty, Celia received a sentence of thirty-nine lashes administered immediately, another thirty-nine lashes received the following Saturday, and transportation away from Virginia. Where she ended up is unclear, but her owner went to great lengths to explain her history of good behavior. Sallie Law even testified that Celia gave her no problems during the time she worked in the household. But the Confederacy was at war, resources proved increasingly scarcer, and perhaps Celia's survival no longer hinged on her agreeable behavior, and, instead, she saw another future on the horizon.[103]

Acts of grand larceny became a common occurrence throughout the course of the conflict as the coffers and estates of slaveholders remained vulnerable to the plunders of war. For instance, Henrietta stood trial on charges of grand larceny for stealing "divers paper writings of value commonly called Confederate notes for the payment of money and of the value of fifty-eight dollars" belonging to Leigh Burton. Never mind that Confederate banknotes continued to plummet in value, the charges still stood, and her enslaver paid $200 for her bail.[104] The court docket included another enslaved woman, Melvina, for charges of grand larceny involving the theft of $150 in Confederate currency. The court sentenced her to thirty-nine lashes.[105] Similarly, Sarah, an enslaved woman claimed by James Powers of Richmond, stood trial for helping herself to "one gold ring of the value of thirty dollars" belonging to Lawrence S. Cohen.[106] One woman, Margaret, appeared before the court for stealing $100 belonging to John W. Davis. The court found her guilty of grand larceny, and she received twenty-five lashes for the offense.[107] Some women caught wind of the changing political tides and capitalized on the distractions that the war created to collect a number of items, perhaps in preparation for a life beyond bondage. One woman, Virginia, carried away one trunk, a carpet bag, one white silk shawl, two pairs of pants, one pair of shoes, four shirts, two pairs of socks, one silk cap, six shirt collars, and a pair of shears. For the goods collected, the court deemed Virginia guilty of grand larceny and sentenced her to thirty-nine lashes.[108] Accusations of violent crimes also abounded during the war as the commonwealth became an active site of war and served as the central hub of a new government struggling to maintain its grip.

Emma Jane appeared before the courts in the fall of 1862 for the murder of an infant. Emma Jane faced accusations of "violently assaulting the infant child of Ellen Phaley, a white person and using to the said child and to Ellen Phaley provoking and menacing language." The court found her guilty and sentenced her, not to death or transportation, but to twenty lashes to be administered publicly. Edward D. Eacho claimed ownership of Emma Jane, and he submitted an appeal in which he agreed to pay the court $150 for her release. He also took responsibility for ensuring that she appeared before the court on the day that officials decided on the results of her appeal. Since she faced a sentence of twenty lashes, a sentence unlike sale and transportation and execution, Eacho likely preferred to handle the matter himself. Slaveholders administered lashes of twenty and much more to discipline enslaved people, and the costs of the court and the time away from labor proved too costly for many Virginians who experienced financial losses during the war. It is also possible that Eacho did not believe Emma Jane to be guilty or that the accusation appeared out of character for her. Regardless, his appeal, which the court approved, meant that any discipline returned under the jurisdiction of his authority.[109] Similarly, the court tried Martha, an enslaved woman accused of attempting to murder Anna S. Vaughn, a white infant for whom she was charged with nursing. The records show that the child grew ill after

Martha administered morphine. It was not uncommon to find morphine locked up in the medicine cabinets of nineteenth-century Southern homes, and, as discussed in chapter 2, the use of morphine on infants did not appear outside the realm of possibility. It is likely that court officials understood that infants responded differently to the consumption of morphine, and since the child did not die as a result, Martha's case might be read as an accident. Moreover, the court records do not include a deposition of any witnesses or medical experts but note that Martha received thirty-nine lashes as a sentence.[110] Countless enslaved women remained in bondage, often with the same slaveholders until legal emancipation took effect.

During the winter months of 1862, Abraham Lincoln appeared closer to a finished draft of the proclamation designed to set scores of enslaved people free in Confederate territories. Enslaved people throughout the 1850s and the beginning of the war already showed signs of restlessness, finding opportunities for refusal that came with wartime conditions. As the threat of emancipation loomed large in the deliberations of Confederate officials, the need to maintain control on the home front, particularly with regard to preserving slavery in the South, became a priority. Confederates straddled the competing demands of demonstrating a firm and convincing sense of intolerance toward the resistance of the enslaved and the need to protect the economic value of the enslaved and the financial interests of slaveholders. The disruptions of war, and the demands of establishing a legitimate nation-state, meant that the sentencing practices of the courts remained unpredictable.

On December 3, 1862, Margaret faced murder charges for the death of Francis Dean Tardy, the infant child belonging to Samuel C. Tardy. Like countless enslaved women, Margaret served as the nurse to the child, a responsibility that might involve wet nursing; regular care such as bathing, clothing, and feeding the child; and also tending to the child when he fell ill. An enslaved woman deposed as a witness testified that she heard groans from the child near the privy and that "the child was very bloody" and Margaret seemed to be "blowing the child in the face." She also observed that the child seemed "perfectly well and healthy" prior to Margaret's trip to the privy. She noticed Margaret giving the child air through the mouth, and Margaret explained that she believed the child experienced a spasm or seizure. The Tardys sent for doctor Dinwiddie B. Philips, who found the child suffering from "violent convulsions" with "blood about the mouth" and a bruise on the forehead. While the skin did not appear broken, the doctor observed several bruises that appeared on the ears, temples, forehead, and hip of the child. He opined that the child died of "compression of the brain," but noted that "there was every indication that violence had been sued to the child." A second doctor followed up with another examination and testified that he noticed blood in the child's mouth along with bruises on the head. While the Tardys' older twins suffered from convulsions, the doctor explained, "The convulsions of the deceased were not such as are produced by disease but were such as are produced by violence." The court found Margaret guilty of murder in the first degree. Just days after Lincoln signed the Emancipation Proclamation, Margaret died on the gallows in the Confederate capital.[111]

The court tried a case involving Eliza, an enslaved woman accused of administering laudanum to Augustus Kuper, the child belonging to Frederick Kuper, for whom she worked. Frederick Swift claimed ownership of Eliza and likely hired her out to the Kupers. The issue central to cases such as these focused on the "intent to kill" qualifier of the charge, particularly those involving substances such as laudanum, which enslaved nurses and white mothers typically gave infants to address ailments and distress. The record, hastily written, indicates that Eliza was discharged, with no evidence or testimony referred to in the deliberations. The infant survived the incident, and given the common practice of administering laudanum and, subsequently, the harmful side effects of the treatment, the court likely decided that the case did not warrant the sentence typically executed in infanticide cases.[112] Some cases did not reflect acts of insurgency but certainly stoked the fires of vulnerability and alarm that made Virginians conscious of an enemy within as they struggled to protect the commonwealth they made painstaking efforts to build.

In February 1864, Fanny, an enslaved woman on the estate belonging to John Cary, must have heard news from afar of the developments of the war. She now lived within the legal jurisdiction of the Confederate States of America and the court fixed her value at $800. This was no small figure in antebellum or wartime terms, but in the Confederacy this amount was particularly significant, if not inflated. Moreover, just as Washington, D.C., was the citadel of the Union, Richmond, where Fanny lived, became the stronghold of the Confederacy. She undoubtedly learned of the advances made by Lee's Army of Northern Virginia, the strategic gains at the beginning of the war, and the losses that smattered throughout in neighboring battles. Word of emancipation in the District of Columbia certainly spread among enslaved women in Richmond, and yet they waited in the grip of bondage, where the laws of the antebellum era remained and the demands of labor were ever present in their day-to-day lives.

In 1864, emancipatory transformations seemed to unfold everywhere but in Richmond, and much to John Cary's dismay, Fanny set one of the buildings on his estate on fire.[113] Arson occurred regularly before the war, but at a time when locals struggled to overcome increasingly depleted resources, Fanny's alleged actions exacerbated existing tensions within the Confederacy. Her testimony is absent in the historical record, but we can infer a number of motivations. To begin, it is possible that Fanny was not the culprit or, if she was, it was an accident. The scholarship on slave resistance, however, confirms the persistence of intentional acts of arson committed by enslaved people, particularly during times of war. While the hustings court had a history of issuing clemency in cases where the governor deemed it appropriate, more measures such as lashes and labor on the public works became a possible outcome geared toward protecting the *property* that remained. In Fanny's case, however, the court sentenced her to sale and transportation beyond the limits of the Confederacy. Interestingly, the state penitentiary purchased Fanny at the sum of $800, and she remained there for the duration of the war. Fanny's experience was not defined by flight or a willingness to remain but reveals the ways that enslaved women might find themselves confined within the bastion of the Confederate territory with limited recourse beyond geographically contained retaliation.

Later that same year, the governor did commute the sentence of an enslaved woman accused of arson. Jane, living in Goochland County, pleaded not guilty to setting ablaze the dwelling home of her owner, Charles R. Woodson, and subsequently received a sentence of death by hanging.[114] The governor, however, commuted the sentence to sale and transportation outside the limits of the Confederacy, and the penitentiary in Virginia purchased Jane at the sum of $2,000, which is not completely surprising given the currency inflation that came toward the close of the war. By 1864, enslaved women learned of how wartime legislation freed thousands of former slaves, and how Union armies increasingly encroached on Southern territories and brought news of emancipation, but for these women, who lived within the final stronghold of Lee's Army of Northern Virginia and the seat of the Confederate government, freedom did not appear within reach—even if it did appear in view. Fanny's and Jane's experiences illuminate the ways that reactions to the war could be circumscribed by varying conditions of war and legal customs of sovereign nations, which were complex in and of themselves.

The war brought to light the incendiary possibilities of enslaved and free Black women acting on their own terms. The breakdown of slaveholder authority that came with the war was directly linked to the dismantling of slave society and the presence of Black troops. In one incident, a group of Black soldiers took possession of the local courthouse across the Potomac in Prince

George County, Maryland. During this raid, they released twenty prisoners, all of whom were Black and "chiefly women and children."[115] One of the prisoners was convicted of arson, and others awaited sentencing for larceny. Most of them were runaways held in jail for safekeeping until slaveholders returned to the area to retrieve them. Interestingly, the soldiers released all of the prisoners but left one white man confined to his cell. News of this incident spread throughout the region and was headlined in the *Alexandria Gazette*, an organ that provided key information pertinent to white Virginians seeking wartime updates near the citadel of the Union war. These acts of collective defiance among soldiers and enslaved women convicted and imprisoned for various crimes tapped into the root fears of white Southerners and in particular Virginians who sided with the Confederacy. Arson, grand theft, attempted murder, and flight, perceived as acts of rebellion, illuminated this point in more ways than one. To begin, the very presence of Black soldiers slowly encroaching on Virginia soil ignited anxieties about a society in complete disarray and an upending of the old order. Moreover, to release enslaved women and children imprisoned with the intention of being returned to former owners signaled the precarity of their financial investments in slavery. Their financial futures, social position, and political power in that moment went up in flames the moment that Black Union troops assumed their positions in the military ranks.

It is no coincidence that Sherman's March was a proliferation of acts of arson as the soldiers scorched the most vital parts of the South. This was a tactic stealthily wielded by the enslaved for centuries before the American Civil War. This quick and destructive act became the new military strategy of the Union army and served multiple purposes, including the ruin of significant structures vital to everyday life in the South, but also the value lost in property by eliminating access to estates, supplies, furniture, crops, and, most importantly, the enslaved. With each wave of arson and rampage came the looming reality of what it would take to rebuild the South. And along the way, enslaved people did their part to contribute to these losses. They acted with their feet and with their willingness to deploy some of the warfare tactics they learned from surviving the violence of slavery many decades before the firing at Fort Sumter.

Right off the heels of Sherman's March, and just north of the James River within a mile of Richmond, Vina and Mary were guided by a white person who helped them maneuver through the picket lines of Confederate military encampments near the Confederate capital. In Henrico County, Union forces assembled with plans to build on the momentum generated by Sherman's army. In the frigid conditions of Virginia in early January, the women made their way to Union lines. John D. Holstead claimed ownership of Vina, and Catherine Gamble likewise claimed Mary as her property. Much to their consternation, the women left with the aid of Ann Perrin, a white woman whom Mary and Vina paid for her assistance with a silk dress and a set of six silver spoons. Once they arrived at Perrin's home, a free Black man, who went by the name of Childress, took the women "about 2 1/2 miles from the city from where they went to the enemy." The court accused Perrin of "advising" and "convincing" the women to escape to Union lines, but it is also possible that the women devised the plans themselves and Perrin appeared as a willing accomplice in exchange for the items she received. These were desperate times in the Confederacy, particularly for white women left on the home front with deteriorating resources as a result of the financial toll of the war.[116] Officials arrested Perrin along with Mary. According to Holstead, "[Vina] made her escape and has never been heard of since she left."[117]

Warfare shaped the contours of resistance that enslaved women and girls deployed against their former owners in order to pursue new possibilities. The promise that the Confederate government could protect the property of slaveholders proved to be one critical failure among many in the new nation. Enslaved women and girls, however, quickly became students of the possibilities and opportunities presented by the war. They acted on their own politics and on the understanding that slavery produced a society rife with injustice, and, as Thavolia Glymph reminds us, they were Unionists. The brush of fire set against the structures of local homesteads, or the plot to leave and locate kin, set in motion the political sensibilities of enslaved women and girls who did their part to undermine the seceded states. As the cases of women and girls reveal in this chapter, they not only made their way to Union lines, but most of them left for counties in Virginia in search of family and friends. Freedom began with kinship and the reconstitution of ties that played such a critical part in how they envisioned new lives. Insurgency came with grave risks and costs, and belonging and freedom, although imperfect, became its sweet rewards.

Conclusion

There is a nexus between the brutal centuries of colonial slavery and the racial polarization and anxieties of today. The poisonous legacy of legalized oppression based upon the matter of color can never be adequately purged from our society if we act as if slave laws had never existed.

—A. Leon Higginbotham Jr., *In the Matter of Color*

By the end of the nineteenth century, counties throughout Virginia showed signs of recovery from a domestic war that ravaged the landscape of the now truncated commonwealth, set apart from its former western counterpart. If one looks carefully, one will find the remnants of endless toil in the exhausted dirt and among the grand and at one time elegant homes that adorned plantation estates. Today, a number of historic houses, plantations, and sites welcome visitors curious about the origins of Americans, and some might even inquire about the Native and African people who lived on the land. The land tells a story of violence, community, and complexity and of people who continue to live with the enduring legacies of what Anglo-American society and its laws had wrought. Black, Indigenous, and European people would continue the struggle to claim and reclaim life on these lands that ultimately became Virginia through imposed and layered acts of violent theft. Before the nineteenth century came to a close, and not long after wartime emancipation, the formerly enslaved and their descendants lived amid new sets of laws based on racial segregation. Just as quickly as the legislature dismantled slave codes, new laws regarding the separation of the races gave the New South a reconstituted legal framework from which to organize southerners along lines of race and gender. Indigenous peoples appeared scattered, some near and many far from the ancestral lands violently taken from them. Virginia invokes a history of peoples barely noticeable in our histories of the region, until recently. To consider how Virginia became an important place for the ruminations of justice, there are many actors to consider, and here we have contemplated what enslaved women and girls might tell us.

The arrival of Africans on the shores of Point Comfort and the scheme of colonial settlement forever changed the genealogy of justice as a legal concept and a lived reality in North America. English common law failed to accommodate what colonists had in mind for the organization of labor in

Virginia. While they remained aware of the moral and political burden of slavery, their appetite for unlimited supplies of labor and the vast amounts of Indigenous lands they hoped to conquer seemed insatiable. One way to ensure the constant access and flow of labor appeared in colonial law and the passage of statutes that ensured the inheritability of slavery. Enslaved women gave birth to children from an ethics of love and communal belonging, but slaveholders and non-slaveholders alike possessed the legal power to cull their sexual and reproductive labor for the purposes of profit. Racial and gendered distinctions explicated in the laws of the colony worked in tandem with emerging theories about the hierarchy and distinct characteristics of the races. These intellectual queries made famous by a man like Thomas Jefferson did not quite capture his own discomfort, and those of his generation, when the liabilities and contradictions of slavery loomed ever present. Jefferson, and others, understood the nuisance of slavery, but slavery and the labor of enslaved women made a man of his stature possible and irresistible for aspiring men of Virginia. To perform the backbreaking work of labor that the colonies demanded, the labor of enslaved people and indentured servants propped up the generation that eventually received their education at institutions such as the College of William and Mary, inherited vast amounts of stolen land, and married into newly established genteel families. Behind the scenes or even at the forefront of Virginian luxuries were the enslaved people who made it all possible and the laws that made bondage sustainable.

Virginians across race and legal status forged ties, whether through consent or force, in ways that required trust and varying degrees of intimacy. While the capital offenses of enslaved women and girls did not appear prominent in relation to their demographic presence, moments emerged where they exploited these assumptions of trust and intimacy. Incidents of poisoning remind us that enslaved women and girls drew from the stores of knowledge about plants and medicines extracted from elders, forests, and years of healing experience. The medical profession in the United States fell short of any reputable standing among European nations and emerged in nascent form throughout the South. Reliance on midwives, conjurers, elderly women and men, and nurses emphasized the intellectual economy of the enslaved, thus enslaved, free, and slaveholding Virginians collectively relied on this pharmacopoeia. Even as white Virginians depended on this knowledge, they also held their suspicions of it knowing that the trust required to cook, nurse, and administer medicine also underscored their own vulnerability to the deadly risks of becoming victim to attempted poisoning. Still, jurists struggled to prove any motive without the testimony of locals and witnesses, and the general ignorance about the harmful effects of commonly used substances made evidence that much more difficult to consider. Some motives, however, came through clearly in the form of confessions and through the testimony of multiple witnesses ranging from other enslaved people to free Black and white neighbors. In addition to exploring possible motivations for committing capital crimes, I am interested in the contexts in which the alleged acts occurred and the legal concept of clemency as it is applied in cases involving enslaved women and girls who committed these acts against white Virginians.

Jurists, petitioners, and Virginia governors invoked the legal idea of clemency in instances when they deemed that circumstances demanded a modified outcome. In murder trials, the cases under consideration often reminded locals of all that could go wrong for the enslaved but mostly for the white men, women, and children in their vicinity. Murder cases did not let Virginians dismiss the threat that groupings of enslaved people posed to the broader peace of the commonwealth or rest on the faulty assumption of the "contented slave." But as details of these cases appeared in the newspaper, the violence and death implicated the locale in which it took place. Locals felt compelled to submit petitions to offer broader context, to intervene on the authority of their proximity to the incident, and to bring order to what the enslaved left undone. Many petitioners were apprised of instances in which enslaved women and girls were brought to a point of resistance. They alluded to episodes of sadistic violence, the disturbing knowledge of sexual exploitation, or the tender age at which an enslaved girl found no other form of recourse. Clemency offered a nod to what everyone knew about life on these homesteads. If neighbors understood this, imagine what the women and girls experienced firsthand. The trauma of the body in bondage appeared in cases of infanticide.

Infanticide occurred roughly every two years from the period of 1799 to 1860 according to one estimate.[1] The complications that came with pregnancy in the nineteenth century undoubtedly had an impact on the fertility of enslaved women, especially on considerations of the conditions of bondage. Most enslaved women who delivered children who grew beyond their infant years reared them with an ethos of love, cautiously instructing them in the lessons of survival, but also sharing knowledge of the wonders of plants, food, songs, and stories. The cases involving infanticide do not appear to be a common occurrence but were regular enough to warrant an examination of the lives of these women and girls and the legal contexts in which the courts determined their postpartum futures. Many of these cases reveal the painful details of rape, invasive medical experimentation and investigation, and the profound rejection of motherhood in the face of chattel slavery. These are not easy stories to decipher, especially given the pervasive silences in the record, but they temper discussions of clemency in ways that force us to consider what precisely clemency means to the enslaved women and girls in this book. The legal technologies of the South invoked alternative meanings of reprieve that dictated the terms of exoneration with specific limits. *Reprieve* for the enslaved women and girls in the courts might seem limited since the measure resulted in death or the continued exploitation of their lives and labors at best.

By the time of the Civil War, the courts expanded the concept of clemency to include labor on the public works, in addition to whippings, sales beyond the state, and executions. Virginia became an important site of political contestation beginning in the 1850s, and these clashes between Unionists and secessionists, western and eastern residents of Virginia, and the enslaved people and white Virginians who inhabited its environs represented the range of political inclinations that shaped wartime transformations. With the western half of the commonwealth severed from the east, a new state within Union territory reflected the culmination of a longtime split along regional and slaveholding and nonslaveholding lines. Richmond became the capital of the Confederacy, and as the new government went about the work of war and governance, enslaved men made their way to Union lines and enslaved women and girls set houses ablaze, escaped, and stole valuable goods during a time of unprecedented scarcity. The continuity of insurgency from the antebellum era to the Civil War reveals a political struggle that took shape before emancipation became a possibility. Most enslaved women remained in the homes of their enslavers until the bitter end, but not without appearing in court for any number of infractions, ranging from arson to grand larceny, poisoning, and murder. Their stories reveal that insurgency did not appear to be the exclusive domain of men.

Enslaved women and girls cultivated attitudes and ideas about justice and their personal limits with regard to slavery's reach and power. These gestures and ruptures of refusal conveyed their rejection of what they believed to be wrong. This does not mean that the women, men, and girls who do not appear in the court documents lacked any conceptions of justice or found resistance unappealing in any way. For some, survival involved strategies typically outside the purview of historical treatments of resistance. Enslaved women and girls made decisions informed by the collective knowledge produced by those around them. Just as we see with the petitioners, enslaved people formulated their own ideas about justice among their respective networks of kin. This helps us understand why many of these cases include enslaved accomplices, but the political diversity of these communities also points us toward those willing to testify against enslaved defendants. The complexities of thought meant that enslaved women and girls were motivated by a variety of factors and circumstances that landed them in court. These wrongdoings perpetrated by enslavers, overseers, and hirers of the enslaved included the withholding of small but meaningful and expected privileges, physical brutality, intimidation, sexual violence, the sale of loved ones, the nagging demands of the white families they served, to name but a few outside of the wholesale rejection of slavery itself. What the court deemed capital crimes often functioned as one of the few avenues of recourse that protected the investments of slaveholders yet placed incredible burdens on those convicted of the offenses. Enslaved Virginians understood this, and, to a degree, these laws allowed slaveholders and lawmakers to profitably enforce the consequences of these actions. But what about the enslaved people who comprehended the full extent of these consequences and confessed to these crimes anyway? What is clemency to the enslaved person who would rather meet her end than to suffer one more day under the watchful eye of her enslaver? What might this tell us about the limits of justice and enslaved people's efforts to convey a different understanding of it? This question is a difficult one to consider, and much of this book offers an unfinished account of what we might glean from the cases. Given that many of the enslaved women and girls punished for infractions suffered at the discretion of slaveholders, the cases represent a limited portrait of what we can know about the outcomes of their lives. How many more were sold, executed, whipped, and maimed?

For the enslaved women and girls who appear throughout this book, justice meant more than Southern law and clemency allowed for. For Southerners, the rule of law, as lawmakers constituted it for the protection of property, represented a sacred trust and social contract that ensured the possibilities of their prosperity on the basis of slavery. The law could not serve the purposes of justice that these women yearned for. Justice meant the abolishment of slavery and the recognition of their equal humanity and entitlements to freedom. Justice could also mean the power to protect her person or the modest but meaningful privileges that made life bearable. No matter how she viewed it, justice, as administered by Virginia courts, remained insufficient. Dynamics between white and Black Southerners brought ideas about right and wrong to the forefront of debate and contestations over cases that involved what white Virginians believed to be displays of violent excess. Slaveholders recognized the humanity of the enslaved even as they exploited it and actively sought to reconstitute the lives of the enslaved to be equivalent to

Slave pen in Alexandria, Virginia, 1860s (glass, stereograph, wet collodion). Civil War
Photographs, 1861–1865, Library of Congress Prints and Photographs Division.

chattel. The cases that appear in this book reveal more than legal outcomes;
they show the violent ruptures, tensions, forced intimacy, and power dynamics that shaped the world that slavery made.

The legal commitment to slavery meant that lawmakers in the commonwealth continued to think through the most effective ways to ensure that the
property interest in the enslaved remained secure and that the courts upheld
the political ambitions of white Southerners. Matters of justice were considered in the intellectual contexts of law and medicine, as well as the local

understandings of white and Black Virginians. Within these cases, competing ways of knowing emerged. Different perspectives, shaped by dynamics of power, meant that what we can know about the motivations and culpability of enslaved women can be obstructed by the legal system that subjected Black women to slavery and a discriminating application of criminal law. The basis of these determinations about the culpability and criminality of enslaved women can be found in the earliest writings of Thomas Jefferson to antebellum intellectuals such as Thomas Roderick Dew. Leading thinkers in politics, law, and medicine put forth ideas to define the behavior and biology of Black women as both deviant, inferior, and incapable of offering unvarnished testimony. Racialized perceptions about the criminality and culpability of Black women critically shaped legal outcomes and informed how they navigated the criminal justice system in years to come.

After the Civil War, Congress passed the Civil Rights Act of 1866, which declared all persons born in the United States citizens, "of every race and color, without regard to any previous condition of slavery or involuntary servitude."[2] The measure excluded Native Americans, many of whom desired citizenship within their own respective polities, but the well-known Reconstruction measure overturned the legal precedents that excluded Black people on the basis of race and any previous legal condition determined by slavery. The bill accomplished little in the effort to check American seizure of Native lands. Historians note primarily how the law changed the status of African Americans. The measure stipulated that Black people possessed access to "full and equal benefit of all laws and proceedings for the security of person and property, as is enjoyed by white citizens, and shall be subject to like punishment, pains, and penalties." In theory, the Civil Rights Act made the crimes of Black people synonymous with the crimes of white persons. Throughout the history of Virginia and the American South, criminal laws applied differently among the races. The women appeared in this book, because gender, race, and slavery shaped the criminalized contexts of their actions. The Civil Rights Act and the Fourteenth Amendment offered the possibility that formerly enslaved women might access the equal protection and application of the laws as everyone else. The Reconstruction amendments and legislation signaled a watershed moment in American legal history and demonstrated ways to leverage legal technologies to account for a more inclusive framework of citizenship.

The Reconstruction era promised to fundamentally alter the nation's relationship to slavery with the innovative use of the law and the expanded use and interpretation of the Constitution. To include formerly enslaved and free Black people into the fold meant that the nation made important strides toward the arc of justice. The realization of this promise, however, remained an ongoing process, one that Black women continued to pursue through activism and political organization, but also everyday acts of insisting on their rights. Moreover, Sarah Haley's work reminds us that the continued commodification and exploitation of Black women's labor was made possible through convict leasing and the presumption of their criminality. These women were forced to help build the new South.[3] Segregation perpetuated a policing and paternalist state on the basis of race and gender and the assumption that Black women's bodies must be surveilled and supervised under the law.[4] The relationship between Black women and crime also remains one that we confront in the twenty-first century with Black women funneled into American prisons. The specter of slavery, and the legal culpability that came with being an enslaved woman, understood through the lens of race and gender, tempered the gains made by the laws of Reconstruction and the criminality assigned to Blackness remained. Still, Black women discovered ways to define and make meaning of their lives that set in motion epistemologies of Blackness and womanhood that contradicted the centuries-old constructions of race. This does not mean that they were immune to the impact of this legacy and the reconstitution of the police state and criminal legal system. I wrote this book during a time characterized by persistent police brutality, the murders of innocent Black women, the era of #SayHerName. The workings of profiling, injustice, and death preceded our current climate of police brutality. The historian Talitha LeFlouria gave us a thorough study of the Black women funneled into the convict leasing system, toiling in the New South and "chained in silence," as she reminds us.[5] Crystal Feimster provided us with insights about the manner in which rape and lynching shaped the transition from slavery to freedom in the segregated South.[6] What were the possibilities of freedom in a policing state and a nation that continued to deprive Black women of political inclusion?

Black women in Virginia labored alongside loved ones and others in their milieu to begin to build new lives in a place largely shaped by centuries of bondage. Had they imagined what life might look like beyond the contexts of chattel slavery prior to the war? We know that formerly enslaved people performed the important work of building communities, households, businesses, churches, organizations, and schools of their own. Often with the aid of northern donors, but also through the miraculous work of bringing together the modest earnings of freedpeople, Black women set in motion an ethics of care that originated well before the war. Still, some freedpeople worked on the same estates, working for former owners who reluctantly paid wages or issued contracts that obligated them to work under exploitative conditions. Many

Black southerners found themselves in an endless cycle of debt peonage in a sharecropping system that ensured they would never get ahead. Much of Virginia needed to be reimagined if the stain of slavery were to be removed.

Virginians attempted to rebuild a state that now included scores of free African Americans who could trace their lineages back to the colonial era. Some scraped away every bit of their earnings into the Freedman's Savings Bank, others toiled away at their modest plots of land, and some might even have attended classes in the freedmen's schools or the Hampton Institute, not far from Point Comfort, where Angela, Margaret, and Isabella arrived in 1619. Some of the descendants of this charter generation remained in Virginia, while countless others were forcibly taken to other parts of the South when the demand for more exploitable labor reached its peak in the domestic slave trade. African and African-descended women breathed life into generations to follow, and even as they faced the stale horrors of bondage, they and theirs became a people. They were a people with ideas, experiences, and centuries of history. They leave us with many questions, but one in particular stays close. What limits and demands of justice remain?

Acknowledgments

Nearly ten years ago, I worked as a public history fellow at the Prince William County Office of Historic Preservation. The summer program gave me an opportunity to work with the wonderful staff at the office and to dive into the exciting work of local history. I was also a resident of Prince William County at the time, making the experience that much more meaningful to me. It was during my time with the Office of Historic Preservation that I learned about the story of Agnes and Katy, who appear in chapter 3. I will be forever grateful for that experience and for the encounter with the stories that brought me to this project about enslaved women and girls in Virginia.

Working on a project about Virginia gave me the great privilege of conducting archival research at the Library of Virginia, a place with rich holdings and incredibly helpful and collegial librarians and archivists such as Kenneth Forest and Cara Griggs. I am grateful for their help, especially for assistance with hustings court records. The staff at the Albert and Shirley Small Special Collection at the University of Virginia, the Virginia Museum of History and Culture, and the John D. Rockefeller Jr. Library at the Colonial Williamsburg Foundation were especially helpful. Research for this book was supported by critical funding from Oberlin College and Conservatory and Cornell University.

Many colleagues read sections and versions of this book, and to them I owe a tremendous debt. These generous scholars include Cynthia Greenlee, Vanessa M. Holden, Wendy Kozol, Jennifer L. Morgan, Alan Taylor, and the first cohort of fellows at the Bright Institute at Knox College. Chapter 3 appeared in the *Journal of Southern History* (*JSH*) and won the Letitia Woods Brown Prize for best article in African American women's history. I am grateful to editors and readers at the *JSH* and to the Association of Black Women Historians for their support and recognition of the research in this book. Additionally, I would like to thank Catherine Adams, Christian Crouch, Catherine Denial, Kellie Carter Jackson, Courtney Joseph, and Danielle Terrazas Williams for their scholarship and friendship, which has sustained me through the process of writing this book. I would also like to express my gratitude for Gary Gallagher and Elizabeth Varon, two wonderful and inspiring mentors who generously give of their time to support my work and career.

The reviewers of this book painstakingly read through proposals and drafts, and I am grateful for their insights and careful consideration of the work presented here. I am particularly appreciative because the readers agreed to review the book during a global pandemic, amid all the ways that this historic event has had an impact on our lives. I was incredibly fortunate to work with Debbie Gershenowitz, a generous and attentive editor who stewarded this project through a pandemic and helped me work through revisions. I am so grateful for Debbie's support and enthusiasm for this book. I have learned so much from publishing with the University of North Carolina Press and appreciate all the ways my work has been supported by the editors, staff, and reviewers.

From the beginning of my journey as a historian, I have been supported by a vibrant village of kin. I am always grateful to my parents, Lewis and Micha, and my godmother Barbara, who always take an interest in my work and provide tremendous support that allows me to pursue this career. My siblings, Angela, Lewis, Kelly Ann, and now Grace, Johnson, John, my mother in love, Adeline, and all of my nieces and nephews anchor me in love and sweet fellowship. Conversations and life with Angela sustain me on a daily basis; thank you always for your friendship and guidance. Many thanks to Marques Hillman Richeson, an expert editor who read earlier versions of chapter 3 and allowed me to indulge him in questions about the law. To both Marques and Charles Hillman, I so value our friendship, our sweet family, and our mutual devotion to Nari and each other. Thank you for your support and encouragement along the way. To Tim and Daisy Lovelace, our kinfolk and dearest friends, I am so fortunate to do this work with such wonderful and inspiring people. Your presence in my life has sustained me since the beginning of this journey at the University of Virginia, and I could not imagine this season, or any other, without our vibrant friendship. Daisy is my sister from another mother, and I am so grateful for our conversations, laughter, and many adventures.

I started this book with an amazing little person in my life, and now I am so fortunate to bring this project to the finish line with two daughters. Nari and Sophie Grace, thank you for being the most wonderful motivators for putting this work out into the world.

Ambrose, my love and partner in life, thank you for your unwavering support. Whether I deserve it or not, you are my biggest cheerleader. Thank you for always taking an interest in this book, for asking engaging questions, and for helping me carve out time to research and write. Your love and encouragement sustained me as I brought this book to the finish line.

Thavolia, you have supported my growth as a scholar when the ideas in this book existed in the barest and most undeveloped form. For your willingness to see potential in my work and for your ongoing support of my career, I am most grateful. Your scholarship, mentoring, and inspiring example paved the way for an entire generation of scholars like me. This book is for you.

Notes

Prelude

1. Kingsbury, ed. *The Records of the Virginia Company of London*, III, 243; Sluiter, "New Light on the '20," 395–398.
2. Berry, *Their Pound of Flesh*, chap. 1; Morgan, *Reckoning with Slavery*, 39.
3. Mustakeem, *Slavery at Sea*, 24–25.
4. Newby-Alexander, "The Arrival of the First Africans," 193–194.
5. Berlin, "From Creole to African."

Introduction

1. Berry, *"Swing the Sickle,"* 15–16; Morgan, *Laboring Women*, 7, 27, 95.
2. Johnson, *Soul by Soul*, 23.
3. Miles, *All That She Carried*, xiv.
4. Spillers, "Mama's Baby, Papa's Maybe," 69; see also McKittrick, "Mathematics of Black Life."
5. See Fuentes, *Dispossessed Lives*.
6. Hartman, "Venus in Two Acts."
7. Gross, *Colored Amazons*, 4.
8. Haley, *No Mercy Here*, 5.
9. Johnson, "To Remake the World."
10. Bynum, *Unruly Women*, 114.
11. Camp, *Closer to Freedom*, 7.
12. Glymph, *House of Bondage*, 2–4; also see Jones-Rogers, *They Were Her Property*.
13. Bauer and Bauer, "Day to Day Resistance"; Morgan, *Laboring Women*, 166–167; Ellison, "Resistance to Oppression"; Kaye, *Joining Places*, 169–171; Rugemer, *Politics of Resistance*, 174–178.
14. Schwarz, *Twice Condemned*, 139, 232; Stevenson, *Life in Black and White*, 164.
15. Rugemer, *Politics of Resistance*, 10, 260.
16. The legal historian Hendrik Hartog discusses this dynamic in the context of pig keepers. Hartog explains the presence of pluralism in the law, or the "implicit acceptance of customs founded on multiple sources of legal authority," not necessarily "a practice confirmed by judicial doctrine or statute." Hartog, "Pigs and Positivism," 935. But by virtue of their unfreedom and their presumed criminality, enslaved women and girls accused of violent crimes were not viewed as authorities by the American public or the courts.
17. Schwarz, *Slave Laws in Virginia*, 71.
18. Schwarz, 64.
19. Schwarz, 74.
20. Schwarz, 72.

21. Shepherd, *Statutes at Large of Virginia*, vol. 2, 279–280.

22. Schwarz, *Slave Laws in Virginia*, 86; Egerton, *Gabriel's Rebellion*.

23. Egerton, *Gabriel's Rebellion*, 210.

24. Schwarz, *Slave Laws in Virginia*, 77; see also Ayers, *Vengeance and Justice*, 134–135.

25. Edwards, *People and Their Peace*, 42.

26. Ayers, *Vengeance and Justice*, 38.

27. Edwards, *People and Their Peace*, 231–232.

28. Kaye, *Joining Places*, 12.

29. Gross, *Double Character*, 76; Schwarz, *Slave Laws in Virginia*, 107–111.

30. Johnson, *Soul by Soul*, 107.

31. Schwarz, *Twice Condemned*, 3–4.

32. Gross, *Double Character*, 3–5.

33. Ghachem, "Slave's Two Bodies," 811–812.

34. Schwarz, *Twice Condemned*, 26.

35. Davis, "Black Woman's Role," 84; Hine, *Hine Sight*, 28–34; White, *Ar'n't I a Woman?*, 79; Stevenson, "Gender Convention, Ideals, and Identity," 174–175, 180.

36. Gross, *Double Character*; Gross, *What Blood Won't Tell*; de la Fuente and Gross, *Becoming Free, Becoming Black*.

37. Edwards, *People and Their Peace*.

38. Schweninger, *Appealing for Liberty*; Thomas, *Question of Freedom*.

39. See also Millward, *Finding Charity's Folk*; Myers, *Forging Freedom*.

40. Schweninger, *Appealing for Liberty*; Thomas, *Question of Freedom*.

41. Twitty, *Before Dred Scott*, 75.

42. Thomas, *Question of Freedom*, 149.

43. Welch, *Black Litigants*, 11.

44. Welch, 133.

45. Kennington, *Shadow of Dred Scott*, 5.

46. Merry, *Getting Justice and Getting Even*, 5, 62.

47. Johnson, *Wicked Flesh*, 151.

48. In the North, Black girls also did not receive protection from execution even though they lived in closer proximity to reform and abolitionist movements. See Webster, "Hanging Pretty Girls," 255.

49. Morris, *Southern Slavery and the Law*.

50. Higginbotham, *In the Matter of Color*.

51. Robinson, *Black Marxism*.

52. Morgan, *Reckoning with Slavery*, 19.

53. Morgan, *Reckoning with Slavery*, 16; Berry, *Their Pound of Flesh*, 12–13.

54. Haley, *No Mercy Here*, 4–5.

55. Davis, "Black Woman's Role," 87.

56. Johnson, *Wicked Flesh*, 173.

57. Holden, *Surviving Southampton*, 120.

58. Glymph, *House of Bondage*, 30, 68; Camp, *Closer to Freedom*, 141; Hine, *Hine Sight*, 37–39; Jones-Rogers, "'[S]he Could . . . Spare One Ample Breast'"; King, "'Prematurely Knowing of Evil Things,'" 173; Morgan, *Laboring Women*, 95; Stevenson, "What's Love Got to Do with It?," 102–103.

59. Dunaway, *African-American Family*, 117, 121–123; Fede, *Homicide Justified*, 111–112; White, *Ar'n't I a Woman?*, 67, 113–114, 121.

60. King, "'Mad' Enough to Kill"; McNair, "Slave Women, Capital Crime"; Hadden, *Slave Patrols*.

61. Brown, *Reaper's Garden*, 242; Brown, "Social Death and Political Life," 1249; Scott, *Arts of Resistance*, 183; Kelley, *Race Rebels*, 5–9; Kolchin, *American Slavery*, 161–165, 240–243; Camp, *Closer to Freedom*, xi–xiv.

62. Forret, *Slave against Slave*.

63. Von Daacke, *Freedom Has a Face*, 7; Flanigan, "Criminal Procedure in Slave Trials," 538, 551–553; Sommerville, "Rape Myth," 483.

64. Bardaglio, "Rape and the Law," 763; Brophy, *University, Court, and Slave*, 160–163; Maris-Wolf, *Family Bonds*, 22, 35; Morris, *Southern Slavery and the Law*, 105–106; Schweninger, *Appealing for Liberty*, 3, 288; Taylor, *Internal Enemy*, 63–67; Tushnet, *American Law of Slavery*, 23–26.

65. Schwarz, *Twice Condemned*, 24–25; Schweninger, "Vass Slaves," 488.

66. Brophy, *University, Court, and Slave*, 59, 206–207.

67. Bardaglio, "Rape and the Law," 752; Flanigan, "Criminal Procedure in Slave Trials," 547, 551–553. For the argument for greater "proportionality in the law," see Preyer, "Criminal Law and Reform," 55–56.

68. Dusinberre, *Strategies for Survival*, 85; Rugemer, *Politics of Resistance*, 298.

69. Ayers, *Vengeance and Justice*, 135; Bardaglio, "Rape and the Law," 760; Flanigan, "Criminal Procedure in Slave Trials," 546; Schweninger, "Vass Slaves," 488; Ghachem, "Slave's Two Bodies," 811–812.

70. Harris, "Whiteness as Property," 1716; Brown, *Good Wives, Nasty Wenches*, 5–7; Sommerville, "Rape Myth," 489; Stevenson, *Life in Black and White*, 323.

71. Fede, *Homicide Justified*, 112.

72. Fede, *Homicide Justified*, 109–110; Hening, *Statutes at Large*, vol. 12, 681.

73. Shepherd, *Statutes at Large of Virginia*; Morris, *Southern Slavery and the Law*, 307.

74. Schwarz, *Twice Condemned*, 17.

75. Virginia, *Code of Virginia*, 49, 55; Flanigan, "Criminal Procedure in Slave Trials," 544.

76. Schwarz, *Twice Condemned*, ix, 80.

77. Taylor, *Internal Enemy*, 67, 80–83.

78. Edwards, *People and Their Peace*, 13–15, 29, 62.

79. Bogin, "Petitioning," 395; Morgan, *Inventing the People*, 224–228.

80. Fede, *Homicide Justified*, 129. For "certificates of character," see Maris-Wolf, *Family Bonds*, 50–51.

81. Ely, *Israel on the Appomattox*; Von Daacke, *Freedom Has a Face*.

82. Edwards, *People and Their Peace*, 60, 91–92, 212; Maris-Wolf, *Family Bonds*, 11.

83. Reinhardt, *Who Speaks for Margaret Garner?*; Taylor, *Driven toward Madness*.

84. The historian Thavolia Glymph first introduced the idea of enslaved women's acts of wartime insurgency, among additional scholarship cited throughout the book. See Glymph, "Rose's War."

85. Hening, *Statutes at Large*, vol. 1, iii.

86. Jefferson, *State of Virginia*, 150.

Chapter One

1. *Virginian Luxuries*, ca. 1825, Abby Aldrich Rockefeller Folk Art Center, Williamsburg, Va.
2. Bushman, *Refinement of America*, xviii; Kulikoff, *Tobacco and Slaves*, 262.
3. Woodard, *Delectable Negro*, 18, 40, 157.
4. Gikandi, *Slavery and the Culture of Taste*, 30.
5. Hening, *Statutes at Large*, vol. 1, xiv.
6. Tomlins, *Freedom Bound*, 155.
7. Hening, *Statutes at Large*, vol. 1, xvi.
8. Taylor, *American Colonies*, 134; Kulikoff, *Tobacco and Slaves*, 30–31.
9. Jarvis, "Bermuda and the Beginnings of Black Anglo-America," 108.
10. Morgan, "Virginia Slavery in Atlantic Context," 87.
11. Taylor, *American Colonies*, 133.
12. Kulikoff, *Tobacco and Slaves*, 29.
13. Taylor, *American Colonies*, 136.
14. Ostler, *Surviving Genocide*.
15. De la Fuente and Gross, *Becoming Free, Becoming Black*, 95.
16. De la Fuente and Gross, *Becoming Free, Becoming Black*, 27; Kulikoff, *Tobacco and Slaves*, 44.
17. Brown, *Good Wives, Nasty Wenches*, 7.
18. Brown, 5.
19. Jennifer L. Morgan is the exception here. See Morgan, *Reckoning with Slavery*, chap. 2.
20. Kulikoff, *Tobacco and Slaves*, 62–64.
21. Brown, *Good Wives, Nasty Wenches*, 116–117.
22. Hening, *Statutes at Large*, vol. 2, 170; Morgan, "*Partus sequitur ventrem.*"
23. Morgan, "*Partus sequitur ventrem*," 2.
24. Billings, *Old Dominion*, 8–9.
25. Kulikoff, *Tobacco and Slaves*, 31.
26. Coombs, "Phases of Conversion," 346–347.
27. Kulikoff, *Tobacco and Slaves*, 47.
28. Kulikoff, 40–41.
29. British colonies in the Caribbean primarily employed the labor of enslaved Africans with an uneven ratio, whereas indentured servants, Native Americans, and Africans constituted the labor force with varying ratios over time. See Berlin, *Many Thousands Gone*, 32–34; Morgan, *Laboring Women*, 56–60; Rugemer, *Politics of Resistance*, 45–49.
30. Swinburne, *Testaments and Last Wills*, 43–44.
31. Morris, *Southern Slavery and the Law*, 44.
32. Morris, 44.
33. Stevenson, "What's Love Got to Do with It?," 102.
34. Hening, *The Statutes at Large*, vol. 1, 226.
35. Berlin, *Many Thousands Gone*, 45.
36. Morgan, *American Slavery, American Freedom*, 264.
37. Morgan, 266–269.
38. Morgan, 257.
39. Kulikoff, *Tobacco and Slaves*, 35–37; Taylor, *American Colonies*, 149–150.

40. Morgan, *American Slavery, American Freedom.*

41. Hening, *Statutes at Large*, vol. 2, 270.

42. Taylor, *American Colonies*, 153.

43. Morgan, *Slave Counterpoint*, 81.

44. Morgan, 81.

45. Morgan, 81; Kulikoff, *Tobacco and Slaves*, 72.

46. Clark, *American Quadroon*, 9–12, 70; Winters, *Mulatta Concubine*, 3–10, 20–25.

47. Taylor, *American Colonies*, 155.

48. Berlin, *Many Thousands Gone*, 24; Sweet, *Domingos Álvares*, 4–5.

49. Taylor, *American Colonies*, 154.

50. Berlin, "From Creole to African"; Sweet, "Defying Social Death."

51. McKinley, *Fractional Freedoms*, 36.

52. Snyder, *Brabbling Women*, 114; Goetz, *Baptism of Early Virginia*, 164.

53. Governor William Gooch to Edmund Gibson, *Virginia Magazine of History and Biography* 32 (July 1924): 324.

54. Snyder, *Brabbling Women*, 114.

55. Hening, *Statutes at Large*, vol. 4, chap. 7, 325.

56. Hening, 326–327.

57. Hening, 327.

58. Brown, *Tacky's Revolt*, 227; Rugemer, *Politics of Resistance*, 131–140.

59. Hening, *Statutes at Large*, vol. 4, chap. 7, 327.

60. Hening, *Statutes at Large*, vol. 4, chap. 4, 126.

61. Peters and Peters, *Virginia's Historic Courthouses*; Lounsbury, *Courthouses of Early Virginia.* While these works are devoted largely to courthouses, the authors provide discussion of jails since most jails were built near courthouses.

62. Schwarz, *Slave Laws in Virginia*, 71–72.

63. Hening, *Statutes at Large*, vol. 4, chap. 4, 128.

64. Hening, 126.

65. Campbell, "'Victim of Prejudice'"; Von Daacke, *Freedom Has a Face*, 7; Flanigan, "Criminal Procedure in Slave Trials," 538, 551–553; Sommerville, "Rape Myth," 483.

66. Hening, *Statutes at Large*, vol. 4, chap. 4, 126.

67. For more research on mutilation as a form of punishment, see Forret, *Slave against Slave*, 123–126.

68. Hening, *Statutes at Large*, vol. 4, chap. 4, 132.

69. Hening, 132–133.

70. Hening, 133.

71. Adams and Pleck, *Love of Freedom*; Bell, *Running from Bondage*; Horne, *Counter-Revolution of 1776.*

72. Jefferson, *State of Virginia*, query 14.

73. Jefferson, 144–145.

74. Jefferson, 145.

75. Jefferson, 146.

76. Gomez, *Exchanging Our Country Marks*, 107, 115–117.

77. Gomez, 151.

78. Hening, *Statutes at Large*, vol. 4, chap. 4, 129.

79. Hening, 128.

80. Hening, 128.

81. Jefferson, *State of Virginia*, query 14, 146.

82. Jefferson, 147.

83. Onuf, *Jefferson's Empire*, 15.

84. Jefferson, *State of Virginia*, query 14, 151.

85. Fabian, *Skull Collectors*.

86. Merkel, "Jefferson's Failed Anti-slavery Proviso," 559–560.

87. *Commonwealth v. Daphney*, July 16, 1793, Auditor of Public Accounts, Condemned Blacks Executed or Transported, Records—Bonds for the Transportation of Condemned Slaves, 1806–1857, Reel 2549, Library of Virginia (hereinafter cited as LOV); Palmer, McRae, and Flournoy, *Calendar of Virginia State Papers*, vol. 6, 532–543.

88. *Commonwealth v. Nelly*, June 8, 1793, Auditor of Public Accounts, Condemned Blacks Executed or Transported, Records—Bonds for the Transportation of Condemned Slaves, 1806–1857, Reel 2549, LOV.

89. *Commonwealth v. Polly*, February 19, 1798, Auditor of Public Accounts, Condemned Blacks Executed or Transported, Records—Bonds for the Transportation of Condemned Slaves, 1794–1809, Reel 2550, LOV.

90. *Commonwealth v. Milly*, August 1, 1798, Auditor of Public Accounts, Condemned Blacks Executed or Transported, Records—Bonds for the Transportation of Condemned Slaves, 1794–1809, Reel 2550, LOV; *Commonwealth v. Milly*, August 1, 1790, Monongalia County Court Records, West Virginia Microfilm, Reel 1, LOV.

91. *Commonwealth v. Amey*, June 15, 1799, Auditor of Public Accounts, Condemned Blacks Executed or Transported, Records—Bonds for the Transportation of Condemned Slaves, 1794–1809, Reel 2550, LOV.

92. "Ran Away—Temp," *Virginia Argus* (Richmond), February 14, 1797, Library of Congress (hereinafter cited as LOC).

93. "Ran Away—Creasy," *Virginia Argus* (Richmond), December 6, 1799, LOC.

94. "Ran Away—Biddy," *Virginia Argus* (Richmond), December 6, 1799, LOC.

95. *Commonwealth v. Nancy*, September 27, 1809, Auditor of Public Accounts, Condemned Blacks Executed or Transported, Records—Condemned Slaves, Court Orders, and Valuations, 1794–1809, Reel 2550, LOV.

Chapter Two

1. *Commonwealth v. Charity*, September 6, 1803, Auditor of Public Accounts, Condemned Blacks Executed or Transported, Records—Bonds for the Transportation of Condemned Slaves, 1794–1809, Reel 2550, LOV.

2. War Department Collection of Revolutionary War Records, 1709–1939, Record Group 93, M881, Roll 1084, National Archives, Washington, D.C.

3. Morris, *Southern Slavery and the Law*, 253.

4. Morris, 164, 232–233.

5. Hening, *Statutes at Large*, vol. 2, 170; Morgan, "*Partus sequitur ventrem*."

6. Schwarz, *Twice Condemned*, 92.

7. Schwarz, *Slave Laws in Virginia*, 7.

8. Hening, *Statutes at Large*, vol. 5, 104–112; Hening, *Statutes at Large*, vol. 8, 137–138.

9. Fett, *Working Cures*, 2; Gómez, *Experiential Caribbean*; Sweet, *Domingos Álvares*, 63, 69; Strang, *Frontiers of Science*, 87–88; Turner, *Contested Bodies*, chap. 4.

10. Sweet, *Domingos Álvares*, 69.

11. Sweet, 55; Turner, *Contested Bodies*, 115.

12. Hicks, "Blood and Hair," 63.

13. Owens, *Medical Bondage*, 52. In other locations in the Atlantic, men also served as the purveyors of knowledge, as shown in Sweet, *Domingos Álvares*, and Gómez, *Experiential Caribbean*.

14. Fett, *Working Cures*, 130–131.

15. Fett, *Working Cures*, 12.

16. Examples of men doing this work in the early Atlantic are offered in Sweet, *Domingos Álvares*, and Gómez, *Experiential Caribbean*. See Fett, *Working Cures*, 112.

17. Fett, *Working Cures*, 112.

18. *Journal of the House of Delegates of Virginia, Session 1842–43*, 58.

19. *Journal of the House of Delegates of Virginia, Session 1842–43*, 58.

20. *Acts Passed at a General Assembly of the Commonwealth of Virginia, 1842–43*, 59–60.

21. Scott, *Criminal Law in Colonial Virginia*, 196–197; Lowe, *Murder in the Shenandoah*, 80–82.

22. *Supplement to the Revised Code of the Laws of Virginia*, 147–234.

23. *Commonwealth v. Fanny*, February 28, 1806, Auditor of Public Accounts, Condemned Blacks Executed or Transported, Records—Condemned Slaves, Court Orders, and Valuations, 1794–1809, Reel 2550, LOV.

24. *Commonwealth v. Fanny*, February 28, 1806, Auditor of Public Accounts.

25. Glymph, *House of Bondage*, 37; Jones-Rogers, *They Were Her Property*, 78–79.

26. *Commonwealth v. Delphy*, August 10, 1818, Auditor of Public Accounts, Condemned Blacks Executed or Transported, Records—Condemned Slaves, Court Orders, and Valuations, 1810–1822, Reel 2551, LOV.

27. *Commonwealth v. Hannah*, January 1822, Auditor of Public Accounts, Condemned Slaves and Free Blacks Executed or Transported, Records—Condemned Slaves, Court Orders, and Valuations, 1823–1832, Misc. Reel 2552, LOV.

28. Barclay, "Mothering the 'Useless,'" 128–133.

29. *Commonwealth v. Mariah*, December 5, 1823, Auditor of Public Accounts, Condemned Slaves and Free Blacks Executed or Transported, Records—Condemned Slaves, Court Orders, and Valuations, 1823–1832, Misc. Reel 2552, LOV.

30. "Amelia County Marriage Bonds," 39.

31. *Commonwealth v. Mariah*, December 5, 1822, Amelia County Court Order Book, 1819–1825, Reel 48, LOV.

32. Morris, *Southern Slavery and the Law*, 220.

33. Von Daacke, *Freedom Has a Face*, 7; Flanigan, "Criminal Procedure in Slave Trials," 538, 551–553; Sommerville, "Rape Myth," 483; Taylor, *Internal Enemy*, 63–67; Tushnet, *American Law of Slavery*, 23–26.

34. Morris, *Southern Slavery and the Law*, 241; Campbell, "'Victim of Prejudice,'" 74, 84.

35. Savage, "'Black Magic' and White Terror"; McNair, "Slave Women, Capital Crime."

36. *Commonwealth v. Susan and Kesiah*, February 3, 1829, Auditor of Public Accounts, Condemned Slaves and Free Blacks Executed or Transported, Records—Condemned Slaves,

Court Orders, and Valuations, 1823–1832, Misc. Reel 2552, LOV; *Commonwealth v. Susan and Kesiah*, March 14, 1829, Virginia Governor's Office, William B. Giles (1827–1830), Executive Papers, Reel 6312, State Government Records Collection, LOV; *Commonwealth v. Susan and Kesiah*, January 13, 1829, Henrico County Court Minute Book, 1827–1831, Reel 80, LOC.

37. For more on the political diversity of enslaved testimony and fractures within enslaved communities, see Berry, "Poisoned Relations" 46–48.

38. *Commonwealth v. Susan and Kesiah*, Auditor of Public Accounts; *Commonwealth v. Susan and Kesiah*, Giles Executive Papers; *Commonwealth v. Susan and Kesiah*, Henrico County Court Minute Book.

39. Baptist, *Half Has Never Been Told*, 29.

40. *Commonwealth v. Annie*, May 25, 1829, Amelia County Court Order Book, 1846–1855, Reel 52, LOV; *Commonwealth v. Annie*, April 21, 1829, Auditor of Public Accounts, Condemned Slaves and Free Blacks Executed or Transported, Records—Condemned Slaves, Court Orders, and Valuations, 1823–1832, Misc. Reel 2552, LOV.

41. *Commonwealth v. Annie*, Amelia County Court Order Book; *Commonwealth v. Annie*, Auditor of Public Accounts.

42. *Commonwealth v. Annie*, April 21, 1829, Giles Executive Papers, Reel 6313; *Commonwealth v. Annie*, Amelia County Court Order Book; *Commonwealth v. Nanny*, May 29, 1829, Amelia County Court Order Book, 1846–1855, Reel 52, LOV; *Commonwealth v. Annie*, Auditor of Public Accounts.

43. West and Fauntleroy, "Muse (Mewes) Family," 316.

44. *Commonwealth v. Peggy*, March 19, 1829, Auditor of Public Accounts, Condemned Slaves and Free Blacks Executed or Transported, Records—Condemned Slaves, Court Orders, and Valuations, 1823–1832, Misc. Reel 2552, LOV.

45. Beck, *Botany of the United States*, 367.

46. *Commonwealth v. Susan*, March 18, 1852, Virginia Governor's Office, Joseph Johnson (1852–1856), Executive Papers, Misc. Reel 6384, State Government Records Collection, LOV; *Commonwealth v. Susan*, March 15, 1852, Auditor of Public Accounts, Condemned Slaves and Free Blacks Executed or Transported, Records—Condemned Slaves, Court Orders, and Valuations, 1846–1857, Misc. Reel 2554, LOV; *Commonwealth v. Susan*, March 1852, Prince Edward County Court Orders, 1841–1853, Reel 31, LOV.

47. Schwarz, *Twice Condemned*, 208–209.

48. *Commonwealth v. Fanny*, August 21, 1832, Auditor of Public Accounts, Condemned Slaves and Free Blacks Executed or Transported: Records, 1779–1865, Folder 8, Box 3, LOV.

49. *Commonwealth v. Nelly*, June 23, 1834, Auditor of Public Accounts, Condemned Slaves and Free Blacks Executed or Transported, Records—Condemned Slaves, Court Orders, and Valuations, 1833–1845, Misc. Reel 2553, LOV.

50. *Commonwealth v. Eliza*, August 28, 1849, Auditor of Public Accounts, Condemned Slaves and Free Blacks Executed or Transported, Records—Condemned Slaves, Court Orders, and Valuations, 1846–1857, Misc. Reel 2554, LOV; *Commonwealth v. Roberta*, August 28, 1849, Auditor of Public Accounts, Condemned Slaves and Free Blacks Executed or Transported, Records—Condemned Slaves, Court Orders, and Valuations, 1846–1857, Misc. Reel 2554, LOV; *Commonwealth v. Eliza*, August 28, 1849, Brunswick County Court Minute Book, 1824–1852, Reel 45, LOV; *Commonwealth v. Roberta*, August 28, 1849, Brunswick County Court Minute Book, 1824–1852, Reel 45, LOV.

51. Fett, *Working Cures*, 130–131.

52. *Commonwealth v. Eliza*, Brunswick County Court Minute Book; *Commonwealth v. Roberta*, Brunswick County Court Minute Book; *Commonwealth v. Eliza*, Auditor of Public Accounts.

53. Stuart, "Use of Slave Produce," 161. For more on the boycott of goods associated with slavery, see Everill, *Not Made by Slaves.*

54. Stuart, "Use of Slave Produce," 161–162.

55. "SLAVERY," *Richmond (Va.) Daily Whig*, July 1, 1845, LOC.

56. "GLORIOUS VIRGINIA," *Richmond (Va.) Enquirer*, May 22, 1849, LOC.

57. "GLORIOUS VIRGINIA."

58. Rosso, "Poppy and Opium," 82–83; Obladen, "Lethal Lullabies."

59. Obladen, "Lethal Lullabies."

60. "Hustings Court," *Richmond (Va.) Enquirer*, June 22, 1852, LOC; *Commonwealth v. Phillis*, June 16, 1852, Auditor of Public Accounts, Condemned Slaves and Free Blacks Executed or Transported, Records—Condemned Slaves, Court Orders, and Valuations, 1846–1857, Misc. Reel 2554, LOV.

61. "Hustings Court"; *Commonwealth v. Phillis*, Auditor of Public Accounts.

62. "Hustings Court."

63. Link, *Roots of Secession*, 81; Takagi, *"Rearing Wolves,"* 112; Ward, *Public Executions in Richmond*, 58.

64. "The Commutation of Death-Penalty," *Richmond (Va.) Enquirer*, May 11, 1852, LOC; *Commonwealth v. Jordan Hatcher*, March 12, 1852, Auditor of Public Accounts, Condemned Slaves and Free Blacks Executed or Transported, Records—Condemned Slaves, Court Orders, and Valuations, 1846–1857, Misc. Reel 2554, LOV.

65. "The Commutation of Death-Penalty," *Richmond (Va.) Enquirer*, May 11, 1852, LOC.

66. "The Commutation of Death-Penalty," *Richmond (Va.) Enquirer*, May 11, 1852, LOC.

67. "Commutation of Death-Penalty"; *Commonwealth v. Jordan Hatcher*, Auditor of Public Accounts.

68. Ailes and Tyler-McGraw, "Leaving Virginia for Liberia"; Mills, *The World Colonization Made*, 15–17, 30.

69. "A Terrible Broad-Side," *Richmond (Va.) Enquirer*, June 22, 1852, LOC.

70. "Governor Johnson," *Staunton (Va.) Spectator*, June 9, 1852, LOC.

71. "Governor Johnson."

72. "Henrico County Meeting," *Daily Dispatch* (Richmond, Va.), June 8, 1852, LOC.

73. Link, *Roots of Secession*, 85.

74. Takagi, *"Rearing Wolves,"* 31.

75. Campbell, "'Victim of Prejudice,'" 82–84.

76. Link, *Roots of Secession*, 82.

77. Link, 82.

78. "The Boot on the Other Leg," *Richmond (Va.) Enquirer*, June 22, 1852, LOC.

79. "Local Matters: The Case of Poisoning," *Daily Dispatch* (Richmond, Va.), June 4, 1852, LOC.

80. Stevens, *Anthony Burns*, 189.

81. Stevens, 188.

82. Stevens, 189.

83. Stevens, 192–193.

84. "Local Matters: The Case of Poisoning."

85. "Local Matters: The Case of Poisoning."

86. Jones-Rogers, *They Were Her Property*, 15–17.

87. Glymph, *House of Bondage*, 25; Jones-Rogers, *They Were Her Property*, 10.

88. "Local Matters: The Case of Poisoning."

89. "Local Matters: The Case of Poisoning."

90. "Local Matters: The Case of Poisoning."

91. "Messrs. Editors," *Richmond (Va.) Enquirer*, June 22, 1852, LOC.

92. "Messrs. Editors."

93. "Messrs. Editors."

94. "Jordan Hatcher Again," *Richmond (Va.) Enquirer*, June 4, 1852, LOC.

95. "Jordan Hatcher Again."

96. "Charge of Poisoning," *Daily Dispatch* (Richmond, Va.), March 3, 1854, LOC.

97. "Poisoning," *Daily Dispatch* (Richmond, Va.), April 14, 1855, LOC; "Hustings Court," *Richmond Enquirer*.

98. *Lynchburg (Va.) Daily*, May 30, 1857, LOC.

99. "Incendiary Visitants and How to Treat Them," *Richmond (Va.) Enquirer*, February 17, 1857, LOC.

100. "Incendiary Visitants."

101. "Communications," *Alexandria (Va.) Gazette*, February 14, 1861, LOC.

102. Peters, *Slave and Free Negro Records*, 58; "Prince William Items," *Alexandria (Va.) Gazette*, February 12, 1859, LOC.

103. *Commonwealth v. Amelia*, August 1, 1860, Auditor of Public Accounts, Condemned Slaves and Free Blacks Executed or Transported: Records, 1779–1865, Folder 8, Box 3, LOV.

104. *Daily Dispatch* (Richmond, Va.), February 18, 1865, LOC.

105. "Alleged Poisoning by Slaves," *Richmond (Va.) Daily Whig*, March 5, 1861, LOC.

106. "The School Girl," *Daily Dispatch* (Richmond, Va.), October 29, 1864, LOC.

107. "School Girl."

108. "Hustings Court."

Chapter Three

1. *Commonwealth v. Nelly, James, Elias, Newman, and Ellen*, December 26, 1856, Statements of Nelly, James, Elias, Newman, and Eliza, Coroner's Inquest, Prince William County Court Minute Book, 1856–1861, 70, LOV; *Commonwealth v. Nelly and Others*, April 29, 1857, Auditor of Public Accounts, Condemned Slaves and Free Blacks Executed or Transported: Records, 1779–1865, Misc. Reel 2554, LOV.

2. Flanigan, *Criminal Law of Slavery*.

3. Edwards, *People and Their Peace*, 13–15, 29, 62; also see Kaye, *Joining Places*, 121–124.

4. Bogin, "Petitioning," 395; Morgan, *Inventing the People*, 224–228.

5. Fede, *Homicide Justified*, 129. For "certificates of character," see Maris-Wolf, *Family Bonds*, 50–51.

6. Edwards, *People and Their Peace*, 60, 91–92, 212; Maris-Wolf, *Family Bonds*, 11.

7. Schwarz, *Twice Condemned*, 106; Holden, "Generation, Resistance, and Survival," 687.

8. *Commonwealth v. Nelly, James, Elias, Newman, and Ellen*, December 26, 1856, Virginia Governor's Office, Henry A. Wise (1856–1860), Executive Papers, Reel 4199, State Government Records Collection, LOV.

9. Statements of Nelly, James, Elias, Newman, and Eliza, Coroner's Inquest.

10. Kaye, *Joining Places*, 11.

11. Dusinberre, *Strategies for Survival*, 110–113; Genovese, *Roll, Jordan, Roll*, 3–8, 321–322; Penningroth, *Claims of Kinfolk*, 6, 46–49, 96–99.

12. Statements of Nelly, James, Elias, Newman, and Eliza, Coroner's Inquest.

13. Statements of Nelly, James, Elias, Newman, and Eliza, Coroner's Inquest.

14. Statements of Nelly, James, Elias, Newman, and Eliza, Coroner's Inquest.

15. *Commonwealth v. Nelly, James, Elias, Newman, and Ellen*, Wise Executive Papers.

16. *Commonwealth v. Nelly, James, Elias, Newman, and Ellen*, Wise Executive Papers.

17. Statements of Nelly, James, Elias, Newman, and Eliza, Coroner's Inquest.

18. King, "'Prematurely Knowing of Evil Things,'" 174; Stevenson, "What's Love Got to Do with It?," 106.

19. Statements of Nelly, James, Elias, Newman, and Eliza, Coroner's Inquest.

20. Statements of Nelly, James, Elias, Newman, and Eliza, Coroner's Inquest.

21. *Commonwealth v. Nelly, James, Elias, Newman, and Ellen*, Wise Executive Papers.

22. Bush, "Slave Mothers and Children"; Holden, "Generation, Resistance, and Survival," 675.

23. *Commonwealth v. Nelly, James, Elias, Newman, and Ellen*, Wise Executive Papers.

24. Von Daacke, *Freedom Has a Face*, 182; Wilder, *Ebony and Ivy*, 60.

25. King, *Stolen Childhood*, xx.

26. Morris, *Southern Slavery and the Law*, 306–307; Rugemer, *Politics of Resistance*, 129.

27. The terms *girl* and *boy* can be used as a pejorative reference to adult enslaved women and men; however, the antebellum legal record in Virginia does not consistently support such informal usage of the terms. I interpret the use of these terms to reflect a reference to younger age rather than stereotypical usages to ridicule women and men. More specifically, the age of the white children defended in these cases also places enslaved children in the purview of white children as playmates.

28. *Commonwealth v. Caroline*, May 21, 1832, Auditor of Public Accounts, Condemned Slaves and Free Blacks Executed or Transported: Records, 1779–1865, Reel 2552, LOV. Age is not specified; Caroline is referred to as "slave girl" rather than "woman slave."

29. *Commonwealth v. Rebecca*, May 28, 1825, Auditor of Public Accounts, Condemned Slaves and Free Blacks Executed or Transported: Records, 1779–1865, Folder 3, Box 3, LOV.

30. *Commonwealth v. Caroline*, May 31, 1832, Fauquier County Court Order Book, 1832–1835, Reel 58, LOV.

31. *Commonwealth v. Judy*, September 25, 1827, Virginia Governor's Office, William B. Giles (1827–1830), Executive Papers, Reel 6307, State Government Records Collection, LOV; *Commonwealth v. Judy*, September 25, 1827, Auditor of Public Accounts, Condemned Slaves and Free Blacks Executed or Transported, Records—Condemned Slaves, Court Orders, and Valuations, 1823–1832, Misc. Reel 2552, LOV.

32. For more on cursory testimony, see Campbell, "'Victim of Prejudice,'" 74.

33. *Commonwealth v. Judy*, June 5, 1827, Fluvanna County Court Order Book, 1820–1828, Reel 20, LOV; *Commonwealth v. Judy*, Auditor of Public Accounts.

34. *Commonwealth v. Pat*, September 20, 1821, Auditor of Public Accounts, Condemned Blacks Executed or Transported, Records—Condemned Slaves, Court Orders, and Valuations, 1810–1822, Reel 2551, LOV.

35. *Commonwealth v. Nelly*, January 16, 1827, Auditor of Public Accounts, Condemned Slaves and Free Blacks Executed or Transported, Records—Condemned Slaves, Court Orders, and Valuations, 1823–1832, Misc. Reel 2552, LOV.

36. *Commonwealth v. Nelly*, Auditor of Public Accounts.

37. Glymph, *House of Bondage*, 37.

38. *Commonwealth v. Mary*, May 1833, Auditor of Public Accounts, Condemned Slaves and Free Blacks Executed or Transported, Records—Condemned Slaves, Court Orders, and Valuations, 1833–1845, Misc. Reel 2553, LOV.

39. *Commonwealth v. Phoebe*, April 6, 1836, Auditor of Public Accounts, Condemned Slaves and Free Blacks Executed or Transported, Records—Condemned Slaves, Court Orders, and Valuations, 1833–1845, Misc. Reel 2553, LOV.

40. *Commonwealth v. Andrew, Lucinda, and Caroline*, August 22, 1838, Auditor of Public Accounts, Condemned Slaves and Free Blacks Executed or Transported, Records—Condemned Slaves, Court Orders, and Valuations, 1833–1845, Misc. Reel 2553, LOV.

41. "The Bath Tragedy," *Staunton (Va.) Spectator, and General Advertiser*, September 6, 1838, LOC; "The Horrible Murders," *Richmond (Va.) Enquirer*, September 7, 1838, LOC; *Commonwealth v. Andrew, Lucinda, and Caroline*, Auditor of Public Accounts.

42. "Bath Tragedy"; "Horrible Murders"; *Commonwealth v. Andrew, Lucinda, and Caroline*, Auditor of Public Accounts.

43. Forret, *Slave against Slave*, 357.

44. "Bath Tragedy"; "Horrible Murders"; *Commonwealth v. Andrew, Lucinda, and Caroline*, Auditor of Public Accounts.

45. *Commonwealth v. Andrew, Lucinda, and Caroline*, Auditor of Public Accounts.

46. Gross, *Colored Amazons*, chap. 4.

47. "Horrible Murders."

48. *Commonwealth v. Andrew, Lucinda, and Caroline*, Auditor of Public Accounts.

49. "Horrible Murders."

50. *Commonwealth v. Andrew, Lucinda, and Caroline*, Auditor of Public Accounts.

51. *Commonwealth v. Catherine*, June 27, 1857, Auditor of Public Accounts, Condemned Slaves and Free Blacks Executed or Transported, Records—Condemned Slaves, Court Orders, and Valuations, 1846–1857, Misc. Reel 2553, LOV.

52. *Commonwealth v. Peggy*, August Term 1853, Auditor of Public Accounts, Condemned Slaves and Free Blacks Executed or Transported, Records—Condemned Slaves, Court Orders, and Valuations, 1846–1857, Misc. Reel 2554, LOV.

53. *Commonwealth v. Betsey*, August 12, 1840, Auditor of Public Accounts, Condemned Slaves and Free Blacks Executed or Transported, Records—Condemned Slaves, Court Orders, and Valuations, 1833–1845, Misc. Reel 2553, LOV.

54. *Commonwealth v. Margaret*, June 23, 1853, Auditor of Public Accounts, Condemned Slaves and Free Blacks Executed or Transported, Records—Condemned Slaves, Court Orders, and Valuations, 1846–1857, Misc. Reel 2554, LOV; "The Execution," *Richmond (Va.) Daily Whig*, August 24, 1853, LOC.

55. *Commonwealth v. Jane*, August 6, 1852, Auditor of Public Accounts, Condemned Slaves and Free Blacks Executed or Transported, Records—Condemned Slaves, Court Orders, and Valuations, 1846–1857, Misc. Reel 2554, LOV; "Another Shocking Murder," *Alexandria (Va.) Gazette*, July 12, 1852, LOC.

56. *Commonwealth v. Molly*, August Term 1852, Auditor of Public Accounts, Condemned Slaves and Free Blacks Executed or Transported, Records—Condemned Slaves, Court Orders, and Valuations, 1846–1857, Misc. Reel 2554, LOV.

57. "Local Matters—Murder," *Daily Dispatch* (Richmond, Va.), July 20, 1852, LOC.

58. Williams et al., *Dreadful Tragedy in Richmond*, 24.

59. Williams et al., 15.

60. Williams et al., 17.

61. *Commonwealth v. Jane Williams*, August 9, 1852, Auditor of Public Accounts, Condemned Slaves and Free Blacks Executed or Transported: Records, 1846–1857, Misc. Reel 2554, LOV.

62. "Local Matters—the Case of John Williams," *Daily Dispatch* (Richmond, Va.), August 13, 1852, LOC.

63. Williams et al., *Dreadful Tragedy in Richmond*, 12.

64. "The Trial of Jane and John Williams for the Murder of the Winston Family," *Daily Dispatch* (Richmond, Va.), October 25, 1852; *Commonwealth v. Jane Williams*, Auditor of Public Accounts.

65. Williams et al., *Dreadful Tragedy in Richmond*, 19.

66. Williams et al., 20.

67. Williams et al., 20.

68. Williams et al., 23.

69. Barclay, "Mothering the 'Useless,'" 120.

70. Williams et al., *Dreadful Tragedy in Richmond*, 18.

71. Williams et al., 19.

72. Schwarz, *Twice Condemned*, 234–235; Dusinberre, *Strategies for Survival*, 154–155.

73. Williams et al., *Dreadful Tragedy in Richmond*, 30.

74. Williams et al., 27.

75. Williams et al., 28.

76. Williams et al., 36.

77. Williams et al., 37; Von Daacke, *Freedom Has a Face*, 7.

78. Maris-Wolf, *Family Bonds*, 3, 47; Ely, *Israel on the Appomattox*.

79. Williams et al., *Dreadful Tragedy in Richmond*, 1.

80. Williams et al., 29–30.

81. Williams et al., 30.

82. *Baltimore Sun*, December 21, 1849, LOC.

83. *Alexandria (Va.) Gazette*, January 10, 1850, LOV.

84. Copeland and McMaster, *Five George Masons*.

85. Wilder, *Ebony and Ivy*, 139; White, "Introduction: Scarlet and Black," 4.

86. Virginia, *Acts of the General Assembly*, 131.

87. Farrand, *Federal Convention of 1787*, vol. 2, 370.

88. "PUBLIC SALE," *Alexandria (Va.) Gazette*, January 17, 1850; "VALUABLE FARM FOR SALE," *Alexandria (Va.) Gazette*, LOC, January 12, 1852.

89. Kaye, *Joining Places*, 129; Franklin and Schweninger, *Runaway Slaves*, 209–210.

90. "Twenty Dollars Reward," *Alexandria (Va.) Gazette*, LOC, October 21, 1822.

91. "$25 Reward," *Alexandria (Va.) Gazette*, LOC, February 4, 1823.

92. "Fifty Dollars Reward," *Alexandria (Va.) Gazette*, January 22, 1840.

93. *Commonwealth v. Agnes*, January 8, 1850, Auditor of Public Accounts, Condemned Slaves and Free Blacks Executed or Transported, Records—Condemned Slaves, Court Orders, and Valuations, 1846–1857, Misc. Reel 2554, LOV; *Commonwealth v. Agnes*, trial transcript, January 7, 1850, Virginia Governor's Office, John Buchanan Floyd (1849–1852), Executive Papers, Misc. Reel 6370, State Government Records Collection, LOV.

94. *Commonwealth v. Agnes*, Auditor of Public Accounts; *Commonwealth v. Agnes*, trial transcript.

95. *Commonwealth v. Agnes*, trial transcript.

96. For more information regarding community participation in local jurisprudence, see Edwards, *People and Their Peace*.

97. *Commonwealth v. Agnes*, Auditor of Public Accounts; *Commonwealth v. Agnes*, trial transcript.

98. Schwarz, *Twice Condemned*, 253; Dusinberre, *Strategies for Survival*, 74–75.

99. *Commonwealth v. Agnes*, Auditor of Public Accounts; *Commonwealth v. Agnes*, trial transcript.

100. Stevenson, *Life in Black and White*, 246.

101. Owens, *Medical Bondage*, 106–107; Schwartz, *Birthing a Slave*, 116–120, 137.

102. *Commonwealth v. Agnes*, Auditor of Public Accounts; *Commonwealth v. Agnes*, trial transcript.

103. *Commonwealth v. Agnes*, Auditor of Public Accounts; *Commonwealth v. Agnes*, trial transcript.

104. *Commonwealth v. Agnes*, Auditor of Public Accounts; *Commonwealth v. Agnes*, trial transcript.

105. Stevenson, *Life in Black and White*, 236.

106. *Commonwealth v. Agnes*, Auditor of Public Accounts; *Commonwealth v. Agnes*, trial transcript.

107. *Commonwealth v. Agnes*, Auditor of Public Accounts; *Commonwealth v. Agnes*, trial transcript.

108. See also Matthews, *Middling Folk*, 191.

109. *Commonwealth v. Agnes*, Auditor of Public Accounts; *Commonwealth v. Agnes*, trial transcript.

110. *Commonwealth v. Gerard Mason*, Testimony of William Johnson, October 1845, Virginia Governor's Office, James McDowell (1843–1846), Executive Papers, Misc. Reel 6355, State Government Records Collection, LOV; *Commonwealth v. Gerard Mason*, October 1845, Prince William County Court Minute Book, 1843–1846, Reel 28, LOV.

111. *Commonwealth v. Gerard Mason*, Testimony of William Johnson; *Commonwealth v. Gerard Mason*, Prince William County Court Minute Book.

112. *Commonwealth v. Gerard Mason*, Testimony of James Foster, October 1845, McDowell Executive Papers, Misc. Reel 6355; *Commonwealth v. Gerard Mason*, Prince William County Court Minute Book.

113. *Commonwealth v. Gerard Mason*, Testimony of William Bates, October 1845, McDowell Executive Papers, Misc. Reel 6355; *Commonwealth v. Gerard Mason*, Prince William County Court Minute Book.

114. *Commonwealth v. Gerard Mason*, Testimony of Henry Duvall, October 1845, McDowell Executive Papers, Misc. Reel 6355; *Commonwealth v. Gerard Mason*, Prince William County Court Minute Book.

115. *Commonwealth v. Gerard Mason*, Testimony of Henry Duvall; *Commonwealth v. Gerard Mason*, Prince William County Court Minute Book.

116. *Commonwealth v. Gerard Mason*, Coroner's Inquest, October 1845, McDowell Executive Papers, Misc. Reel 6355; *Commonwealth v. Gerard Mason*, Prince William County Court Minute Book.

117. *Commonwealth v. Gerard Mason*, Coroner's Inquest; *Commonwealth v. Gerard Mason*, Testimony of William Johnson; *Commonwealth v. Gerard Mason*, Prince William County Court Minute Book.

118. Wyatt-Brown, *Southern Honor*, 363, 373–380; Dusinberre, *Strategies for Survival*, 88–94.

119. Fede, *Homicide Justified*, 129; Gross, *Double Character*, 47–49.

120. King, "'Prematurely Knowing of Evil Things,'" 178–179; Jennings, "'Us Colored Women'"; Stevenson, "What's Love Got to Do with It?," 116.

121. Schwarz, *Twice Condemned*, 159. Georgia revised state laws to acknowledge the rape of enslaved women in 1861. See Bardaglio, "Rape and the Law," 760.

122. Higginbotham, "Race, Sex, Education," 682–694. The laws are less clear when the perpetrators are enslaved men. See Forret, *Slave against Slave*, 352–354; King, "'Prematurely Knowing of Evil Things,'" 181–184.

123. *The Revised Statutes of the State of Missouri*, 170; McLaurin, *Celia, a Slave*, for an overview of the case, see 14–32.

124. Hartman, "Ruses of Power."

125. Hartman, "Ruses of Power," 541.

126. Hine, *Hine Sight*, xxviii.

127. Fuentes, *Dispossessed Lives*, 102.

128. Jennings, "'Us Colored Women.'"

129. Peters and Peters, *Virginia's Historic Courthouses*, 1, 7–8.

130. For more on public memory and slavery, see Araujo, *Public Memory of Slavery*, specifically chaps. 2 and 7.

131. For more examples, see *Commonwealth v. Richard Turner*, 5 Rand. 678 (Va., 1827); *State v. John Mann*, 13 N.C. 263 (North Carolina Supreme Court, 1829).

132. Schwarz, *Twice Condemned*, 52, 79.

133. Kaye, *Joining Places*, 170.

Chapter Four

1. "From Beck's Medical Jurisprudence," *Phenix Gazette* (Alexandria, Va.), July 26, 1827, LOC; "Medical Text-Books," *Richmond (Va.) Enquirer*, October 28, 1845, LOC.

2. Owens, *Medical Bondage*, 53.

3. Owens, 84; Hogarth, *Medicalizing Blackness*, 135; Savitt, *Medicine and Slavery*, 290.

4. Wecht, "History of Legal Medicine," 245.

5. During the nineteenth century, the term *infant* might be used to capture a broader age range than contemporary usage of the term. Here, I use the term for cases that pertain to children younger in age.

6. Schwartz, *Birthing a Slave*, 139.

7. Wecht, "History of Legal Medicine," 247.

8. Wecht, "History of Legal Medicine," 247; Turner, *Contested Bodies*, 135.

9. Gómez, *Experiential Caribbean*, 164.

10. Act XVI, in Hening, *Statutes at Large*, vol. 3, 86–88.

11. Act XVI, in Hening, 86–88.

12. Act XIX, in Hening, 453–454.

13. Hening, *Statutes at Large*, vol. 3, 459; Hening, *Statutes at Large*, vol. 9, 358.

14. Hening, *Statutes at Large*, vol. 3, 461.

15. For more on the ramifications of Black male castration, see Richeson, "Race-to-Castrate."

16. "University of Virginia," *Richmond (Va.) Enquirer*, August 10, 1827, LOC; "University of Virginia," *Constitutional Whig* (Richmond, Va.), August 18, 1831, LOV.

17. "A Public Examination of the Students of the University of Virginia," *Central Gazette* (Charlottesville, Va.), January 5, 1827, LOC.

18. "Staunton Law School," *Staunton (Va.) Spectator*, August 17, 1832, LOC.

19. Gross, *Double Character*, 134.

20. Schwartz, *Birthing a Slave*, 92.

21. Owens, *Medical Bondage*, 7.

22. Beck, *Elements of Medical Jurisprudence*, 460.

23. Beck, 466.

24. Beck, 467–469.

25. Schwartz, *Birthing a Slave*, 120.

26. Beck, *Elements of Medical Jurisprudence*, 472.

27. Bush, "Hard Labor," 204; Turner, *Contested Bodies*, 180.

28. Perrin, "Resisting Reproduction."

29. Beck, *Elements of Medical Jurisprudence*, 481–483.

30. Schwartz, *Birthing a Slave*, 96–97.

31. Beck, *Elements of Medical Jurisprudence*, 472.

32. Hine, "Inner Lives of Black Women." Although Hine's analysis applies to Black women in the American Midwest during later decades, a perusal of the extant testimony that appears throughout this study reveals a similar approach that enslaved women employ when presented with the task of disclosing intimate details of their lives.

33. Turner, *Contested Bodies*, 253.

34. "Infanticide," *Alexandria (Va.) Gazette*, September 27, 1820, LOV; "Catherine Scott," *Daily Dispatch* (Richmond, Va.), March 8, 1854, LOV; "Acquittal," *Daily Dispatch* (Richmond, Va.), August 7, 1854, LOV; "Infanticide," *Daily Dispatch* (Richmond, Va.), October 13, 1857, LOV.

35. Miscarriage, abortion, and infanticide also appear in a different context for white and Black women after the Civil War. See Turner, "Ambiguities of Law."

36. White, *Ar'n't I a Woman?*, 84.

37. Beck, *Elements of Medical Jurisprudence*, 460.

38. Savitt, *Medicine and Slavery*, 117.

39. Stevenson, *Life in Black and White*, 101.

40. Savitt, *Medicine and Slavery*, 182.

41. Savitt, *Medicine and Slavery*, 127; Cody, "Cycles of Work and of Childbearing"; Johnson, "Smothered Slave Infants."

42. Beck, *Elements of Medical Jurisprudence*, 461.

43. Savitt, *Slavery and Medicine*, 127, 136.

44. *Commonwealth v. Jenny*, September 20, 1815, Auditor of Public Accounts, Condemned Blacks Executed or Transported, Records—Condemned Slaves, Court Orders, and Valuations, 1810–1822, Reel 2551, LOV.

45. For more analysis on Jenny's case, see Forret, *Slave against Slave*, 163.

46. *Commonwealth v. Letty*, July 24, 1822, Auditor of Public Accounts, Condemned Blacks Executed or Transported, Records—Condemned Slaves, Court Orders, and Valuations, 1810–1822, Reel 2551, LOV; Virginia Governor's Office, Thomas Mann Randolph Jr. (1819–1822), Executive Papers, Misc. Reel 6282, State Government Records Collection, LOV; see also King, "'Mad' Enough to Kill," 42–43.

47. *Commonwealth v. Lucy*, November 4, 1819, Auditor of Public Accounts, Condemned Slaves and Free Blacks Executed or Transported, Records—Condemned Slaves, Court Orders, and Valuations, 1823–1832, Misc. Reel 2552, LOV.

48. "Murder and Sentence of Death," *Alexandria (Va.) Gazette and Daily Advertiser*, November 18, 1819, LOC.

49. "Murder and Sentence of Death." Turner, "Ambiguities of Law," shows how Black women were criminalized and constructed as murderous mothers after the Civil War.

50. "Murder and Sentence of Death."

51. *Commonwealth v. Polly*, November 9, 1819, Auditor of Public Accounts, Condemned Blacks Executed or Transported, Records—Condemned Slaves, Court Orders, and Valuations, 1810–1822, Reel 2551, LOV.

52. *Commonwealth v. Mary*, August 7, 1819, Auditor of Public Accounts, Condemned Blacks Executed or Transported, Records—Condemned Slaves, Court Orders, and Valuations, 1810–1822, Reel 2551, LOV.

53. *Commonwealth v. Milly*, June 16, 1826, Auditor of Public Accounts, Condemned Slaves and Free Blacks Executed or Transported: Records—1779–1865, Folder 4, Box 3, LOV.

54. *Commonwealth v. Martha*, May 21, 1827, Auditor of Public Accounts, Condemned Slaves and Free Blacks Executed or Transported, Records—Condemned Slaves, Court Orders, and Valuations, 1823–1832, Misc. Reel 2552, LOV; *Commonwealth v. Martha*, May 21, 1827, Prince Edward County Court Orders, 1824–1832, Reel 29, LOV.

55. For other instances of slaveholders locking up pregnant enslaved women, see Perrin, "Resisting Reproduction," 262.

56. *Commonwealth v. Martha*, Prince Edward County Court Orders.

57. Edwards, *People and Their Peace*.

58. *Commonwealth v. Ally*, February 18, 1833, Auditor of Public Accounts, Condemned Slaves and Free Blacks Executed or Transported, Records—Condemned Slaves, Court Orders, and Valuations, 1833–1845, Misc. Reel 2553, LOV.

59. *Commonwealth v. Kesiah*, May 5, 1834, Auditor of Public Accounts, Condemned Slaves and Free Blacks Executed or Transported, Records—Condemned Slaves, Court Orders, and Valuations, 1833–1845, Misc. Reel 2553, LOV; *Commonwealth v. Kesiah*, May 5, 1834, Henrico County Court Minute Book, 1833–1835, Reel 81, LOV.

60. For more on abolitionist responses, see Sinha, *Slave's Cause*; Everill, *Not Made by Slaves*.

61. Stowe, *Uncle Tom's Cabin*.

62. Taylor, *Driven toward Madness*; Lubet, *Fugitive Justice*, 241–244.

63. *Richmond (Va.) Enquirer*, January 3, 1854, LOC.

64. "The Fugitive Slave Case," *Carroll (Ohio) Free Press*, February 21, 1856, LOC.

65. Weisenburger, *Modern Medea*, 164; "Fugitive Slave Case."

66. Stone, quoted in Coffin, *Reminiscences*, 565.

67. "Fugitive Slave Case."

68. "The Wicked—the Disgraceful End," *Anti-slavery Bugle* (Salem, Ohio), March 8, 1856, LOC; "No Slavery Outside of the Slave States," *Anti-slavery Bugle* (Salem, Ohio), March 8, 1856, LOC.

69. Sharpe, *In the Wake*, 104.

70. "The Cincinnati Slave Case," *Richmond (Va.) Enquirer*, May 2, 1856, LOC.

71. Blackett, *Captive's Quest for Freedom*, 252; Weisenburger, *Modern Medea*, 224–225; Reinhardt, *Who Speaks for Margaret Garner?*, chap. 3.

72. *Commonwealth v. Caroline*, April 23, 1851, Auditor of Public Accounts, Condemned Slaves and Free Blacks Executed or Transported, Records—Condemned Slaves, Court Orders, and Valuations, 1846–1857, Misc. Reel 2554, LOV.

73. *Commonwealth v. Caroline*, Auditor of Public Accounts.

74. Davis, "Black Woman's Role," 87.

75. *Commonwealth v. Fannie*, August 3, 1852, Auditor of Public Accounts, Condemned Slaves and Free Blacks Executed or Transported, Records—Condemned Slaves, Court Orders, and Valuations, 1846–1857, Misc. Reel 2554, LOV; Virginia Governor's Office, Joseph Johnson (1852–1856), Executive Papers, August–October 1852, Misc. Reel 6389, State Government Records Collection, LOV.

76. "The Case of Infanticide," *Daily Dispatch* (Richmond, Va.), September 9, 1852, LOC.

77. "Case of Infanticide."

78. "Case of Infanticide"; *Commonwealth v. Lucy*, September 16, 1852, Auditor of Public Accounts, Condemned Slaves and Free Blacks Executed or Transported, Records—Condemned Slaves, Court Orders, and Valuations, 1846–1857, Misc. Reel 2554, LOV.

79. "Local Matters," *Daily Dispatch* (Richmond, Va.), October 22, 1852, LOC; *Commonwealth v. Lucy*, September 16, 1852, Auditor of Public Accounts.

80. "Local Matters"; "Infanticide," *Staunton (Va.) Spectator*, September 29, 1852, LOC.

81. *Commonwealth v. Lucy*, September 16, 1852, Auditor of Public Accounts.

82. "Local Matters."

83. Lebsock, "Free Black Women," 281–282. For more on the economic activity of free and enslaved Black people, see Schweninger, "Roots of Enterprise"; Hill Edwards, *Unfree Markets*.

84. Forret, *Slave against Slave*, 335.

85. "The Stethoscope," *Daily Dispatch* (Richmond, Va.), October 5, 1854, LOV.

86. Shanks, "Uterine and Constitutional Disorders," 605.

87. Shanks, 606.

88. Shanks, 603.

89. Washington, *Medical Apartheid*, 110–113.

90. Shanks, "Uterine and Constitutional Disorders," 607.

91. Shanks, 607.

92. "Creosote for Warts," *Daily Dispatch* (Richmond, Va.), January 28, 1856, LOC; "Howard's Compound Creosote Tooth Wash," *Alexandria (Va.) Gazette*, February 7, 1845, LOC; "Fresh Drugs," *Alexandria (Va.) Gazette*, April 17, 1850, LOC; "Drugs, Chemicals, Paints, Oils, Window Glass, Putty, Dyestuffs," *Alexandria (Va.) Gazette*, June 25, 1846, LOC; "Drugs, Chemicals," *Alexandria (Va.) Gazette*, June 10, 1858, LOC.

93. Bos et al., "Genotoxic Exposure."

94. "Local Matters."

95. "Infanticide," *Alexandria (Va.) Gazette*, August 11, 1853, LOC; *Commonwealth v. Lucy*, September 16, 1852, Auditor of Public Accounts, Condemned Blacks Executed or Transported, Records—Condemned Slaves, Court Orders, and Valuations, 1846–1857, Misc. Reel 2554, LOV.

96. "Infanticide," *Daily Dispatch* (Richmond, Va.), August 9, 1853, LOC.

97. "Infanticide," *Daily Dispatch* (Richmond, Va.), August 11, 1853, LOC.

98. "Infanticide," August 11, 1853.

99. "Hustings Court," *Daily Dispatch* (Richmond, Va.), September 15, 1853, LOC.

100. "Infanticide—Sentence of Death," *Daily Dispatch* (Richmond, Va.), April 18, 1856, LOV; "Message IV: Relative to Reprieves and Pardons, to the General Assembly of Virginia," December 7, 1857, in *Journal of the House of Delegates of the Commonwealth of Virginia, for the Session of 1857–58*, Doc. No. 1, clxxviii; *Commonwealth v. Opha Jane*, June 7, 1856, Auditor of Public Accounts, Condemned Blacks Executed or Transported, Records—Bonds for the Transportation of Condemned Slaves, 1806–1857, Reel 2549, LOV; *Commonwealth v. Opha Jane*, May 19, 1856, Auditor of Public Accounts, Condemned Slaves and Free Blacks Executed or Transported, Records—Condemned Slaves, Court Orders, and Valuations, 1846–1857, Misc. Reel 2554, LOV.

101. Virginia Governor's Office, Henry A. Wise (1856–1860), Executive Papers, Misc. Reel 4202, State Government Records Collection, LOV; "Conviction," *Alexandria (Va.) Gazette*, June 19, 1857, LOV; "Message IV: Relative to Reprieves and Pardons," clxxxv; Beck, *Elements of Medical Jurisprudence*, 156–163.

102. "Attempted Infanticide," *Daily Dispatch* (Richmond, Va.), September 29, 1857, LOC.

103. "The Infanticide Case," *Staunton (Va.) Spectator*, March 4, 1857, LOV.

104. "Transportation," *Daily Dispatch* (Richmond, Va.), October 7, 1857, LOV.

105. "Drowned Her Child," *Alexandria (Va.) Gazette*, August 7, 1858, LOC.

106. Commonwealth v. Ellen, August 15, 1858, Auditor of Public Accounts, Condemned Blacks Executed or Transported, Misc. Reel 2555, LOV.

107. "Infanticide," *Daily Dispatch* (Richmond, Va.), June 15, 1860, LOC.

Chapter Five

1. Brown, *Tacky's Revolt*, 4.

2. Camp, *Closer to Freedom*, 89–92.

3. Glymph, *Women's Fight*, 99.

4. *Commonwealth v. Peggy, Patrick, Franky, and Caroline*, September 10, 1830, Auditor of Public Accounts, Condemned Slaves and Free Blacks Executed or Transported, Records—Condemned Slaves, Court Orders, and Valuations, 1823–1832, Misc. Reel 2552, LOV; *Commonwealth v. Peggy, Patrick, Franky, and Caroline*, December 8, 1830, Virginia Governor's Office, John Floyd (1830–1834), Executive Papers, Misc. Reel 6319, State Government Records Collection, LOV.

5. *Commonwealth v. Peggy, Patrick, Franky, and Caroline*, Auditor of Public Accounts; *Commonwealth v. Peggy, Patrick, Franky, and Caroline*, John Floyd Executive Papers.

6. *Commonwealth v. Peggy, Patrick, Franky, and Caroline*, Auditor of Public Accounts; *Commonwealth v. Peggy, Patrick, Franky, and Caroline*, John Floyd Executive Papers.

7. For earlier scholarly treatment of enslaved women and insurgency, see Glymph, "Rose's War."

8. Turner, *Confessions of Nat Turner*.

9. "Capture of Nat Turner," *Constitutional Whig* (Richmond, Va.), November 7, 1831, LOC.

10. Dew, "Nat Turner's Insurrection," 6.

11. Holden, *Surviving Southampton*, 36, 107; Tragle, *Southampton Slave Revolt*, 208–209; Kaye, "Neighborhoods and Nat Turner."

12. "Insurrection in Southampton," *Richmond (Va.) Enquirer*, August 30, 1831, LOC.

13. *Staunton (Va.) Spectator*, September 9, 1831, LOC; *Commonwealth v. Lucy*, September 19, 1831, Auditor of Public Accounts, Condemned Slaves and Free Blacks Executed or Transported, Records—Condemned Slaves, Court Orders, and Valuations, 1823–1832, Misc. Reel 2552, LOV.

14. *Commonwealth v. Lucy*, September 22, 1831, Southampton County Court Minute Book, 1830–1842, Reel 34, LOV.

15. Drewry, *Southampton Insurrection*, 85.

16. Holden, *Surviving Southampton*, 27–28; Drewry, *Southampton Insurrection*, 47–48.

17. *Constitutional Whig* (Richmond, Va.), January 12, 1832, LOC; Allmendinger, *Nat Turner*; Breen, *Deluged in Blood*.

18. Randolph, quoted in Faulkner, *Speech of Charles Jas. Faulkner*, 3.

19. Dew, "Nat Turner's Insurrection," 5.

20. *Southern Planter* (Woodville, Miss.), January 26, 1832, LOC.

21. "To the People of Virginia," *Richmond (Va.) Enquirer*, February 4, 1832, LOC.

22. Dew, *Review of the Debates*, 67; see also Root, *Sons of the Fathers*.

23. Dew, 12.

24. Brophy, *University, Court, and Slave*, 36.

25. Dew, *Review of the Debates*, 30.

26. Dew, 30.

27. Dew, 48.

28. Dew, 95.

29. Dew, 95.

30. See Phillips, *American Negro Slavery*; Stampp, *Peculiar Institution*; Elkins, *Slavery*.

31. Dew, *Review of the Debates*, 96.

32. Link, *Roots of Secession*, 179–182, 248; Oates, *To Purge This Land*, 243–247.

33. *Staunton (Va.) Spectator*, December 13, 1859, LOC.

34. *Staunton (Va.) Spectator*, December 13, 1859, LOC.

35. Link, *Roots of Secession*, 191; McPherson, *Battle Cry of Freedom*, 231–232.

36. See theses exceptions in the following work: Glymph, *Women's Fight*; McCurry, *Women's War*; Taylor, *Embattled Freedom*.

37. "From South Carolina," *Richmond (Va.) Whig*, February 3, 1865, LOC.

38. Taylor, *Embattled Freedom*.

39. Camp, *Closer to Freedom*, 65.

40. "Advice to Slaveholders," *Alexandria (Va.) Gazette*, December 22, 1856, LOC.

41. Link, *Roots of Secession*, 45.

42. "Advice to Slaveholders."

43. "Advice to Slaveholders."

44. "Arson," *Daily Dispatch* (Richmond, Va.), June 8, 1855, LOC.

45. Peters, *Slave and Free Negro Records*, 37.

46. "Arson," *Daily Dispatch* (Richmond, Va.), March 14, 1854, LOC.

47. "Charge of Arson," *Daily Dispatch* (Richmond, Va.), February 16, 1854, LOC.

48. "Charge of Arson."

49. *Commonwealth v. Fanny*, February 15, 1849, Auditor of Public Accounts, Condemned Slaves and Free Blacks Executed or Transported: Records, 1779–1865, Folder 8, Box 3, LOV.

50. Johnson, *Soul by Soul*, 107.

51. "Charge of Arson," *Daily Dispatch* (Richmond, Va.), August 7, 1857, LOV.

52. *Commonwealth v. Nancy*, July 17, 1824, Auditor of Public Accounts, Condemned Slaves and Free Blacks Executed or Transported: Records, 1779–1865, Folder 8, Box 3, LOV.

53. *Commonwealth v. Lucy Barker*, March 6, 1851, Auditor of Public Accounts, Condemned Slaves and Free Blacks Executed or Transported, Records—Condemned Slaves, Court Orders, and Valuations, 1846–1857, Misc. Reel 2554, LOV.

54. Berry, *The Price for Their Pound of Flesh*, 112–113.

55. *Commonwealth v. Lucy Barker*, Auditor of Public Accounts.

56. "Acquittal of a Prisoner," *Daily Dispatch* (Richmond, Va.), September 29, 1857, LOC.

57. Campbell, "'Victim of Prejudice,'" 85; Forret, *Slave against Slave*, 146.

58. *Commonwealth v. Alberta*, December 10, 1859, Auditor of Public Accounts, Condemned Slaves and Free Blacks Executed or Transported: Records, 1779–1865, Folder 8, Box 3, LOV.

59. "Mayor's Court," *Richmond (Va.) Whig*, January 16, 1865, LOC.

60. "Mayor's Court," *Daily Dispatch* (Richmond, Va.), March 13, 1865, LOC.

61. Nunley, *At the Threshold of Liberty*, 163.

62. Takagi, *"Rearing Wolves,"* 141.

63. Oakes, *Freedom National*, 225–230; Edwards, *Legal History*, 83; Siddali, *From Property to Person*, 37, 175, 233, 259.

64. "A Girl for Hire," *Abingdon Virginian*, March 20, 1863, LOC.

65. Feimster, *Southern Horrors*, 22.

66. Glymph, *Women's Fight*, 223; Glymph, "Rose's War," 520.

67. "RANAWAY," *Alexandria (Va.) Gazette*, May 11, 1861, LOC.

68. "TWENTY DOLLARS REWARD," *Daily Dispatch* (Richmond, Va.), September 30, 1862, LOC.

69. "TWENTY DOLLARS REWARD."

70. Franklin and Schweninger, *Runaway Slaves*, 210, 237, 239–240; White, *Ar'n't I a Woman?*, 70, 79.

71. Glymph, *Women's Fight*, 226.

72. "RANAWAY," *Daily Dispatch* (Richmond, Va.), November 1, 1862, LOC.

73. Hunter, *Bound in Wedlock*, 210–211.

74. "RUNAWAY—FIFTY DOLLARS REWARD," *Daily Dispatch* (Richmond, Va.), October 14, 1861, LOC.

75. "RANAWAY," *Daily Dispatch* (Richmond, Va.), June 28, 1862, LOC.

76. For more on the rituals of freedom, see Nunley, *At the Threshold of Liberty*, chap. 2.

77. "ONE HUNDRED DOLLARS REWARD," *Daily Dispatch* (Richmond, Va.), July 5, 1862, LOC.

78. "$15 REWARD," *Daily Dispatch* (Richmond, Va.), December 25, 1861, LOC.

79. Nunley, *At the Threshold of Liberty*, chap. 2.

80. "FIFTY DOLLARS REWARD," *Daily Dispatch* (Richmond, Va.), November 19, 1862, LOC.

81. "ONE HUNDRED DOLLARS REWARD," *Daily Dispatch* (Richmond, Va.), December 27, 1864, LOC.

82. "RANAWAY—$10 REWARD," *Daily Dispatch* (Richmond, Va.), December 19, 1861, LOC.

83. "FIVE HUNDRED DOLLARS REWARD," *Daily Dispatch* (Richmond, Va.), January 30, 1865, LOC.

84. "RAN AWAY," *Daily Dispatch* (Richmond, Va.), May 13, 1864, LOC.

85. "TWENTY-FIVE DOLLARS REWARD," *Daily Dispatch* (Richmond, Va.), September 23, 1862, LOC.

86. "RUNAWAY—$100 REWARD," *Daily Dispatch* (Richmond, Va.), September 23, 1862, LOC.

87. "TWENTY-FIVE DOLLARS REWARD."

88. "TWENTY-FIVE DOLLARS REWARD," *Daily Dispatch* (Richmond, Va.), November 1, 1862, LOC.

89. "RAN-AWAY," *Daily Dispatch* (Richmond, Va.), November 1, 1862, LOC.

90. "$50 AND TEN DOLLARS REWARD FOR A RUNAWAY," *Daily Dispatch* (Richmond, Va.), April 14, 1862, LOC.

91. "TWENTY-FIVE DOLLARS REWARD," *Daily Dispatch* (Richmond, Va.), August 26, 1862, LOC.

92. "300 DOLLARS REWARD," *Daily Dispatch* (Richmond, Va.), January 7, 1864, LOC.

93. "RUNAWAY," *Daily Dispatch* (Richmond, Va.), January 7, 1864, LOC.

94. For more on the geographical diversity of fugitive slave escapes, see Baumgartner, *South to Freedom*.

95. "$150 REWARD," *Richmond (Va.) Whig*, August 10, 1863, LOC.

96. Williams, *Help Me Find My People*, 13, 153–159.

97. "ONE THOUSAND DOLLARS," *Daily Dispatch* (Richmond, Va.), December 27, 1864, LOC.

98. "TWO HUNDRED DOLLARS REWARD," *Daily Dispatch* (Richmond, Va.), December 27, 1864, LOC.

99. "$500 REWARD," *Richmond (Va.) Whig*, July 7, 1864, LOC.

100. *Commonwealth v. Lavinia*, September 8, 1862, Richmond Circuit Court, Court Records and Ended Causes, 1862–1863, LOV.

101. *Commonwealth v. Lavinia*, Richmond Circuit Court.

102. *Commonwealth v. Celia*, February 13, 1865, Richmond Circuit Court, Court Records and Ended Causes, 1865–1866, LOV.

103. *Commonwealth v. Celia*, Richmond Circuit Court.

104. *Commonwealth v. Henrietta*, August 16, 1862, Richmond Circuit Court, Court Records and Ended Causes, 1862–1863, LOV.

105. *Commonwealth v. Melvina*, April 15, 1863, Richmond Circuit Court, Court Records and Ended Causes, 1862–1863, LOV.

106. *Commonwealth v. Sarah*, August 24, 1862, Richmond Circuit Court, Court Records and Ended Causes, 1862–1863, LOV.

107. *Commonwealth v. Margaret*, March 10, 1863, Richmond Circuit Court, Court Records and Ended Causes, 1862–1863, LOV.

108. *Commonwealth v. Virginia*, April 16, 1863, Richmond Circuit Court, Court Records and Ended Causes, 1862–1863, LOV.

109. *Commonwealth v. Emma Jane*, September 9, 1862, Richmond Circuit Court, Court Records and Ended Causes, 1862–1863, LOV.

110. *Commonwealth v. Martha*, March 13, 1863, Richmond Circuit Court, Court Records and Ended Causes, 1862–1863, LOV.

111. *Commonwealth v. Margaret*, December 8, 1862, Richmond Circuit Court, Court Records and Ended Causes, 1862–1863, LOV.

112. *Commonwealth v. Eliza*, February 17, 1865, Richmond Circuit Court, Court Records and Ended Causes, 1865–1866, LOV.

113. *Commonwealth v. Fanny*, February 10, 1864, Auditor of Public Accounts, Condemned Slaves and Free Blacks Executed or Transported: Records, 1858–1865, Misc. Reel 2555, LOV.

114. *Commonwealth v. Jane*, October 10, 1864, Auditor of Public Accounts, Condemned Slaves and Free Blacks Executed or Transported: Records, 1858–1865, Misc. Reel 2555, LOV.

115. "Negro Troops—Jail Delivery," *Alexandria (Va.) Gazette*, March 12, 1864, LOC.

116. McCurry, *Confederate Reckoning*, 175–181.

117. *Commonwealth v. Ann Perrin*, February 16, 1865, Richmond Circuit Court, Court Records and Ended Causes, 1865–1866, LOV.

Conclusion

1. Forret, *Slave against Slave*, 365.

2. *Statutes at Large* 27, 39th Congress, 1st Sess., chap. 31 (1866).

3. Haley, *No Mercy Here*, 157–161.

4. Gross, *Colored Amazons*, 141.

5. LeFlouria, *Chained in Silence*.

6. Feimster, *Southern Horrors*, chap. 2.

Bibliography

Primary Sources

ARCHIVES

Auditor of Public Accounts, Condemned Blacks Executed or Transported, Records—
Bonds for the Transportation of Condemned Slaves, Library of Virginia, Richmond

Auditor of Public Accounts, Condemned Blacks Executed or Transported, Records—
Condemned Slaves, Court Orders, and Valuations, Library of Virginia, Richmond

Auditor of Public Accounts, Condemned Slaves and Free Blacks Executed or Transported,
Records—Condemned Slaves, Court Orders, and Valuations, Library of Virginia,
Richmond

Auditor of Public Accounts, Condemned Slaves and Free Blacks Executed or Transported,
Records, 1779–1865, Library of Virginia, Richmond

Richmond Circuit Court, Court Records and Ended Causes, Library of Virginia

Virginia County Court Minute and Order Books, Library of Virginia

Accomack	Cumberland	Madison
Albemarle	Dinwiddie	Monongalia
Amelia	Fairfax	New Kent
Amherst	Fauquier	Norfolk
Appomattox	Fluvanna	Nottaway
Arlington	Franklin	Powhatan
Bath	Gloucester	Prince Edward
Bedford	Goochland	Prince William
Botetourt	Henrico	Pulaski
Brooke	Isle of Wight	Rappahannock
Brunswick	James City	Richmond
Buckingham	King and Queen	Roanoke
Cabell	King William	Southampton
Campbell	Lancaster	Spotsylvania
Caroline	Lewis	Surry
Clarke	Loudoun	Sussex
Culpeper	Lunenburg	Westmoreland

Virginia Governor's Office, Executive Papers, State Government Records Collection,
Library of Virginia, Richmond

Thomas Mann Randolph Jr. (1819–1822)	John Floyd (1830–1834)
James Pleasants (1822–1825)	Littleton Waller Tazewell (1834–1836)
John Tyler (1825–1827)	Wyndham Robertson (1836–1837)
William B. Giles (1827–1830)	David Campbell (1837–1840)

Thomas Walker Gilmer (1840–1841)
John M. Patton (1841)
John Rutherfoord (1841–1842)
John Munford Gregory (1842–1843)
James McDowell (1843–1846)
William Smith (1846–1849)

John Buchanan Floyd (1849–1852)
Joseph Johnson (1852–1856)
Henry A. Wise (1856–1860)
John Letcher (1860–1861)
William Smith (1864–1865)

War Department Collection of Revolutionary War Records, National Archives, Washington, D.C.

NEWSPAPERS

Abingdon Virginian
Alexandria (Va.) Daily Advertiser
Alexandria (Va.) Gazette
Alexandria (Va.) Gazette and Daily Advertiser
Anti-slavery Bugle (Salem, Ohio)
Baltimore Sun
Central Gazette (Charlottesville, Va.)
Constitutional Whig (Richmond, Va.)
Daily Dispatch (Richmond, Va.)

Daily Richmond (Va.) Whig
Lynchburg (Va.) Daily
Phenix Gazette (Alexandria, Va.)
Richmond (Va.) Daily Whig
Richmond (Va.) Enquirer
Southern Planter (Woodville, Miss.)
Staunton (Va.) Spectator
Staunton (Va.) Spectator, and General Advertiser
Virginia Argus (Richmond, Va.)

Published Primary Sources

Acts Passed at a General Assembly of the Commonwealth of Virginia, 1842–43. Richmond, Va.: Samuel Shepherd, 1843.

Beck, Lewis Caleb. *Botany of the United States North of Virginia; Comprising Descriptions of the Flowering and Fern-Like Plants Hitherto Found in Those States, Arranged according to the Natural System. With a Synopsis of the Genera according to the Linnean System, a Sketch of the Rudiments of Botany, and a Glossary of Terms.* New York: Harper & Brothers, 1848.

Beck, Theodoric Romeyn. *Elements of Medical Jurisprudence.* 2nd ed. London: Printer for John Anderson, Medical Bookseller, West-Smithfield; S. Highley, 174, Fleet-Street, and Webb-Street, Borough; W. Blackwood, Edinburgh, and Hodges and McArthur, Dublin, 1825.

Bos, R. P., C. T. J. Hulshof, J. L. G. Theuws, and P. Th. Henderson. "Genotoxic Exposure of Workers Creosoting Wood." *British Journal of Industrial Medicine* 41, no. 2 (1984): 260–262.

Cobb, Thomas R. R. *An Inquiry into the Law of Negro Slavery in the United States of America. To Which Is Prefixed, An Historical Sketch of Slavery.* Vol. 1. Savannah, Ga.: W. Thorne Williams, 1858.

Coffin, Levi. *Reminiscences of Levi Coffin, the Reputed President of the Underground Railroad; Being a Brief History of the Labors of a Lifetime in Behalf of the Slave, with the Stories of Numerous Fugitives, Who Gained Their Freedom through His Instrumentality, and Many Other Incidents.* Cincinnati: Robert Clarke, 1880.

Dew, Thomas Roderick. *Review of the Debate in the Virginia Legislature of 1831 and 1832.* Richmond: T.W. White, 1832.

Farrand, Max, ed. *The Records of the Federal Convention of 1787.* 4 vols. New Haven, Conn.: Yale University Press, 1837.

Hening, William Waller. *The Statutes at Large; Being a Collection of All the Laws of Virginia, from the First Session of the Legislature, in the Year 1619.* 13 vols. Richmond, Va.: J. & G. Cochran, 1809–1823.

Jefferson, Thomas. *Notes on the State of Virginia.* London: Printed for John Stockdale, Opposite Burlington-House, Piccadilly, 1787.

Journal of the House of Delegates of the Commonwealth of Virginia, for the Session of 1857–58. Richmond, Va.: William F. Ritchie, public printer, 1857.

Journal of the House of Delegates of Virginia, Session 1842–43. Richmond, Va.: Samuel Shepherd, printer to the Commonwealth, 1842.

Missouri. *The Revised Statutes of the State of Missouri: Revised and Digested by the Eighth General Assembly During the Years One Thousand Eight Hundred and Thirty-four, and One Thousand Eight Hundred and Thirty-five: Together with the Constitutions of Missouri and of the United States.* Printed at the Argus Office, 1835.

Palmer, William Pitt, Sherwin McRae, and Henry W. Flournoy. *Calendar of Virginia State Papers and Other Manuscripts.* 11 vols. Richmond, 1875–1893.

Shanks, L. "On the Relation of Uterine and Constitutional Disorders, as Cause and Effect—Their Pathology, Diagnosis and Treatment, Illustrated by Cases." *Stethoscope: A Monthly Journal of Medicine and the Collateral Sciences* (Medical Society of Virginia) 4 (1854): 596–608.

Shepherd, Samuel, ed. *The Statutes at Large of Virginia, from October Session 1792, to December Session 1806, Inclusive, in Three Volumes, (New Series,) Being a Continuation of Hening.* Richmond, Va.: Samuel Shepherd, 1835.

Supplement to the Revised Code of the Laws of Virginia. Richmond, Va., 1833.

Swinburne, Henry. *A Brief Treatise of Testaments and Last Willes, Very profitable to be understood of all the Subjects of this Realme of England, (desirous to know, Whether, Whereof, and How, they may make their Testaments: and by what meanes the same may be effected or hindered,) and no lesse delightfull, aswell for the rareness of the worke, as for the easiness of the stile, and method: Compiled of such lawes Ecclesiasticall and Ciuill, as be not repugnant to the lawes, customes, or statutes of this Realme, nor dero/gatorie to the Prerogatiue Royall.* London: John Windet, 1590.

Tate, Joseph. *Digest of the Laws of Virginia, Which Are of a Permanent Character and General Operation; Illustrated by Judicial Decisions: To Which Is Added, An Index of the Names of the Cases in the Virginia Reporters.* 2nd ed. Richmond, Va.: Smith and Palmer, 1841.

Turner, Nat. *The Confessions of Nat Turner, the Leader of the Late Insurrection in Southampton, Va. as Fully and Voluntarily Made to Thomas R. Gray, in the Prison Where He Was Confined, and Acknowledged by Him to Be Such, When Read before the Court of Southampton; With the Certificate, under Seal of the Court Convened at Jerusalem, Nov. 5, 1831, for His Trial. Also, an Authentic Account of the Whole Insurrection, with Lists of the Whites Who Were Murdered, and of the Negroes Brought before the Court of Southampton, and There Sentenced, &c.* Baltimore: Thomas R. Gray; Lucas & Deaver, printer, 1831.

Virginia. *Acts of the General Assembly of the Commonwealth of Virginia.* Richmond, Va., 1829.
———. *The Code of Virginia: With the Declaration of Independence and Constitution of the United States; and the Declaration of Rights and Constitution of Virginia.* Richmond, Va.: William F. Ritchie, 1849.

Williams, Jane, John Williams, T. V. Moore, and Robert Ryland. *Particulars of the Dreadful Tragedy in Richmond, on the Morning of the 19th July, 1852: Being a Full Account of the Awful Murder of the Winston Family: Embracing All the Particulars of the Discovery of the Bloody Victims, the Testimony before the Coroner's Jury, and the Evidence on the Final Trials of the Murderess and Murderer. Jane and John Williams: Their Sentence, Confessions, and Execution upon the Gallows: Together with the Funeral Sermon of the Rev. Mr. Moore, on the Death of Mrs. Winston and Daughter, and the Sermon of the Rev. Robert Ryland on the Subject of the Murders.* Richmond, Va.: John D. Hammersley, 1852.

Secondary Sources

Adams, Catherine, and Elizabeth H. Pleck. *Love of Freedom: Black Women in Colonial and Revolutionary New England.* New York: Oxford University Press, 2010.

Ailes, Jane, and Marie Tyler-McGraw. "Leaving Virginia for Liberia: Western Virginia Emigrants and Emancipators." *West Virginia History* 6, no. 2 (2012): 1–34.

Allmendinger, David F., Jr. *Nat Turner and the Rising in Southampton County.* Baltimore: Johns Hopkins University Press, 2017.

"Amelia County Marriage Bonds." *William and Mary Quarterly* 17, no. 1 (July 1908): 34–49.

Araujo, Ana Lucia. *Public Memory of Slavery: Victims and Perpetrators in the South Atlantic.* Amherst, N.Y.: Cambria Press, 2010.

Ayers, Edward L. *Vengeance and Justice: Crime and Punishment in the 19th-Century American South.* New York: Oxford University Press, 1984.

Baptist, Edward. *The Half Has Never Been Told: Slavery and the Making of American Capitalism.* New York: Basic Books, 2016.

Barclay, Jennifer L. "Mothering the 'Useless': Black Motherhood, Disability, and Slavery." *Women, Gender, and Families of Color* 2, no. 2 (Fall 2014): 115–140.

Bardaglio, Peter W. "Rape and the Law in the Old South: 'Calculated to Excite Indignation in Every Heart.'" *Journal of Southern History* 60, no. 4 (November 1994): 749–772.

Bauer, Raymond A., and Alice H. Bauer. "Day to Day Resistance to Slavery." *Journal of Negro History* 27 (October 1942): 388–419.

Baumgartner, Alice L. *South to Freedom: Runaway Slaves to Mexico and the Road to the Civil War.* New York: Basic Books, 2020.

Bell, Karen Cook. *Running from Bondage: Enslaved Women and Their Remarkable Fight for Freedom in Revolutionary America.* New York: Cambridge University Press, 2021.

Berlin, Ira. "From Creole to African: Atlantic Creoles and the Origins of African-American Society in Mainland North America." *William and Mary Quarterly* 53, no. 2 (April 1996): 251–288.

———. *Many Thousands Gone: The First Two Centuries of Slavery in North America.* Cambridge, Mass.: Belknap Press of Harvard University Press, 1998.

Berry, Chelsea. "Poisoned Relations: Medical Choices and Poison Accusations within Enslaved Communities." In *Medicine and Healing in the Age of Slavery*, edited by Sean

Morey Smith and Christopher D.E. Willoughby. Baton Rouge: Louisiana State University Press, 2021.

Berry, Daina Ramey. *The Price for Their Pound of Flesh: The Value of the Enslaved, from Womb to Grave, in the Building of a Nation*. Boston: Beacon Press, 2017.

———. *"Swing the Sickle for the Harvest Is Ripe": Gender and Slavery in Antebellum Georgia*. Urbana: University of Illinois Press, 2007.

Billings, Warren M. "The Cases of Fernando and Elizabeth Key: A Note on the Status of Blacks in Seventeenth-Century Virginia." *William and Mary Quarterly* 30, no. 3 (July 1973): 467–474.

———, ed. *The Old Dominion in the Seventeenth Century: A Documentary History of Virginia, 1606–1689*. Chapel Hill: Published for the Institute of Early American History and Culture at Williamsburg, Va., by the University of North Carolina Press, 1975.

Blackett, Richard J. M. *The Captive's Quest for Freedom: Fugitive Slaves, the 1850 Fugitive Slave Law, and the Politics of Slavery*. New York: Cambridge University Press, 2018.

Bogin, Ruth. "Petitioning and the New Moral Economy of Post-Revolutionary America." *William and Mary Quarterly* 45, no. 3 (July 1988): 391–425.

Breen, Patrick H. *The Land Shall Be Deluged in Blood: A New History of the Nat Turner Revolt*. New York: Oxford University Press, 2016.

Brophy, Alfred L. *University, Court, and Slave: Pro-slavery Thought in Southern Colleges and Courts and the Coming Civil War*. New York: Oxford University Press, 2016.

Brown, Kathleen. *Good Wives, Nasty Wenches, and Anxious Patriarchs: Gender, Race, and Power in Colonial Virginia*. Chapel Hill: The University of North Carolina Press, 1996.

Brown, Vincent. *The Reaper's Garden: Death and Power in the World of Atlantic Slavery*. Cambridge, Mass.: Harvard University Press, 2008.

———. "Social Death and Political Life in the Study of Slavery." *American Historical Review* 14, no. 5 (December 2009): 1231–1249.

———. *Tacky's Revolt: The Story of an Atlantic Slave War*. Cambridge, Mass.: Belknap Press of Harvard University Press, 2020.

Bush, Barbara. "African Caribbean Slave Mothers and Children: Traumas of Dislocation and Enslavement across the Atlantic World." *Caribbean Quarterly* 56, no. 1/2 (2010): 69–94.

———. "Hard Labor: Women, Childbirth, and Resistance in British Caribbean Slave Societies." In *More than Chattel: Black Women and Slavery in the Americas*, edited by David Barry Gaspar and Darlene Clark Hine, 193–217. Bloomington: Indiana University Press, 1996.

Bushman, Richard L. *The Refinement of America: Persons, Houses, Cities*. New York: Knopf, 1992.

Bynum, Victoria. *Unruly Women: The Politics of Social and Sexual Control in the Old South*. Chapel Hill: The University of North Carolina Press, 1992.

Camp, Stephanie M. H. *Closer to Freedom: Enslaved Women and Everyday Resistance in the Plantation South*. Chapel Hill: The University of North Carolina Press, 2004.

Campbell, James. "'The Victim of Prejudice and Hasty Consideration': The Slave Trial System in Richmond, Virginia, 1830–61." *Slavery and Abolition* 26, no. 1 (April 2005): 71–91.

Clark, Emily. *The Strange History of the American Quadroon: Free Women of Color in the Revolutionary Atlantic World*. Chapel Hill: The University of North Carolina Press, 2013.

Cody, Cheryll Ann. "Cycles of Work and of Childbearing." In *More than Chattel: Black Women and Slavery in the Americas*, edited by David Barry Gaspar and Darlene Clark Hine, 61–78. Bloomington: Indiana University Press, 1996.

Coombs, John C. "The Phases of Conversion: A New Chronology for the Rise of Slavery in Early Virginia." *William and Mary Quarterly* 68, no. 3 (July 2011): 332–360.

Copeland, Pamela C., and Richard K. MacMaster. *The Five George Masons: Patriots and Planters of Virginia and Maryland*. 2nd ed. Fairfax, Va.: George Mason University Press, 2016.

Davis, Angela. "Reflections on the Black Woman's Role in the Community of Slaves." *Black Scholar* 3, no. 4 (December 1971): 81–100.

de la Fuente, Alejandro, and Ariela Gross. *Becoming Free, Becoming Black: Race, Freedom, and Law in Cuba, Virginia, and Louisiana*. Cambridge: Cambridge University Press, 2020.

Drewry, William Sidney. *The Southampton Insurrection*. Washington, D.C.: Neale Company, 1900.

Dunaway, Wilma A. *The African-American Family in Slavery and Emancipation*. Cambridge: Cambridge University Press, 2003.

Dusinberre, William. *Strategies for Survival: Recollections of Bondage in Antebellum Virginia*. Charlottesville: University of Virginia Press, 2009.

Edwards, Laura F. *A Legal History of the Civil War and Reconstruction: A Nation of Rights*. New York: Cambridge University Press, 2015.

———. *The People and Their Peace: Legal Culture and the Transformation of Inequality in the Post-Revolutionary South*. Chapel Hill: The University of North Carolina Press, 2009.

Egerton, Douglas R. *Gabriel's Rebellion: The Virginia Slave Conspiracies of 1800 and 1802*. Chapel Hill: The University of North Carolina Press, 1993.

Elkins, Stanley. *Slavery: A Problem in American Institutional and Intellectual Life*. Chicago: University of Chicago Press, 1959.

Ellison, Mary. "Resistance to Oppression: Black Women's Response to Slavery in the United States." *Slavery and Abolition* 4, no. 1 (May 1983): 56–63.

Ely, Melvin. *Israel on the Appomattox: A Southern Experiment in Black Freedom from the 1790s through the Civil War*. New York: Vintage Books, 2004.

Everill, Bronwen. *Not Made by Slaves: Ethical Capitalism in the Age of Abolition*. Cambridge, Mass.: Harvard University Press, 2020.

Fabian, Ann. *The Skull Collectors: Race, Science, and America's Unburied Dead*. Chicago: University of Chicago Press, 2010.

Faulkner, Charles James. *The Speech of Charles Jas. Faulkner, of Berkeley in the House of Delegates of Virginia, on the Policy of the State with Respect to Her Slave Population. Delivered*. Richmond, Va.: T. W. White, printer, 1832. Library of Congress.

Fede, Andrew T. *Homicide Justified: The Legality of Killing Slaves in the United States and the Atlantic World*. Athens: University of Georgia Press, 2017.

Feimster, Crystal. *Southern Horrors: Women and the Politics of Rape and Lynching*. Cambridge, Mass.: Harvard University Press, 2009.

Fett, Sharla. *Working Cures: Healing, Health, and Power on Southern Slave Plantations*. Chapel Hill: The University of North Carolina Press, 2002.

Flanigan, Daniel J. *The Criminal Law of Slavery and Freedom, 1800–1868*. New York: Garland, 1987.

———. "Criminal Procedure in Slave Trials in the Antebellum South." *Journal of Southern History* 40, no. 4 (November 1974): 537–564.

Forret, Jeff. *Slave against Slave: Plantation Violence in the Old South*. Baton Rouge: Louisiana State University Press, 2015.

———. *William's Gang: A Notorious Slave Trader and His Cargo of Black Convicts*. New York: Cambridge University Press, 2020.

Franklin, John Hope. *The Militant South, 1800–1861*. Cambridge, Mass.: Belknap Press of Harvard University Press, 1956.

Franklin, John Hope, and Loren Schweninger. *Runaway Slaves: Rebels on the Plantation*. New York: Oxford University Press, 1999.

Fuentes, Marisa J. *Dispossessed Lives: Enslaved Women, Violence, and the Archive*. Philadelphia: University of Pennsylvania Press, 2016.

Genovese, Eugene. *Roll, Jordan, Roll: The World the Slaves Made*. New York: Vintage Books, 1976.

Ghachem, Malick. "The Slave's Two Bodies: The Life of an American Legal Fiction." *William and Mary Quarterly* 60, no. 4 (October 2003): 809–842.

Gikandi, Simon. *Slavery and the Culture of Taste*. Princeton, N.J.: Princeton University Press, 2011.

Glymph, Thavolia. *Out of the House of Bondage: The Transformation of the Plantation Household*. New York: Cambridge University Press, 2008.

———. "Rose's War and the Gendered Politics of a Slave Insurgency in the Civil War." *Journal of the Civil War Era* 3, no. 4 (December 2013): 501–532.

———. *The Women's Fight: The Civil War's Battles for Home, Freedom, and Nation*. Chapel Hill: The University of North Carolina Press, 2020.

Goetz, Rebecca Anne. *The Baptism of Early Virginia: How Christianity Created Race*. Baltimore: Johns Hopkins University Press, 2012.

Gomez, Michael. *Exchanging Our Country Marks: The Transformation of African Identities in the Colonial and Antebellum South*. Chapel Hill: The University of North Carolina Press, 1998.

Gómez, Pablo F. *The Experiential Caribbean: Creating Knowledge and Healing in the Early Modern Atlantic*. Chapel Hill: The University of North Carolina Press, 2017.

Gross, Ariela. *Double Character: Slavery and Mastery in the Antebellum Southern Courtroom*. Princeton, N.J.: Princeton University Press, 2000.

———. *What Blood Won't Tell: A History of Race on Trial in America*. Cambridge, Mass.: Harvard University Press, 2008.

Gross, Kali N. *Colored Amazons: Crime, Violence, and Black Women in the City of Brotherly Love, 1880–1910*. Durham, N.C.: Duke University Press, 2006.

Hadden, Sally. *Slave Patrols: Law and Violence in Virginia and the Carolinas*. Harvard Historical Studies. Cambridge, Mass.: Harvard University Press, 2001.

Haley, Sarah. *No Mercy Here: Gender, Punishment, and the Making of Jim Crow Modernity*. Chapel Hill: The University of North Carolina Press, 2016.

Harris, Cheryl. "Whiteness as Property." *Harvard Law Review* 106, no. 8 (June 1993): 1701–1791.

Hartman, Saidiya. "Seduction and the Ruses of Power." *Callaloo* 19, no. 2 (1992): 537–560.

———. "Venus in Two Acts." *Small Axe: A Caribbean Journal of Criticism* 12, no. 2 (June 2008): 1–14.

Hartog, Hendrik. "Pigs and Positivism." *Wisconsin Law Review*, no. 4 (1985): 899–936.

Hicks, Mary E. "Blood and Hair: Barbers, Sangradores, and the West African Corporeal Imagination in Salvador da Bahia, 1793–1843." In *Medicine and Healing in the Age of Slavery*, edited by Sean Morey Smith and Christopher D.E. Willoughby. Baton Rouge: Louisiana State University Press, 2021.

Higginbotham, A. Leon, Jr. *In the Matter of Color: The Colonial Period.* Vol. 1 of *Race and the American Legal Process.* New York: Oxford University Press, 1978.

———. "Race, Sex, Education, and Missouri Jurisprudence: *Shelley v. Kraemer* in a Historical Perspective. *Washington University Law Quarterly* 67, no. 3 (1989): 673–708.

Hill Edwards, Justene. *Unfree Markets: The Slaves' Economy and the Rise of Capitalism in South Carolina.* New York: Columbia University Press, 2021.

Hine, Darlene Clark. *Hine Sight: Black Women and the Re-construction of American History.* Bloomington: Indiana University Press, 1994.

———. "Rape and the Inner Lives of Black Women in the Middle West: Preliminary Thoughts on the Culture of Dissemblance." *Signs: Journal of Women in Culture and Society* 14, no. 4 (1989): 912–920.

Hogarth, Rana. *Medicalizing Blackness: Making Racial Difference in the Atlantic World, 1780–1840.* Chapel Hill: The University of North Carolina Press, 2017.

Holden, Vanessa M. "Generation, Resistance, and Survival: African-American Children and the Southampton Rebellion of 1831." *Slavery and Abolition* 38, no. 4 (2017): 673–696.

———. *Surviving Southampton: African American Women and Resistance in Nat Turner's Community.* Urbana: University of Illinois Press, 2021.

Horne, Gerald. *The Counter-Revolution of 1776: Slave Resistance and the Origins of the United States of America.* New York: New York University Press, 2016.

Hunter, Tera. *Bound in Wedlock: Slave and Free Black Marriage in the Nineteenth Century.* Cambridge, Mass.: Belknap Press of Harvard University Press, 2017.

Jackson, Kellie Carter. *Force and Freedom: Black Abolitionists and the Politics of Violence.* Philadelphia: University of Pennsylvania Press, 2019.

Jarvis, Michael J. "Bermuda and the Beginnings of Black Anglo-America." In *Virginia 1619: Slavery and Freedom in the Making of English America*, edited by Paul Musselwhite, Peter C. Mancall, and James Horn. Williamsburg, Va.: Omohundro Institute of Early American History and Culture; Chapel Hill: The University of North Carolina Press, 2019.

Jennings, Thelma. "'Us Colored Women Had to Go through a Plenty': Sexual Exploitation of African-American Slave Women." *Journal of Women's History* 1, no. 3 (Winter 1990): 45–74.

Johnson, Jessica Marie. *Wicked Flesh: Black Women, Intimacy, and Freedom in the Atlantic World.* Philadelphia: University of Pennsylvania Press, 2020.

Johnson, Michael P. "Smothered Slave Infants: Were Slave Mothers at Fault?" *Journal of Southern History* 47, no. 4 (1981): 493–520.

Johnson, Walter. *Soul by Soul: Life inside the Antebellum Slave Market.* Cambridge, Mass.: Harvard University Press, 1999.

———. "To Remake the World: Slavery, Racial Capitalism, and Justice." In "Race, Capitalism, Justice," edited by Walter Johnson and Robin D. G. Kelley. Forum 1, *Boston Review*, 2017, 11–31.

Jones-Rogers, Stephanie. "'[S]he Could . . . Spare One Ample Breast for the Profit of Her Owner': White Mothers and Enslaved Wet Nurses' Invisible Labor in American Slave Markets." *Slavery and Abolition* 38, no. 2 (2017): 337–355.

———. *They Were Her Property: White Women as Slave Owners in the American South.* New Haven, Conn.: Yale University Press, 2019.

Kaye, Anthony E. *Joining Places: Slave Neighborhoods in the Old South.* Chapel Hill: The University of North Carolina Press, 2007.

———. "Neighborhoods and Nat Turner: The Making of a Slave Rebel and the Unmaking of a Slave Rebellion." *Journal of the Early Republic* 27, no. 4 (2007): 705–720.

Kelley, Robin D. G. *Race Rebels: Culture, Politics, and the Black Working Class.* New York: Free Press, 1996.

Kennington, Kelly. *In the Shadow of Dred Scott: St. Louis Freedom Suits and the Legal Culture of Slavery in Antebellum America.* Athens: University of Georgia Press, 2017.

King, Wilma. "'Mad' Enough to Kill: Enslaved Women, Murder, and Southern Courts." In "Women, Slavery, and Historical Research." *Journal of African American History* 92, no. 1 (Winter 2007): 37–56.

———. "'Prematurely Knowing of Evil Things': The Sexual Abuse of African American Girls and Young Women in Slavery and Freedom." *Journal of African American History* 99, no. 3 (Summer 2014): 173–196.

———. *Stolen Childhood: Slave Youth in Nineteenth-Century America.* Bloomington: Indiana University Press, 1995.

Kolchin, Peter. *American Slavery: 1619–1877.* New York: Macmillan, 2003.

Kulikoff, Allan. *Tobacco and Slaves: The Development of Southern Cultures in the Chesapeake, 1680–1800.* Chapel Hill: The University of North Carolina Press, 1986.

Lebsock, Suzanne. "Free Black Women and the Question of Matriarchy: Petersburg, Virginia 1784–1820." *Feminist Studies* 8, no. 2 (1982): 270–292.

LeFlouria, Talitha. *Chained in Silence: Black Women and Convict Labor in the New South.* Chapel Hill: The University of North Carolina Press, 2015.

Link, William A. *Roots of Secession: Slavery and Politics in Antebellum Virginia.* Chapel Hill: The University of North Carolina Press, 2003.

Lounsbury, Carl R. *The Courthouses of Early Virginia: An Architectural History.* Charlottesville: University of Virginia Press, 2005.

Lowe, Jessica K. *Murder in the Shenandoah: Making Law Sovereign in Revolutionary Virginia.* New York: Cambridge University Press, 2019.

Lubet, Steven. *Fugitive Justice: Runaways, Rescuers, and Slavery on Trial.* Cambridge, Mass.: Belknap Press of Harvard University Press, 2010.

Maris-Wolf, Ted. *Family Bonds: Free Blacks and Re-enslavement Law in Antebellum Virginia.* Chapel Hill: The University of North Carolina Press, 2015.

Matthews, Linda H. *Middling Folk: Three Seas, Three Centuries, One Scots-Irish Family.* Chicago: Chicago Review Press, 2010.

McCurry, Stephanie. *Confederate Reckoning: Power and Politics in the Civil War South.* Cambridge: Harvard University Press, 2010.

———. *Women's War: Fighting and Surviving the American Civil War.* Cambridge, Mass.: Belknap Press of Harvard University Press, 2019.

McKinley, Michelle. *Fractional Freedoms: Slavery, Intimacy, and Legal Mobilization in Colonial Lima, 1600–1700.* New York: Cambridge University Press, 2016.

McKittrick, Katherine. "Mathematics of Black Life." *Black Scholar* 44, no. 2 (June 2014): 16–28.

McLaurin, Melton. *Celia, a Slave: A True Story of Violence and Retribution in Antebellum Missouri.* Athens: University of Georgia Press, 1991.

McNair, Glenn. "Slave Women, Capital Crime, and Criminal Justice in Georgia." *Georgia Historical Quarterly* 93, no. 2 (Summer 2009): 135–158.

McPherson, James. *Battle Cry of Freedom: The Civil War Era.* New York: Oxford University Press, 1988.

Merkel, William G. "Jefferson's Failed Anti-slavery Proviso of 1784 and the Nascence of Free Soil Constitutionalism." *Seton Hall Law Review* 38, no. 2 (2008): 555–603.

Merry, Sally Engle. *Getting Justice and Getting Even: Legal Consciousness among Working-Class Americans.* Chicago: University of Chicago Press, 1990.

Miles, Tiya. *All That She Carried: The Journey of Ashley's Sack, a Black Family Keepsake.* New York: Random House, 2021.

Mills, Brandon. *The World Colonization Made: The Racial Geography of Early American Empire.* Philadelphia: University of Pennsylvania Press, 2020.

Millward, Jessica. *Finding Charity's Folk: Enslaved and Free Black Women in Maryland.* Athens: University of Georgia Press, 2015.

Morgan, Edmund S. *American Slavery, American Freedom: The Ordeal of Colonial Virginia.* New York: W. W. Norton, 2003.

———. *Inventing the People: The Rise of Popular Sovereignty in England and America.* New York: W. W. Norton, 1988.

Morgan, Jennifer L. *Laboring Women: Reproduction and Gender in New World Slavery.* Philadelphia: University of Pennsylvania Press, 2004.

———. *"Partus sequitur ventrem*: Law, Race, and Reproduction in Colonial Slavery." *Small Axe: A Caribbean Journal of Criticism* 22, no. 1 (2018): 1–17.

———. *Reckoning with Slavery: Gender, Kinship, and Capitalism in the Early Black Atlantic.* Durham, N.C.: Duke University Press, 2021.

Morgan, Philip D. *Slave Counterpoint: Black Culture in the Eighteenth Century Chesapeake and Lowcountry.* Chapel Hill: University of North Carolina Press, 1998.

———. "Virginia Slavery in Atlantic Context, 1550 to 1650," in *Virginia 1619: Slavery and Freedom in the Making of English America,* edited by Paul Musselwhite, Peter C. Mancall, and James Horn. Williamsburg, Va.: Omohundro Institute of Early American History and Culture; Chapel Hill: University of North Carolina Press, 2019.

Morris, Thomas D. *Southern Slavery and the Law, 1619–1860.* Chapel Hill: University of North Carolina Press, 1996.

Mustakeem, Sowande M. *Slavery at Sea: Terror, Sex, and Sickness in the Middle Passage.* Urbana: University of Illinois Press, 2016.

Myers, Amrita Chakrabarti. *Forging Freedom: Black Women and the Pursuit of Liberty in Antebellum Charleston*. Chapel Hill: University of North Carolina Press, 2011.

Nunley, Tamika Y. *At the Threshold of Liberty: Women, Slavery and Shifting Identities in Washington, D.C.* Chapel Hill: University of North Carolina Press, 2021.

Oakes, James. *Freedom National: The Destruction of Slavery in the United States, 1861–1865*. New York: W. W. Norton, 2013.

Oates, Stephen B. *To Purge This Land with Blood: A Biography of John Brown*. New York: Harper & Row, 1970.

Obladen, Michael. "Lethal Lullabies: A History of Opium Use in Infants." *Journal of Human Lactation* 32, no. 1 (February 2016): 75–85.

Onuf, Peter S. *Jefferson's Empire: The Language of American Nationhood*. Charlottesville: University Press of Virginia, 2000.

Ostler, Jeffrey. *Surviving Genocide: Native Nations and the United States from the American Revolution to Bleeding Kansas*. New Haven, Conn.: Yale University Press, 2019.

Owens, Deirdre Cooper. *Medical Bondage: Race, Gender, and the Origins of American Gynecology*. Athens: University of Georgia Press, 2017.

Penningroth, Dylan C. *The Claims of Kinfolk: African American Property and Community in the Nineteenth-Century South*. Chapel Hill: University of North Carolina Press, 2003.

Perrin, Liese. "Resisting Reproduction: Reconsidering Slave Contraception in the Old South." *Journal of American Studies* 35, no. 2 (2001): 255–274.

Peters, Joan W. *Slave and Free Negro Records from the Prince William County Court Minute and Order Books*. Broad Run, Va.: Albemarle Research, 1996.

Peters, John O., and Margaret T. Peters. *Virginia's Historic Courthouses*. Charlottesville: University Press of Virginia, 1995.

Phillips, Ulrich Bonnell. *American Negro Slavery: A Survey of the Supply, Employment and Control of Negro Labor, as Determined by the Plantation Régime*. New York: D. Appleton, 1918.

Preyer, Kathryn. "Crime, the Criminal Law and Reform in Post-Revolutionary Virginia." *Law and History Review* 1, no. 1 (Spring 1983): 53–85.

Reinhardt, Mark. *Who Speaks for Margaret Garner? The True Story That Inspired Toni Morrison's "Beloved."* Minneapolis: University of Minnesota Press, 2010.

Richeson, Marques P. D. "Sex, Drugs, and . . . Race-to-Castrate: A Black Box Warning of Chemical Castration's Potential Racial Side Effects." *Harvard BlackLetter Law Journal* 25 (2009): 95–131.

Robinson, Cedric J. *Black Marxism: The Making of the Black Radical Tradition*. Chapel Hill: University of North Carolina Press, 2000.

Root, Erik S., ed. *Sons of the Fathers: The Virginia Slavery Debates of 1831–1832*. Lanham, Md.: Lexington Books, 2010.

Rosso, Ana Maria. "Poppy and Opium in Ancient Times: Remedy or Narcotic?" *Biomedicine International* 1 (2010): 81–87.

Rugemer, Edward. *Slave Law and the Politics of Resistance in the Early Atlantic World*. Cambridge, Mass.: Harvard University Press, 2018.

Sanders, Stuart W. *Murder on the Ohio Belle*. Lexington: University Press of Kentucky, 2020.

Savage, John. "'Black Magic' and White Terror: Slave Poisoning and Colonial Society in Early 19th Century Martinique." *Journal of Social History* 40, no. 3 (2007): 635–662.

Savitt, Todd L. *Medicine and Slavery: The Diseases and Health Care of Blacks in Antebellum Virginia.* Urbana: University of Illinois Press, 1981.

Schwartz, Marie Jenkins. *Birthing a Slave: Motherhood and Medicine in the Antebellum South.* Cambridge, Mass.: Harvard University Press, 2010.

Schwarz, Philip J. *Slave Laws in Virginia.* Athens: University of Georgia Press, 1996.

———. *Twice Condemned: Slaves and the Criminal Laws of Virginia, 1705–1865.* Baton Rouge: Louisiana State University Press, 1988.

Schweninger, Loren. *Appealing for Liberty: Freedom Suits in the South.* New York: Oxford University Press, 2018.

———. "The Roots of Enterprise: Black-Owned Businesses in Virginia, 1830–1880." *Virginia Magazine of History and Biography* 100, no. 4 (1992): 515–542.

———. "The Vass Slaves: County Courts, State Laws, and Slavery in Virginia, 1831–1861." *Virginia Magazine of History and Biography* 114, no. 4 (2006): 465–495.

Scott, Arthur Pearson. *Criminal Law in Colonial Virginia.* Chicago: University of Chicago Press, 1930.

Scott, James C. *Domination and the Arts of Resistance: Hidden Transcripts.* New Haven, Conn.: Yale University Press, 1990.

Sharpe, Christina. *In the Wake: On Blackness and Being.* Durham, N.C.: Duke University Press, 2016.

Siddali, Silvana R. *From Property to Person: Slavery and the Confiscation Acts, 1861–1862.* Baton Rouge: Louisiana State University Press, 2005.

Sinha, Manisha. *The Slave's Cause: A History of Abolition.* New Haven, Conn.: Yale University Press, 2016.

Snyder, Terri L. *Brabbling Women: Disorderly Speech and the Law in Early Virginia.* Ithaca, N.Y.: Cornell University Press, 2003.

Sommerville, Diane Miller. "The Rape Myth in the Old South Reconsidered." *Journal of Southern History* 61, no. 3 (August 1995): 481–518.

Spillers, Hortense. "Mama's Baby, Papa's Maybe: An American Grammar Book." *Diacritics* 17, no. 2 (Summer 1987): 64–81.

Stampp, Kenneth. *The Peculiar Institution: Slavery in the Ante-Bellum South.* New York: Vintage Books, 1956.

Stevens, Charles Emery. *Anthony Burns: A History.* Boston: John P. Jewett, 1856.

Stevenson, Brenda E. "Gender Convention, Ideals, and Identity among Antebellum Virginia Slave Women." In *More than Chattel: Black Women and Slavery in the Americas,* edited by David Barry Gaspar and Darlene Clark Hine, 169–190. Bloomington: Indiana University Press, 1996.

———. *Life in Black and White: Family and Community in the Slave South.* New York: Oxford University Press, 1997.

———. "What's Love Got to Do with It? Concubinage and Enslaved Women and Girls in the Antebellum South." In "Women, Slavery and the Atlantic World." Special issue, *Journal of African American History* 98, no. 1 (Winter 2013): 99–125.

Stowe, Harriet Beecher. *Uncle Tom's Cabin.* Boston: John P. Jewett, 1852.

Strang, Cameron B. *Frontiers of Science: Imperialism and Natural Knowledge in the Gulf South Borderlands, 1500–1850.* Williamsburg, Va.: Omohundro Institute of Early American History and Culture; Chapel Hill: University of North Carolina Press, 2018.

Stuart, Charles. "On the Use of Slave Produce." *Quarterly Anti-slavery Magazine* (American Anti-slavery Society) 2 (January 1837): 153–175.

Sweet, James H. "Defying Social Death: The Multiple Configurations of African Slave Family in the Atlantic World." *William and Mary Quarterly* 70, no. 2 (April 2013): 251–272.

———. *Domingos Álvares, African Healing, and the Intellectual History of the Atlantic World.* Chapel Hill: University of North Carolina Press, 2011.

Takagi, Midori. *"Rearing Wolves to Our Own Destruction": Slavery in Richmond, Virginia, 1782–1865.* Charlottesville: University Press of Virginia, 1999.

Taylor, Alan. *American Colonies: The Settling of North America.* New York: Penguin Books, 2001.

———. *The Internal Enemy: Slavery and War in Virginia, 1772–1832.* New York: W. W. Norton, 2013.

———. *Thomas Jefferson's Education.* New York: W. W. Norton, 2019.

Taylor, Amy Murrell. *Embattled Freedom: Journeys through the Civil War's Slave Refugee Camps.* Chapel Hill: University of North Carolina Press, 2018.

Taylor, Nikki M. *Driven toward Madness: The Fugitive Slave Margaret Garner and Tragedy on the Ohio.* Athens: Ohio University Press, 2016.

Thomas, William, III. *A Question of Freedom: The Families Who Challenged Slavery from the Nation's Founding to the Civil War.* New Haven, Conn.: Yale University Press, 2020.

Tomlins, Christopher. *Freedom Bound: Law, Labor, and Civic Identity in Colonizing English America, 1580–1865.* New York: Cambridge University Press, 2010.

Tragle, Henry Irving. *The Southampton Slave Revolt of 1831: A Compilation of Source Material.* Amherst: University of Massachusetts Press, 1971.

Turner, Felicity. "Rights and the Ambiguities of Law: Infanticide in the Nineteenth-Century U.S. South." *Journal of the Civil War Era* 4, no. 3 (September 2014): 350–372.

Turner, Sasha. *Contested Bodies: Pregnancy, Childrearing, and Slavery in Jamaica.* Philadelphia: University of Pennsylvania Press, 2017.

Tushnet, Mark V. *The American Law of Slavery, 1810–1860: Considerations of Humanity and Interest.* Princeton, N.J.: Princeton University Press, 1981.

Twitty, Anne. *Before Dred Scott: Slavery and Legal Culture in the American Confluence, 1787–1857.* New York: Cambridge University Press, 2016.

Von Daacke, Kirt. *Freedom Has a Face: Race, Identity, and Community in Jefferson's Virginia.* Charlottesville: University of Virginia Press, 2012.

Ward, Harry M. *Public Executions in Richmond, Virginia: A History, 1782–1907.* Jefferson, N.C.: McFarland, 2012.

Washington, Harriet A. *Medical Apartheid: The Dark History of Medical Experimentation on Black Americans from Colonial Times to the Present.* New York: Anchor Books, 2006.

Webster, Crystal L. "'Hanging Pretty Girls': The Criminalization of African American Children in Early America." *Journal of the Early Republic* 42, no. 2 (May 2022): 253–276.

Wecht, Cyril H. "The History of Legal Medicine." *Journal of the American Academy of Psychiatry and the Law* 33, no. 2 (June 2005): 245–251.

Weisenburger, Steven. *Modern Medea: A Family Story of Slavery and Child-Murder from the Old South.* New York: Hill and Wang, 1998.

Welch, Kimberly. *Black Litigants in the Antebellum American South*. Chapel Hill: University of North Carolina Press, 2018.

West, Mary Hope, and Juliet Fauntleroy. "The Muse (Mewes) Family of the Northern Neck of Virginia (Concluded)." *Virginia Magazine of History and Biography* 53, no. 4 (October 1945): 312–323.

White, Deborah Gray. *Ar'n't I a Woman? Female Slaves in the Plantation South*. New York: W. W. Norton, 1985.

———. "Introduction: Scarlet and Black—a Reconciliation." In *Scarlet and Black*, vol. 1, *Slavery and Dispossession in Rutgers History*, edited by Marisa J. Fuentes and Deborah Gray White, 1–5. New Brunswick, N.J.: Rutgers University Press, 2016.

Wilder, Craig Steven. *Ebony and Ivy: Race, Slavery, and the Troubled History of America's Universities*. New York: Bloomsbury, 2013.

Williams, Heather Andrea. *Help Me to Find My People: The African American Search for Family Lost in Slavery*. Chapel Hill: The University of North Carolina Press, 2012.

Winters, Lisa Ze. *The Mulatta Concubine: Terror, Intimacy, Freedom, and Desire in the Black Transatlantic*. Athens: University of Georgia Press, 2016.

Woodard, Vincent. *The Delectable Negro: Human Consumption and Homoeroticism within U.S. Slave Culture*. New York: New York University Press, 2014.

Wyatt-Brown, Bertram. *Southern Honor: Ethics and Behavior in the Old South*. New York: Oxford University Press, 1982.

Index

abolition, 44, 74, 81, 83, 128, 130, 144, 150–154

Adaline (slave), 157

Adeline (slave), 169

African-descended women, xii, 1; alleged criminal activity, threat posed by, 2–3; Black radical tradition and, 15, 24; breaking enslaved people and, 10, 159, 161; chattel principle and, 32, 40–41; commodification process and, 1, 14, 20, 117–118; communicative power, loss of, 3–5, 16; criminality, presumption of, 3–4, 9, 10; domestic slave trade and, 2, 7, 8, 9, 44–45, 75, 84; double character paradox, thrice condemned and, 11; gendered experiences of bondage and, 2, 11, 15–16, 17, 23, 53; healers, intellectuals/social leaders and, 57, 59, 72, 85–86; historic records and, 1, 3–4, 181; inherited slavery, enslaved women's reproductive labor and, 29–30, 31, 32, 34, 54, 117–118; kinship, function/meaning of, 9, 14–15, 16, 23, 42–43, 54, 126, 132, 137, 158; legal consciousness, development of, 12–14, 35–36; legal justice, inaccessibility of, 1–2, 3, 20, 28; neighborhoods, political institution/idea of, 9, 16; power dynamics, contested spaces and, 1, 2–3, 5, 24; racial capitalism, property rules and, 14, 15, 17, 18–19; reproductive labor and, 21, 29–30, 31, 32, 34, 41, 54, 56, 117–118, 150; resistance, acts of, 2, 5–6, 7, 10–11, 15, 16–17; slave laws and, 6–7, 10–11, 14, 54, 56; slavery, natural condition of, 31–32; Southern justice ideals and, 17–20, 65, 75, 111; spaces/geographies, strategic understanding of, 5, 9–10; survival orientation, blackness defined and, 15–16; white slaveholders, presumed rights of, 1, 2–3, 5, 6–7, 16–17, 53–56. *See also* Clemency; Colonization; Commonwealth of Virginia; Contemporary racial divisions; Criminal justice system; Infanticide; Justice; Slave insurgency; Slave trade; Slavery; Slaves; Virginia Colony

Algonquian people, 28, 30–31

Allen, Matthew, 68–70

American Confluence, 12

Anti-slavery movement, 74–75, 77–78, 83, 86, 128, 130–131, 143, 144, 153

Arson, 21; accidental arsons, commuted sentences for, 160; Adaline, Stonnell house arson and, 157; Alberta, house arson accusation of, 162; Booton barn arson and, 161–162; Celia, Law house arson and, 173–174; Civil War context and, 22; clemency/commuted sentences and, 126, 160; damage/loss from, 156–157; evidence, insufficiency of, 22; Fanny, arson accusation of, 158–159; Frances, house arson by, 155–158; Jenny, Pickett barn arson and, 157; Lavinia, Hill house arson and, 173; Lucy, Hagerty house arson and, 159–160; Lucy Barker, Raines house arson and, 160–161; Mary, culpability of, 126; Milly, Robe family barn arson and, 47; Nancy, Brooks barn arson and, 160; Nelly, Green house arson and, 87–90; Peggy, Francis house arson and, 146–148; transportation remedy for, 82, 147, 160–161; Virginia vs. West Virginia legal landscape and, 22. *See also* Slave insurgency

Bacon, Nathaniel, 32, 33

Bacon's rebellion, 32–33, 34

Bagby, George W., 163
Baless, Thomas B., 89
Banneker, Benjamin, 43
Barrow, John T., 148–150
Barrow, Mary, 149
Bates, William, 110
Batton, Thomas, 124, 125
Beck, John Brodhead, 115
Beck, Theodoric Romeyn, 115, 119
Benefit of the Clergy provision, 35, 36, 60
Berkeley, William, 32, 33
Booton, John, 161–162
Branson, Sarah, 91
Branson, Stephen, 91
breaking enslaved people, 10, 159, 161
Brightwell, 71
Brooks, William, 160
Brophy, Alfred L., 151
Brown, Kathleen, 29
Brown, Vincent, 145
Buchanan, James, 154
Buckner, Margaret (slave), 99–100
Burns, Anthony (slave), 80
Bush, Barbara, 120
Bushman, Richard L., 26
Butler, Anne, 75
Butler, Patrick, 75, 79
Byrd, Lucy Parke, 51

Camp, Stephanie M. H., 5, 145
Carter, Henry L., 128
Cary, John, 177–178
Champion, Charles B., 100
Chase, Salmon P., 129
chattel principle, 32, 40–41
Chesapeake, xii, 26, 28, 30, 31, 34.
    See also Virginia Colony
Civil Rights Act of 1866, 187
Civil War: Civil Rights Act of 1866 and,
    187; clemency, expanded concept of,
    184; New South, reconstituted legal
    framework and, 181; recovery from, 181;
    slave resistance strategies, development
    of, 22, 84–85, 145, 146, 149; Southern
    states, secession and, 154–155, 163–164;

war conditions, leveraging of, 155,
    162–168, 173, 175; wartime social/
    political transformations and, 184.
    See also Contemporary racial divisions;
    Slave insurgency
clemency, 2, 8–9; acquittals, return to
    slavery and, 98, 114; adulthood status
    and, 90–91; anti-slavery movement and,
    77–78, 128; benefit of the Clergy
    provision and, 35, 36, 60; benevolence/
    evenhandedness, myth of, 8, 17–18, 98,
    114, 157; expanded legal concept of, 184;
    freedom lawsuits and, 11–13, 35; gender
    and, 11, 13–14, 114; girlhood status and,
    126; Hatcher case, Jackson murder and,
    76–78; hearsay evidence/genealogies,
    role of, 12; innocence, capacity for, 37;
    interracial cooperation/support and, 19;
    legal consciousness, development of, 13,
    35–36; legal redress, access to, 12–14, 19,
    28; leniency, varied perspectives on, 162;
    local contexts, communalism and, 11–12,
    17, 18, 19, 87; local petitioners and,
    87–90; malice/intent, felonious charges
    and, 9, 114; mercy, power/logic behind,
    90–91; paternalism, justice ideals and,
    17–18; penal reform movement and, 9;
    performative gesture of, 9; personhood,
    assertion of, 12–13; racial capitalism,
    property rules and, 14, 15, 17, 18–19;
    slaveholders/slave trade, interests of,
    9–10; social hierarchy, maintenance of,
    35–36, 37, 114; transportation remedy
    and, 8, 9–10, 17, 98; violence in slavery
    and, 19–20; Whigs, judicial/political
    influence of, 74, 75–79. *See also* Arson;
    Contemporary racial divisions; Criminal
    justice system; Infanticide; Justice;
    Murder; Poisonings; Reprieve; Slave
    insurgency
Clifford, G. W., 208
Collins, Robert, 163
colonization, xi, 20; African captives,
    commodification of, xi, 1; Atlantic
    world, European power dynamics and,

xi–xii; Bacon's rebellion and, 32–33, 34; colonial economic viability, slave labor and, 30–32, 34; English common law, role of, 14, 31, 122, 181–182; free colonists, protected economic interests of, 33; imperial outposts, slave labor in, xi, 10, 34–35; inherited slavery, enslaved women's reproductive labor and, 29–30, 31, 32, 34; insurrection, capacity for, 32–33; justice, changed genealogy of, 181–182; multiethnic collaboration, rebellion and, 32–33, 34; Native populations, land claims of, xii, 26, 27; secularized law, sustained slavery and, 36, 40; slave importation monopoly, dissolution of, 34; slave resistance, legal response to, 6; slaves' legal status and, xi, xii, 1–2, 3, 31–32, 34; Virginia Colony, charter for, 28; warfare/violence, new dimensions of, 32–34. *See also* African-descended women; Slave trade; Slaves; Virginia Colony

Colton, Joseph Hutchins, 61

Commonwealth of Virginia, 40; African-descended people, slavery and, 40; African-descended people, supposed mental capabilities of, 43–44; African women, status/matrilinarity and, 42; anti-slavery movement and, 74–75, 77–78, 128; Black men's sexuality, legal framework for, 118; bodies of enslaved, collective governance/correction and, 43; Civil War context and, 21–22, 84–85; compliant enslaved people, myth of, 42, 52; Constitution of 1776 and, 44; domestic slave trade, expansion of, 44–45, 46; eastern agricultural region and, 60–61; emancipation, obstacles to, 44, 48; enslaved women, independence of mind and, 45–50, 133; escaped slaves and, 49–50; gatherings/assemblies, illegality of, 43; hired-out slave labor and, 60–61; importation of slaves, prohibition of, 44; indentured servants, pregnancy and, 117–118; infanticide,

reproductive labor and, 47–49; interracial sexual relationships and, 118, 125; kinship/community, multiethnic connections and, 42–43, 49, 50; liberty for the enslaved, idea of, 40; luxury goods/lifestyle and, 52; medical jurisprudence, development of, 119–120; overseers, legal protection of, 46; penitentiary labor, offending slaves and, 162–163; power dynamics, discord/incongruity of, 45–48; propertied white men, liberty for, 40; race distinctions, phenotype and law, 40–41, 44; race epistemologies, legal landscape and, 40–45; racial science, gendered theories about, 41, 42; racial slavery, legal maintenance of, 40, 44–45; regional economy, slave labor and, 54; reproductive labor, slaveholder property interests and, 41, 45, 48, 50, 52; revolutionary rhetoric, language of slavery and, 40; Richmond, Confederate capital and, 22, 184; secularized rights, yeomanry/planter aristocracy and, 40, 60; slave law, logics of, 43, 44–45, 46, 47, 48, 50, 52, 54, 56, 75; slaveholder property interests and, 41, 45, 48, 50, 52; Southern law, supposed Black inferiority and, 41–42; western agricultural region and, 60; Whigs, political/judicial influence of, 74, 75–79. *See also* Contemporary racial divisions; Slave insurgency; Virginia Colony

Commonwealth v. Agnes, 109–110, 111
Commonwealth v. Gerard Mason, 110, 111
communalism, 11–12, 17, 18, 19, 87
Confiscation Act of 1861/1862, 163
contemporary racial divisions, 181; Black women, activism/political organizing of, 188; Black women, perceived criminality of, 188; blackness/womanhood, modern epistemologies of, 188; capital crimes, slaveholder recourse and, 185; Civil Rights Act of 1866 and, 187; Civil War, impact of, 184–185, 187; clemency,

contemporary racial divisions (*Continued*)
legal concept of, 183–184, 185; convict
leasing, exploited Black women's labor
and, 188, 189; criminal law, uneven
application of, 187, 188; English common
law and, 181–182; enslaved women,
culpability/criminality of, 187; Fourteenth
Amendment, equal protection promise
and, 187; free Black communities, building
of, 188–189; Freedman's Savings Bank and,
189; historic plantations/houses, visitors
to, 181; inheritability of slavery and, 182;
justice, slaves' attitudes/ideas about,
184–186; legal outcomes, racialized
perceptions and, 187, 188; legalized
oppression, purging of, 181; Native/
African peoples, neglected historic
presence of, 181; Native lands, theft of, 181,
182, 187; New South, reconstituted legal
framework and, 181–182, 188–189; police
brutality, current climate of, 188; race
ideology, colonial law and, 182; rape/
lynching, transition to freedom and, 188;
Reconstruction era and, 187–188;
reproductive labor, slaveholder profit and,
182; segregation, laws based on, 181, 182,
188; segregation, policing/paternalistic
state and, 188; sharecropping system, debt
peonage and, 188–189; slave insurgency,
continuity of, 182–184, 187; slaveholder
wrongdoings and, 185–186; slaveholding/
non-slaveholding regional split and, 184;
slavery, Southern legal commitment to,
186–187; Southern infrastructure,
rebuilding of, 188, 189; Southern
slaveholder prosperity and, 182, 184–185;
trust/intimacy, enslaved exploitation of,
182–183. *See also* African-descended
women; Commonwealth of Virginia;
Criminal justice system; Justice; Slave
insurgency; Slavery; Slaves; Virginia
Colony
criminal justice system: abortion,
criminalization of, 60; appeals of
convictions and, 8; benefit of the Clergy
provision and, 35, 36, 60; benevolence,
myth of, 8–9; Black criminality,
presumption of, 3–4, 9, 10, 23, 37; Black
men's sexuality, legal framework for, 118;
Christian faith, profession of, 36, 37;
clemency/pardons, rationale for, 2, 4,
8–10, 21; commodification process,
institutionalization of, 4; communicative power, loss of, 3–5, 16; criminal
boundaries, racial/gendered lines and,
53; disciplinary measures and, 6, 39–40;
dismemberment, corrective measure of,
39–40; domestic slave trade and, 2, 7, 8,
9, 10, 44–45, 75, 84; double character
paradox and, 11; English common law,
role of, 14, 28, 31, 37–38, 122; enslaved
women, independence of mind and,
45–49; executed enslaved people and, 8,
9, 17, 22, 53–54, 113; finger screws,
voluntary confessions and, 65; free Black
witnesses and, 91; freedom lawsuits and,
11–13, 48; Gabriel's Conspiracy and, 8;
indentured servants, pregnancy and,
117–118; interracial sexual relations and,
117–118, 125; legal consciousness,
development of, 12–14, 35–36; legal
redress, access to, 1–2, 4, 12–14, 28;
legislative measures, slaveholder
influence and, 54, 56; local contexts and,
11–12, 17, 18, 19, 36; malice/intent,
felonious charges and, 9, 33, 39, 75, 90,
108, 114, 116; medical jurisprudence,
development of, 115–116, 119–120, 137;
penal reform movement and, 9;
personhood, assertion of, 12–13;
petitioning process and, 19–20, 21,
87–90, 144; poisonings and, 59–60;
punishment, racial/gendered logics of,
4, 7–8, 9, 53–54, 117–118; racial capitalism, property rules and, 14, 15, 17, 18–19;
racial identity, conceptualization/
performance of, 11; rape of enslaved
women and, 111–112, 117–118, 188;
reproductive considerations, execution
and, 45, 46, 47, 92, 108–109; resistance,

acts of, 5–6, 7, 10–11, 15, 16–17; rival jurisprudence, enslaved women and, 6; segregated slave courts and, 7, 8, 37; sentencing practices and, 7–8, 18, 19; sexual exploitation, enslaved women/ girls and, 117–118; slave killings, slaveholder rights and, 33, 39–40, 54; slave laws, changes in, 10–11, 54, 56, 59–60; slave laws, development of, 6–7, 11, 14; slaves/minorities, revised legal codes and, 37–39, 54, 56; social engineering, sexual interactions and, 117–119; Southern exploitative culture and, 4, 5, 8, 15; Southern justice ideals and, 17–20, 65, 75, 130, 131; testimonies, bondage experience and, 5–6, 7, 8, 36–37, 54, 96; transportation law and, 8, 9–10, 11, 17; Whigs, judicial/political influence of, 74, 75–79. *See also* African-descended women; Clemency; Commonwealth of Virginia; Justice; Virginia Colony
Crocket, Joseph M., 140
Custis, Mary Anna Randolph, 58

Davis, Angela, 15
Davis, Ann Banks (slave), 168
Davis, Hector, 168
Davis, Jefferson, 172
Davis, Joseph, 166
Davison, Henry, 72
Dearman, James, 127, 128
Dew, Thomas Roderick, 148, 150, 151, 152, 187
double character paradox, 11
Drewry, William Sidney, 150
Duvall, Henry, 110

Eacho, Edward D., 175
Edwards, Laura F., 11, 19
Ely, Melvin, 19
emancipation, 44, 48, 150–154, 163, 176, 181, 184
Emancipation Proclamation of 1863, 163, 176
English common law, 14, 31, 122, 181–182
escape, 21–22, 49–50, 80, 107, 163–172, 179–180. *See also* Slave insurgency; Theft

Fallan, Charles W., 84
Fannie (slave), 133
Fariss, John, 92
Fariss, Martha, 92
Feimster, Crystal, 164, 188
Fett, Sharla, 57, 59
Floyd, John Buchanan, 76, 128
Forbes, Edwin A., 171
Fore, Judith, 134
Forret, Jeff, 17, 135
Foster, James, 110
Fourteenth Amendment, 187
Francis, John, 145, 146–148
Francis, Lavinia, 149–150
Francis, Nathaniel, 149–150
Freedman's Savings Bank, 189; Freedom, xi, xii, Aggie's petition for, 35; benefit of the Clergy provision and, 35; Civil War, enslaved people's participation in, 155; enslaved women's rituals of, 166–167; escaped slaves and, 21–22, 39, 49–50, 129–131; free Black bodies, exploitative examination of, 116; free Black communities, building of, 188–189; free Black people, rights of, 1, 7, 12, 35; free Black witnesses and, 91; free Black women, employment of, 135; free colonists, protected economic interests of, 33; freedom lawsuits and, 11–13, 48; hearsay evidence/genealogies, role of, 12; John Brown's raid and, 153–154; legal consciousness, development of, 12–14, 35–36; liberty concept, germination of, 40; Nat Turner rebellion and, 148–151; rape/lynching, transition to freedom and, 188; theological case for, 148. *See also* Clemency; Contemporary racial divisions; Criminal justice system; Justice; Slave insurgency
Fugitive Slave Act of 1850, 129, 130, 143–144, 163

Gabriel's Conspiracy, 8
Gaines, Archibald K., 129–131
Gaines, Reuben, 99–100

Gamble, Catherine, 180
Garthwright, Samuel, 66
Gaskins, W. E., 90
Gathright, Joel, 45, 46
Ghachem, Mailck, 11
Gikandi, Simon, 26
Giles, William Branch, 67–68
Glymph, Thavolia, 5, 92, 145, 146, 164, 165, 180
Gomez, Michael, 42
Gooch, William, 35, 36
Goode, Thomas, 61
Goode, William Osborne, 150
Grayson, J. B., 89, 90
Green, George E., 87–90
Green, William, 68, 70
Gresham, John, 48
Gross, Ariela, 11
Gross, Kali N., 4

Hagerty, Daniel, 159
Haley, Sarah, 4, 15, 188
Hall, Salena J., 98–99
Hall, William, 111
Hampton Institute, 189
Hanky, Gabriel, 126, 127
Harper's Ferry raid, 153–154
Hartman, Saidiya, 3, 111
Hening, William Waller, 22, 23, 26, 27
Hicks, Mary, 57
Higginbotham, A. Leon, Jr., 14, 181
Higginson, Thomas Wentworth, 153
Hill, Alexander, 173
Hill, Martha, 173
Holden, Vanessa M., 16, 149, 153
Holstead, John D., 180
Homicide. See Infanticide; Murder; Slave
    insurgency
Houslin, James, 49
Howe, Samuel Gridley, 153
Hughes, William, 46–47

indentured servitude, 27, 29, 30, 32, 34, 35,
    37, 117, 182
infanticide, 14, 21, 115; abortion and,
    120–121, 133, 135–137, 139; Ally, commuted

sentence of, 128; anti-slavery movement
and, 128, 130–131, 143, 144; Black/White
sexual interactions, legal context for,
118–119; botanical knowledge, exchange
of, 120, 121, 133; Caroline, suffocated
infant and, 131–132, 133; cause of death,
determination of, 116–117, 121–122;
clemency/commuted sentences and, 21,
123, 124–125, 126, 127, 128, 144; commutation, paternalism ideology/slavery
business and, 128; contented slaves,
myth of, 126, 128; contraceptive practices
and, 120; death, enslaved women's idea
of, 133, 139; definition of, 119; Eliza,
Kuper child death and, 177; Ellen,
drowned child and, 141; Emily, escape
of, 141, 143; Emma Jane, assault of infant
and, 175; English common law and, 122;
enslaved women, therapeutic/medicinal
epistemologies of, 122; evidence,
insufficiency of, 140, 143; Fannie, choked
infant and, 133; Garner family, escape
plot of, 129–131; indentured servants,
pregnancy and, 117–118; intent,
determination of, 140–141, 143, 177;
interracial sexual relationships and,
117–118, 125; investigations of, 115, 116–117,
119–120, 121, 122; Jenny, children's
drownings and, 122–123; Julia, abortion
case study and, 135–137; justice
inaccessibility, silenced voices and, 127,
137–138, 139, 143; Kesiah, commuted
sentence of, 128; kinship bonds, power
of, 126, 132, 137; legal complexities of,
143; Letty, murdered newborn and,
123–124; Lucy, clemency for, 124–125;
Lucy, hidden pregnancy/birth and,
138–139; Lucy Randolph, commuted
sentence for, 134–135; malice, determination of, 132; Margaret, sexual commodification and, 140; Margaret, Tardy infant
death and, 176–177; Martha, attempted
murder charge and, 175–176; Martha,
locals' testimony and, 127; medical
jurisprudence, development of, 115–116,

119–120, 137; Milly, reputation/locals' perception of, 126–127; miscarriage, invasive examinations and, 120, 136; motivations for, 21, 48–49, 116, 121, 123, 130, 132, 133, 137–138, 140; Opha Jane, insufficient evidence and, 140; paternalism, contradictions/inconsistencies of, 126, 128, 130, 132, 135, 138, 144; petitioning process and, 144; Polly, ownership of infant and, 125–126; pregnancy, work conditions during, 122; rape/reproductive exploitation and, 123, 125, 130, 131, 132, 135, 137–138; religious beliefs, influence of, 117, 122; reproductive labor, control over, 21, 118–119, 120, 121, 131, 143–144; reproductive/sexual lives, commodified enslaved women and, 21, 117–118, 121, 130, 131, 132, 143; reputation/deference, factors of, 125, 126–127, 133–134; sentencing, local input into, 123, 124–125, 138, 144; sexual exploitation, consent/culpability paradox and, 117–118, 121; Southern slave law, influence of, 129, 130–131, 143–144; transportation remedy for, 123–124, 125, 127, 128, 131, 133, 138, 140, 141; white children, enslaved women nurses and, 72, 73–74, 75, 91; white males, sexual power of, 117, 118–119, 131; white women, infanticide/abortion by, 121, 133; women's bodies, invasive/violent examinations of, 115–117, 119–120, 121, 122, 139. *See also* Murder; Poisonings; Slave insurgency

insurrection, 21; enslaved/free Black population, expansion of, 78; poisonings by slaves and, 56; volatile colonial landscape and, 32–33. *See also* Slave insurgency

Jackson, Joseph, 167
Jackson, William P., 76–77
Jefferson, Thomas, 23, 40–41, 43, 182, 187
Jennings, Edward, 49
John Brown's raid, 153–154

Johnson, Jessica Marie, 16
Johnson, Joseph, 74, 75, 76, 77, 79
Johnson, Walter, 1, 5, 159
Johnson, William, 110
justice: Bacon's rebellion, white supremacy lessons and, 33; benefit of the Clergy provision and, 35, 36, 60; Black radical tradition and, 15; communicative power, loss of, 3–5; evenhandedness, rule of law and, 17–18, 114, 157; free Black people and, 1, 7; genealogy of, changes in, 181–182; human will, suppressive systems and, 2–4; inaccessibility of, 1–2, 4; legal consciousness, development of, 12–14, 35–36; legal redress and, 1–2, 4, 12–14, 28; medical jurisprudence, development of, 115–116, 119–120, 137; paternalism and, 1–2, 3, 9, 10, 17–18, 111, 114; personhood, assertion of, 12–13; punishment, racial/gendered logics of, 4, 7–8, 9, 53; racial capitalism, property rules and, 14, 15, 17, 18–19; slave killings, slaveholder rights and, 33, 39–40, 54; slaveholders, authority of, 1, 2, 5, 6–7; slavery system, violent nature of, 1, 2, 3, 5, 6, 7; Southern exploitative culture and, 4, 5, 8, 15; Southern justice ideals and, 17–20, 65; Whigs, judicial/political influence of, 74, 75–79. *See also* African-descended women; Clemency; Contemporary racial divisions; Criminal justice system; Slave insurgency

Kaye, Anthony E., 9
Kennington, Kelly, 13
King, Wilma, 90, 91
Kinship ties, 9, 14–15, 16, 23, 42–43, 126, 132, 137
Knapp, Joseph, 70–71
Kuper, Augustus, 84, 177
Kuper, Frederick, 177

Law, Sallie, 173, 174
Law, Theodore, 174
Lawson, Thomas, 53

Lee, Robert E., 165, 166, 177
LeFlouria, Talitha, 188
legal landscapes. *See* African-descended
  Women; Clemency; Commonwealth of
  Virginia; Contemporary racial divisions;
  Criminal justice system; Justice;
  Virginia Colony
Leigh, Benjamin Watkins, 151
Lincoln, Abraham, 154, 176
Link, William A., 78
Lumpkin, Carter, 93

Magee, John R., 100–101
malice, 9, 33, 39, 75, 90, 108, 114, 116
Mann, Rebecca, 69
Mason, David, 53
Mason, George, 67, 107
Mason, Gerard, 106–113, 114
Mayse, Margaret, 94, 96
Mayse, Mary, 94, 96
McKinley, Michelle, 35, 36
Medical jurisprudence, 115–116, 119–120, 137
Meriwether, William H., 119
Merry, Sally Engle, 13
Michie, William, 119
Middle Passage, xi, 42
Miles, Tiya, 1, 3
Miller, Lewis, 55
Mitchell, Isabella, 63
Mitchell, Thomas, 63
Morgan, Edmund S., 32
Morgan, Jennifer L., xi, 14, 15, 29
Morgan, Philip D., 28
Morris, John W., 158
Morris, Thomas D., 14, 31
Morrison, Toni, 25
Moxley, Araminta, 83–84
Moxley, Gilbert, 83–84
mulattoes, 125, 129
murder, 21, 87; age, culpability and, 90–91;
  Agnes, Mason murder and, 106–113, 114;
  attempted murder, punishment for,
  92–93, 99; benevolent master, myth of,
  105, 107; Betsey, Wilson infant murder
  and, 99; Caroline, Smith child murder

and, 91; Catherine, Hall murder and,
  98–99; Celia, Newsom murder and,
  111–112; Charlotte, attempted murder by,
  149–150; clemency/leniency, possibility
  of, 98, 108, 109–110, 111, 114; contented
  slave, myth of, 93–94; enslaved
  children's bodies, slaveholder exploitation of, 90; gendered dynamics,
  response to altercations and, 21;
  Hatcher, Jackson murder and, 76–78, 79;
  inheritance considerations, slave
  transfers and, 99–100; innocence,
  inaccessibility of, 90, 91; Jane Williams,
  Winston family murder and, 101–105,
  114; Jim Phillips, Gaines murder and,
  99–100; Judy, Branson murder and, 91;
  justice, varied conceptualizations of, 21,
  76–77; Katy, Gerard Mason murder of,
  110–111, 112; legal localism, communalism
  and, 87; local interest, petitioning
  process and, 21, 87–90; Lucinda/
  Andrew/Caroline, Mayse children
  murder and, 94–98; Margaret Buckner,
  Gaines murder and, 99–100; Mary, Pond
  attempted murder and, 92–93; mis-
  tresses/slaves, warring intimacy and, 92;
  Molly, Magee murder and, 100–101;
  motivations for, 21, 88, 90, 93, 95, 96–97,
  100, 101, 102, 104, 108; Nelly, Green
  murder and, 87–90; Nelly, Shields
  murder and, 92; Pat, Fariss murder and,
  92; paternalist ethos of moderation and,
  114; Peggy, Pritchard attempted murder
  and, 98; Phoebe, Lumpkin murder and,
  93; punishments, symbolic value of, 90,
  98, 105–106, 112–113; rape of enslaved
  women and, 111–112; Rebecca, child
  Adeline murder and, 91; slavery, terror/
  violence of, 21, 45–47, 76, 88, 92, 93,
  97–98, 104, 106–113; transportation
  remedy for, 82, 90, 91, 97, 98, 99, 108, 111;
  violence, enslaved people's capacity for,
  21, 88, 89–90, 92, 98, 105; Whigs,
  judicial/political influence of, 76–79;
  working conditions/labor disputes,

discontent and, 104–105. *See also* Infanticide; Poisonings; Slave insurgency

Muse, Lawrence, 70, 71

Native Americans: Algonquian people, 28, 30–31; assimilation/religious conversion of, 26; botanical knowledge and, 120, 121; Chesapeake, presence in, xii; Civil Rights Act of 1866 and, 187; European diseases and, 28; land claims of, xii, 28, 181, 187; multiethnic collaboration against and, 32–33; Native lands, theft of, 26, 27, 30–31; population decline and, 28; sovereignty/equality, impossibility of, 26–27; squawroot medicinal plant, 120; testimony, acceptance of, 37

Nat Turner rebellion, 148–151

Newsom, Robert, 111–112

Noble, Mansfield, 73

Owens, Deirdre Cooper, 115

Palmer, Charles, 173, 174

pardons. *See* Clemency

Parker, Theodore, 153

partus sequitur ventrem law, 29–30, 31, 36

paternalism, 1–2, 3, 9, 10, 17–18, 35, 88, 111, 114, 126, 128, 144, 188

Perrin, Liese, 120

Pickett, Robert, 157

Pierce, William, xi

Point Comfort, ix, xii, 181, 189

poisonings, 20, 53; abortion, criminalization of, 60; accusations of, 53, 59, 61, 63, 67, 82; Amanda, Clarke children poisoning and, 84–85; Amelia, attempted poisoning by, 84; Annie, Allen family poisoning and, 68–70; antislavery movement and, 83; Black healers, intellectuals/social leaders and, 57, 59; blame for, 20, 59–60, 72; botanicals, good/bad effects of, 59, 64, 71, 72, 75, 85–86; Charity, Lawson family poisoning and, 53; convictions for, 20, 59–60; criminal boundaries, racial/gendered lines and, 53; Delphy, Isabella Mitchell poisoning and, 63; Eliza, Kuper poisoning and, 84; Eliza/Roberta, Noble infant poisoning and, 73–74; enslaved women/girls, knowledge war and, 53, 56–57, 59; Fanny, Orford poisoning and, 72; Fanny, Thomas Goode poisoning and, 61–62; gendered divisions of labor and, 66; Hannah, Seale family poisoning and, 63–64; hired-out slave laborers and, 60–61, 63, 68, 73; household environs, power/conflict dynamics of, 66, 69–70, 71, 73; interracial trust/compliance, myth of, 20, 59; legislative remedies for, 53–54, 56, 59–60, 65; Lucy, Mrs. Moxley poisoning and, 83–84; Mariah, Townes family poisoning and, 64–66; Martha, Mrs. Tully poisoning and, 82; medicinal/botanical knowledge, exchange of, 56–57, 59, 120, 121; medicinal substances, criminalization of, 59–60, 72; Milly, poisoning attempt by, 47; mistresses, abuse by, 63; motivations/culpability and, 72, 73, 75; Nelly, Wheat child poisoning and, 72; Peggy, Knapp family poisoning and, 70–71; Phillis, Butler infant poisoning and, 75, 76, 79–80, 81; poison, meanings of, 54, 56; punishment for, 53–54, 56, 59–60, 63, 65–66; slave law, expansion/updating of, 53–55, 56, 59–60; slave women's resistance and, 59, 64, 71, 79, 82; slave women's retribution and, 20, 53, 64, 69, 70, 71, 86; Suckey/Kesiah, Garthwright family poisoning and, 66–67; Susan, Judith Brightwell poisoning and, 71; transportation remedy for, 66, 67, 71, 75, 79, 81, 82, 84; wartime resistance and, 84–86; Whigs, judicial/political influence of, 75–79; white children, enslaved women nurses and, 72–73. *See also* Murder; Slave insurgency

Pritchard, John L., 98

Pritchard, Lydia, 98

race ideology, 20, 182. *See also* Commonwealth of Virginia; Contemporary racial divisions; Racial capitalism; Slavery; Slaves; Virginia Colony

racial capitalism, 14, 15, 17, 18–19; abolition war, emancipation and, 150–154; gendered racial capitalism, justice and, 23–24. *See also* African-descended women; Contemporary racial divisions; Slavery; Slaves

Raines, Mary, 160, 161

Raines, William, 161

Randolph, George W., 139

Randolph, Thomas Jefferson, 150, 151

rape, 111–112, 117–118, 123, 125, 130–132, 135, 137–138, 188

Reconstruction era, 187–188

reprieve, 7–8, 9, 10, 35, 98, 126, 128, 144, 160, 184. *See also* Clemency

reproductive labor, 21, 29–30, 31, 32, 34, 41, 54, 56, 117–118, 150

resistance. *See* African-descended women; Arson; Escape; Insurrection; Justice; Slave insurgency

Richardson, Benjamin, 138

Robe, William, Jr., 47

Robinson, Cedric J., 14, 15

Robinson, Helena, 157, 158

Rolfe, John, 28, 30

Rose, Benjamin, 166

Royal African Company, 34

Rugemer, Edward, 6

Said, Edward, 5

Sanborn, Franklin B., 153

Schwartz, Marie Jenkins, 117

Schwarz, Philip J., 7, 11

Schweninger, Loren, 12

Second Battle of Manassas, 172

Secret Six, 153

Seven Days Battles, 166

Sharpe, Christina, 131

Sherman, William Tecumseh, 155, 179

Shields, John, 92

Shields, Sally, 92

Silllers, Hortense, 3

Slave insurgency, 21, 145; abolition war, emancipation and, 150–154; accidental arsons, commuted sentences and, 160, 162; Agnes, escape from slavery and, 165; anti-slavery movement and, 83, 128, 153; benevolence of slavery, myth of, 8–9, 126, 151–152; Black inferiority, claims of, 41–42, 152, 153; Black radical tradition and, 15, 24; Black troops, courthouse raid and, 178–179; breaking enslaved people and, 10, 159, 161; Christmas holiday, opportunity of, 155–156; Civil War conditions, leveraging of, 155, 162–168, 173, 175, 179–180; Civil War, resistance strategy development and, 22, 84–85, 145, 146, 149; Civil War, Southern states secession and, 154–155, 163–164; clemency, petition for, 22, 23–24, 147, 148, 160; collective strategic resistance and, 146, 148–151, 156; Confederate legal regime and, 22; Confederate territory, escape from, 163; Daphney, escaped slave and, 167–168; diasporic warfare, slave resentment/resistance and, 145–146, 148; emancipation and, 150–154, 163, 176; enslaved women, active participation of, 153–154, 155, 164–165; enslaved women, freedom rituals of, 166–167; enslaved women, liberation politics of, 146, 149, 154, 155, 164–165, 180; escaped slaves and, 21–22, 49–50, 80, 107, 163–172, 179–180; Ester, loyalty of, 149–150; federal government, state protections and, 154; freedom, theological case for, 148; gendered racial capitalism, justice and, 23; hired-out slave laborers and, 158, 159–160; intellectual/emotional work, performance of, 23; John Brown's raid and, 153–154; justice, conflicted articulations of, 23, 161–162; kinship/community, significance of, 146, 149, 164, 167–168, 170–172, 180; leniency, varied perspectives on, 162; Lucy, charges of conspiring to rebel and, 148–150; Mary Jane Jackson, escaped slave and, 167; Nat Turner rebellion and, 148–151; offending slaves, harsh treatment of, 159, 161; offending slaves, valuation of, 160–161; paternalist ethic and, 88, 155, 159; paternalistic system, dissolution of, 155, 156, 163–164; Peggy, John Francis assaults of, 145, 146–148; penitentiary labor, sentence of, 162–163; power imbalances and, 24, 155; privileges, withholding of, 88; race epistemologies, legal landscape and, 40–45; reproductive labor, inheritability of slavery and, 150; reputation/character and, 160, 173; resistance, costs of, 24, 88–89, 150; Secret Six, support from, 153; slaveholders, discretionary justice by, 150; slavery, justice/clemency and, 23–24, 147, 148; Southampton Rebellion and, 148–151, 153; Southern fears, slave collective defiance and, 179–180; Southern law, harsh regulations of, 41–42, 151, 155, 156, 159; Southern property interests, protection of, 22, 41, 147–148, 150–151, 152, 154, 160, 176; Southern states secession, threat/danger of, 154–155; theft/grand larceny, plunders of war and, 174–175; transportation remedy for, 147, 159, 160, 161, 162; trials, courts/ slaveholders/slave trade interests and, 160–161; Virginia vs. West Virginia, legal landscapes of, 22; volatile colonial landscape and, 32–33. *See also* Arson; Contemporary racial divisions; Criminal justice system; Infanticide; Insurrection; Murder; Poisonings; Theft

slavery: anti-slavery movement and, 74–75, 77–78, 83, 128; benevolence, myth of, 8–9, 126, 151–152; breaking enslaved people and, 10, 159, 161; colonial economy, viability of, 30–32, 34; contemporary racial polarization and, 181; diffusion thesis and, 68; discipline, social order and, 6; double character paradox and, 11; gendered/sexual dynamics of, 25; hired-out slave laborers and, 60–61, 63, 68, 73; human capacities, profiteering from, 5; inherited slavery, enslaved women's reproductive labor and, 29–30, 31, 32, 34, 117–118; intimate relationships, fluidity in, 34; legal justice, inaccessibility of, 1–2, 3; liberty concept, germination of, 40; local contexts, communalism and, 11–12, 17, 18, 19, 87; moral good/necessity of, 114; natural condition of, 31–32; overseers, role of, 6, 16, 18, 42, 45, 46, 76–77; paternalism and, 1–2, 3, 9, 10; race/gender categories, slave law/medical studies and, 129; racial/gendered hierarchies and, 113–114; racial meaning, enslaved women's reproductive labor and, 29–30, 31, 32; resistance, acts of, 2, 5–6, 7, 10–11, 15, 16; slave laws, changes in, 10–11, 44–45; slave laws, development of, 6–7, 11, 43; slaveholders, presumed rights of, 1, 2, 5, 6–7, 16–17; spaces/geographies, strategic use of, 5; violence and, 1, 2, 3, 5, 6, 7, 16–17, 19. *See also* African-descended women; Clemency; Commonwealth of Virginia; Contemporary racial divisions; Criminal justice system; Slave insurgency; Slave trade; Slaves; Virginia Colony

slaves: adulthood status and, 90–91; Black healers, intellectuals/social leaders and, 53, 56–57, 59, 72; breaking enslaved people and, 10, 159, 161; charter generations of, xii, 35, 189; child slaves, power dynamics of slavery and, 91; commodification process and, xi, 1, 14; contented slaves, myth of, 93–94, 126, 128; criminal justice system, inequities in, 1–2; dehumanization of, 5; domestic slave trade and, 2, 7, 8, 9, 44–45, 75; double character paradox and, 11; elderly enslaved persons, status of, 69, 70; heavenly afterlife, promise of, 103; hired-out slave laborers and, 60–61, 63, 68, 73; illnesses/therapeutics,

slaves (*Continued*)
epistemologies of, 117; intimate relationships, fluidity in, 34; intraracial violent
crime and, 16–17; killing of, slaveholder
rights and, 33, 39–40, 54; legal consciousness, development of, 12–14, 35–36; legal
status of, xi, 1–2, 3, 31–32, 34, 35; multiethnic collaboration, rebellion and, 32–33;
paternalism and, 1–2, 3, 9, 10, 17–18, 35, 88;
Point Comfort, enslaved people in, ix, xii,
181, 189; privileges, withholding of, 88, 185;
religious beliefs, role of, 117; reproductive
labor and, 21, 29–30, 31, 32, 34; slaveholders, authority of, 1–2, 5, 6–7, 16–17, 33;
terms of service and, xi, 1–2; transfer
through owner lines of inheritance and,
99–100; transportation law and, 8, 9–10,
11, 17, 22; work ethic, white expectations
of, 42. *See also* African-descended
women; Clemency; Colonization;
Commonwealth of Virginia; Contemporary racial divisions; Criminal
justice system; Slave insurgency; Slave
trade; Slavery; Virginia Colony
slave ships, xi, xii, 1. *See also* Slave trade;
Virginia Colony
slave trade: Africans, commodification of,
xi–xii, 1; Bermuda, slave labor in, 28;
Chesapeake, early slaves in, 28; domestic
slave trade and, 2, 7, 8, 9, 10, 44–45, 75,
84; importation monopoly, dissolution
of, 34; lifelong bondage, slaveholder
power and, xi, 1, 8, 29, 33, 48, 52, 108, 126.
See also African-descended women;
Colonization; Slave ships; Slavery;
Slaves; Virginia Colony
Smith, Gerrit, 153
Smith, William Ira, 172
Southampton Rebellion, 105, 148–151, 153
Spillers, Hortense, 3
State of Missouri v. Celia, a Slave, 111
Stearns, George L., 153
Stevenson, Brenda E., 31
Stone, Lucy, 130
Stratton, Peter, 122

Sullivant, Anne Marot, 35
Summers, George W., 77, 78
Sweet, James H., 57
Swinburne, Henry, 31

Tardy, Francis Dean, 176–177
Tardy, Samuel C., 176–177
Taylor, Robert, 119
theft, 21; Agnes, escape from slavery and,
165; Celia, Law house theft and, 174; Civil
War context and, 22, 173–175; Daphney,
escape from slavery and, 167–168;
escaped slaves and, 21–22, 49–50, 163–164,
165, 167–168; grand larceny, plunders of
war and, 174–175; Jennie, escape from
slavery and, 165; legal responses to, 22, 36;
local reactions to, 22; Lucy, receiving
stolen goods and, 163; Mary Jane Jackson,
escape from slavery and, 167; punishments for, 22, 175; slaveholder economic
health and, 22; transportation remedy for,
22, 82; valued material goods and, 22;
Virginia, grand larceny by, 175. *See also*
Slave insurgency
Thomas, William, III, 12
Thornton, James, 141
tobacco trade, 28, 30–31, 60
Tomlins, Christopher, 26
Toney, William, 125
Townes, Mary, 64–66
Townes, Paschall, 64–66
transportation law, 8, 9–10, 11, 17, 22; arson
and, 82, 147, 160–161; clemency and, 8,
9–10, 17, 98; domestic slave trade and,
44–45, 75, 84; infanticide and, 123–124,
125, 127, 128, 131, 133, 138, 140, 141; murder
and, 82, 90, 91, 97, 98, 99, 108, 111;
poisonings and, 66, 67, 71, 75, 79, 81, 82,
84; slave insurgency and, 147, 159, 160,
161, 162; theft and, 22, 82. *See also*
Clemency
Travis, Champion, 45, 46
Tucker, William, xi
Twitty, Anne, 12
Tyler, Nathaniel, 167

Virginia Colonization Society, 77

Virginia Colony: Anglo-Americans, protection of the laws and, 27–28; Black radical tradition and, 15; charter for colonization and, 28; court system, segregation and, 7; English common law, role of, 14, 28, 31, 37–38, 122; enslaved population, expansion of, 34; ethnic/racial distinctions, colonial law and, 28–29, 32, 35, 37, 40–41; indentured servitude and, 27, 29, 30, 32, 34, 35, 37, 117; inherited slavery and, 29–30, 31, 32, 34; interracial cooperation/support and, 19, 32–33; legal code, revision of, 37–39; luxury goods, consumption of, 25–26, 52; Native lands, theft of, 26, 27, 30–31; Native nations, resistance by, xii, 27, 28, 29, 32; Native sovereignty/equality, impossibility of, 26–27, 32–33; paternalism and, 1–2, 3, 9, 10, 17–18; penitentiary, establishment of, 9, 38; plantation households, dynamics within, 5–6, 15; property regimes, colonial encroachment and, 27–28, 31–32; racial demarcation and, 29, 30; rebellion, multiethnic collaboration and, 32–33, 34; recorded history, insufficiency of, 3–4; reproductive labor, enslaved women and, 29–30, 31, 32, 34; revolutionary rhetoric, language of slavery and, 40; rule of law, fundamental factors in, 20, 26–28; sentencing practices and, 18, 19, 37–38; servant class, designation of, xi, 32; slave labor, colonial prosperity and, 26, 31, 34; slave law, civil polity/social state and, 23, 26, 28, 29–30; slave laws, changes in, 10–11, 35; slave laws, development of, 6–7, 11, 14, 26–27; slave resistance, acts of, 5–6, 7, 15, 16; slave ships, arrival of, xi,

xii, 26; slaves' legal consciousness and, 13, 35–36; slaves' legal status and, xi, xii, 1–2, 3, 31–32, 34, 35; Southern justice ideals and, 17–20; tax assessment, units of production and, 29; tobacco trade and, 28, 30–31, 60; warfare/violence, colonization pressures and, 32–33. *See also* African-descended women; Colonization; Commonwealth of Virginia; Criminal justice system; Justice; Slave insurgency; Slave trade

Virginia Company, 28

Virginian Luxuries painting, 25, 26, 27, 34

von Daacke, Kirt, 19

Waddle, A., 119

Walker, Thomas, 49, 50

warfare, xi, xii; domestic war, recovery from, 181; English colonization and, 32–34. *See also* Civil War

Washington, Hannibal Bush, 63

Weisenburger, Steven, 130

Welch, Kimberly, 12, 13

West Virginia, 22, 181, 184

Wheat, Forest, 72

Wheat, Joseph H., 72

Wheatley, Phillis, 43

Whig judicial/political influence, 74, 75–79

White, Deborah Gray, 121

White, Nancy, 49

white supremacy: Bacon's rebellion and, 32–33, 34; white Virginians, superiority myth and, 105. *See also* Colonization; Slavery; Virginia Colony

Wilson, John Somerfield, 99

Wilson, Joseph C., 99

Winston, Joseph, 101–105, 114

Winston, Virginia, 101–105, 114

Wise, Henry A., 89, 90, 140, 154

Printed in the USA
CPSIA information can be obtained
at www.ICGtesting.com
CBHW032229080324
5160CB00001B/90